Teaching Reading Shakespeare

Teaching Reading Shakespeare is for all training and practising secondary teachers who want to help their classes overcome the very real difficulties they experience when they have to 'do' Shakespeare.

Providing a practical and critical discussion of the ways in which Shakespeare's plays present problems to the young reader, the book considers how these difficulties might be overcome. It provides guidance on:

- confronting language difficulties, including 'old words', meaning, grammar, rhetoric and allusion;
- reading the plays as scripts for performance at Key Stage 3 and beyond;
- using conversation analysis in helping to read and teach Shakespeare;
- reading the plays in contextual, interpretive and linguistic frameworks required by examinations at GCSE and A Level.

At once practical and principled, analytical and anecdotal, drawing on a wide range of critical reading and many examples of classroom encounters between Shakespeare and young readers, *Teaching Reading Shakespeare* encourages teachers to develop a more informed, reflective and exploratory approach to Shakespeare in schools.

John Haddon has over 30 years' experience of teaching English in the classroom, 17 of them as a Head of Department. He has contributed to a number of titles on A Level teaching practice, English in the National Curriculum and teaching fiction at Key Stage 3.

Teaching Reading
Shakespeare

John Haddon

Routledge
Taylor & Francis Group

LONDON AND NEW YORK

First published 2009
by Routledge
2 Park Square, Milton Park, Abingdon, Oxon OX14 4RN

Simultaneously published in the USA and Canada
by Routledge
270 Madison Avenue, New York, NY 10016

*Routledge is an imprint of the Taylor & Francis Group, an informa
business*

Typeset in Sabon by GreenGate Publishing Services, Tonbridge, Kent
Printed and bound in Great Britain by CPI Antony Rowe,
Chippenham, Wiltshire

British Library Cataloguing in Publication Data
A catalogue record for this book is available
from the British Library

Library of Congress Cataloging in Publication Data
Haddon, John, 1948-
Teaching reading Shakespeare / John Haddon.
p. cm.
Includes bibliographical references and index.
1. Shakespeare, William, 1564-1616--Study and teaching--United
States. 2. Shakespeare, William, 1564-1616--Study and teaching
(Secondary) 3. Education, Secondary--United States. 4. Language arts
(Secondary)--United States. I. Title.
PR2987.H33 2009
822.3'3--dc22
2008033867

ISBN 10: 0-415-47907-X (hbk)
ISBN 10: 0-415-47908-8 (pbk)

ISBN 13: 978-0-415-47907-3 (hbk)
ISBN 13: 978-0-415-47908-0 (pbk)

Contents

Acknowledgements

Earlier versions of parts of this book appeared as articles in *The Use of English*. I am grateful to the editor, Ian Brinton, for permission to make use of them here. Thanks are due to my pupils, students and colleagues over the years, particularly those of Littleover Community School, Derby, where most of the work described here was done. For realistic commentary and encouragement I am grateful to my wife Trish, and for close editorial work to my daughter Ruth.

Prologue

There are quite a few books available on teaching Shakespeare. My aim in this one is to give sustained attention to what is involved in *reading* Shakespeare in the classroom, confronting some of the very real difficulties which our pupils and students encounter in, say, *Romeo and Juliet*, *Richard III* or *Twelfth Night*. Many of the approaches to Shakespeare developed in recent years are inventive, enjoyable, well motivated and potentially very productive. However they can – although they need not – evade or defer engagement with the language (and therefore the substance) of the plays. Thematic and empathic approaches seek to make the plays more relevant to the lives of young people, but at some risk of missing what is distinctive about them. Even those that involve splendidly physical treatments of the language and an awareness of theatre can prove remarkably indifferent to questions of *meaning*.[1]

My main concern in this book is to consider the contributions that can be made by, not to put too fine a point on it, teaching. I've tried to be both principled and pragmatic, with a wide range of practical suggestions and examples, some lightly sketched, some worked out in detail. The approach throughout is informed by literary-critical reading with a strong bias to performance. The chapters can be read independently but are interrelated and cross-referenced and build up into a complete argument concerning what might be involved in the teaching of Shakespeare.

Since the main barrier to Shakespeare for our pupils is his language, Part 1 offers a detailed consideration of the difficulties it presents and some of the ways in which they can be tackled in the classroom. Part 2 discusses five areas of interest which can provide ways of focusing on improving reading in the classroom and beyond. The first discussion concerns how work on the plays' stories might enhance, and be enhanced by, reading. The second focuses on reading Shakespeare's plays as scripts for performance. The next three are concerned with prompts to read within frameworks of understanding insisted on by some examinations: contextual, interpretative and linguistic. The intention here is to be both critical and constructive, focusing on how these frameworks may help or inhibit reading Shakespeare well. Finally, leaving behind any merely pragmatic approaches (we teach Shakespeare because we have to, it's the law), the last chapter considers the question of what it all amounts to: what might be the value to secondary pupils and students of reading or having read Shakespeare? Not in terms of their acquiring qualifications and transferable skills, but in coming to know the plays. What can be said to those people – conceivably ourselves amongst them – who say 'So what?'?

A note on terminology

Although nowadays even primary school children are sometimes referred to as 'students', I've tried to retain 'students' for those who voluntarily attend a course of study and/or those who have developed independently motivated sustained interest in investigating something, and 'pupils' for those in school by law. This leads to some occasional clumsiness in the writing, but I think the distinction is worth hanging on to.

Part I

Language

Chapter 1

Admitting the difficulty

In the 1960s Frank Whitehead posed a question about Shakespeare in secondary schools that continues to deserve consideration: 'how many of his plays ... really come within the linguistic and emotional range of the young adolescent?'[1] While we may feel inclined to retort that education requires us to extend the linguistic and emotional range of our pupils and students precisely by introducing them to texts that lie beyond their present range, or that develop areas of their present intuitions, his question has a real point and should not be evaded. If the text lies too far beyond the linguistic and emotional range of our pupils and students, the connection necessary for development is unlikely to take place. Leaving aside how far 'linguistic' and 'emotional' range can be separated, I want to concentrate in this first chapter on the questions raised for teachers and their classes by the difficulties of Shakespeare's language.

Whatever the difficulties secondary school pupils experience with Shakespeare's language, it is still recognizably continuous with and related to the language that they and their teachers speak. Indeed this is one of the things that we should want to insist on. We should always bear in mind that Eliot's dictum that all genuine poetry can communicate before it is understood might be true. It is possible, even probable, that Shakespeare's language grips at first in particular phrases or passages, sensed as somehow fine or mysterious, or as striking a chord with an individual's feelings or preoccupations (even if, as well may be the case, the words have been misunderstood). It might even be argued that, the story and the dramatic situation having been clearly established, we should to a large extent leave the language to take care of itself. There is a 'never explain' strand in some of the Shakespeare teaching of recent years; however, for all my reservation about some glosses, paraphrases and explanations (see below), I don't feel able to belong to it. Quite apart from any other consideration, pupils are going to face exams on Shakespeare, and we need to take seriously the panic that they feel at times and that tells them that they don't understand *anything* of Shakespeare's language (when actually they understand quite a lot), and which inhibits them and curtails their interest. As with so much in teaching – as I find myself saying again and again in this book – what to explain, how to explain and when are all matters of the teacher's judgement, and beyond a certain point general principles may not be very helpful. It may be, to quote Eliot again, that there is no method other than to be very intelligent. The intelligence will be at work in the judgement and choices made, both in preparation and in the classroom, about what approaches to use when, what to focus on, what to omit.

Over the last twenty years or so there has also been a healthy classroom emphasis on the *physicality* of Shakespeare's language and the importance of getting it onto pupils' tongues as soon as possible. Pupils have been invited to focus on short passages, phrases, even individual words; to realize them in action, play with them, combine them with bodily action, to hurl insults, to use a particular phrase from Shakespeare to say 'hello' or 'I don't trust you' and so on, to speak the words aggressively, kindly, swiftly, etc. While these approaches can be great fun and certainly disarm some of our pupils' hostility to Shakespeare, there is a tendency to use them without complementary attention to *meaning*, which tends to be neglected because it is difficult.

The determined optimism which has rightly driven much of our work over the last twenty years or so, insisting on Shakespeare's accessibility and immediacy, may well have led us to minimize some real impediments to an adequate grasp of Shakespeare. We can be too sanguine about the difficulty of Shakespeare's language for our pupils (even for ourselves). Much of his language is, in all conscience, very (sometimes astonishingly) difficult. Confronted with the text of a Shakespeare play, the sheer *amount* of what is unfamiliar can lead to the feeling of not understanding the text at all. Pupils will often say when asked what in particular they don't understand: '*Any* of it!' When bafflement turns to indifference and hostility, our troubles begin.

It's the difficulty with language – among other factors – that has led to various strategies of delaying or minimizing encounters with it. But it's worth dwelling on what is found difficult and why, and how (at least some of) the difficulties might be met in our planning and teaching.

What pupils find difficult may not always be something we can anticipate. Some years ago, having set groups of Year 9 to work on staging the sleep-walking scene from *Macbeth*, I went round them for the usual reasons – to nudge, prompt, explain, check that they were actually doing anything. Arriving at one group I was dismayed to find that they were completely stuck, had been unable even to get started. 'I don't get it,' said a particularly able girl, to my confusion, 'is she in a wheelchair or something?' When I announced my confusion, she pointed to the line, in the very first speech of the scene: 'When was it she last walk'd?'

Such unforeseeables aside, it is reasonable to anticipate that difficulties with Shakespeare's language will be encountered at the levels of lexis, syntax and discourse organization, with other elements of difficulty being metaphor, allusion and cultural references. Often they will be encountered all together, which makes knowing where to focus our helpful attention difficult. However, for purposes of exposition there is some advantage in considering, as far as is practicable, each level separately, and examining the kinds of problems they present and how we may help our pupils with them as they learn to read Shakespeare. Many teachers' familiarity with early modern English lexis and grammar may well not extend much beyond the knowledge acquired when reading particular Shakespeare plays, and may therefore be in need of enlargement and some degree of organization. In order to write this section I have had to refer to some of the several books that are available on the subject, which are largely written for readers and students of more advanced years and experience than those that secondary school teachers work with. What I try to do in the following chapters is, drawing on my own experience of teaching and reading Shakespeare and referring to some of these works, particularly Charles Barber's *Early Modern English*[2] and N. F. Blake's *Shakespeare's Language: An Introduction*,[3] to work out some observations that may help teachers to be clear about which types of difficulty (usually in combination) are likely to be experienced with particular passages. What's offered in the following chapters is not a *programme*, to be worked through with classes, but some resources to help develop our sympathy with and understanding of our pupils' and students' difficulties, so that we can anticipate questions, make the helpful move without fuss, or make use of an appropriate exercise.

Chapter 2

'All these old words'

Pupils will tell us that Shakespeare wrote in 'Old English' and that he is therefore very hard, if not impossible, to read. They may well add that he also wrote about 'old stuff', and therefore is of no relevance or interest, so the struggle with the language isn't worth the trouble. The short answer, I suppose is: 'What – old stuff like love, death, mystery, treachery, loyalty, honour, anger, happiness, loss and gain, appearance and reality, murderers, ghosts, liars, lovers, wars, shipwrecks, fathers and daughters, rape, magic, courage, politics, etc.; which of these can't we be interested in the twenty-first century?' As to Old English, it's worth showing them some, for instance a version of the Lord's Prayer, so that they can see the difference:

> Fæder ure þu þe eart on heofonum,
> Si þin nama gehalgod.
> To becume þin rice
> gewurþe ð in willa, on eorð an swa swa on heofonum.
> urne gedæghwamlican hlaf syle us todæg,
> and forgyf us ure gyltas, swa swa we forgyfað urum gyltendum.
> and ne gelæd þu us on costnumge, ac alys us of yfele. soþlice.

Old English really *does* pose problems that at first glance seem completely impenetrable: there are letters they may not have seen before, words that look utterly unfamiliar. A little close probing throws up a few likely identifications (or guesses), but on the whole the passage is unreadable without special training.

By contrast an Early Modern English version leaps into focus:

> Our Father which art in heauen, hallowed be thy Name.
> Thy kingdome come. Thy will be done euen in earth, as it is in heauen.
> Giue vs this day our daily bread.
> And forgiue vs our debts, as we also forgiue our debters.

And lead vs not into tentation, but deliuer vs from euill: for thine is the kingdome, and the power, and the glory for euer. Amen.

Of course there remain some difficulties (partly orthographical, and we can remove those easily enough, as they are removed in most modern Shakespeare editions). But we can encourage our pupils to see a continuity between Early Modern English and their own.

When asked 'What do you mean by "all these old words"?' pupils will often cite 'thou' and 'thee' as typical sources of difficulty. Since these are just the subject and object of 'you' in the singular, the real problems with them are probably grammatical rather than lexical, as in agreement they are found in conjunction with earlier (and therefore unfamiliar) verb forms.

These can, however, be simply taught – and then perhaps reinforced by a lesson in which they are to be used by teachers and pupils instead of 'you', etc. ('Sir, thou shouldst not set us homework, thou settedst it on Monday already.' 'Why thou art right, Colin. But thou art out of luck; this week thou hast two homeworks.')

Of more interest is the use of these terms in relation to social and personal relationships. In Early Modern English, 'you' is what the linguists call the *unmarked* form (the usual form that does not draw attention to itself), likely to be used between social equals; 'thou' the *marked* (standing out on some way from the more ordinary). The marked 'thou' can work in one of two ways – it can suggest intimacy (as between close friends or lovers) or condescension (as in talking down to inferiors). There's some useful material on 'thou' in Barber,[1] which pursues the distinction as late as Restoration comedy, and in Sylvia Adamson's essay 'Understanding Shakespeare's grammar: studies in short words',[2] which is particularly good on the social and dramatic nuances created by shifts of usage and how interpretation of these is not always straightforward. Her discussion of the opening of *Measure for Measure* is particularly interesting. It's worth noting that while the *you/thou* distinction is lost to us in our everyday contemporary English, it is still very much alive in other languages[3] which some pupils in multi-cultural classrooms may well be familiar with.

Romeo and Juliet use 'thou' throughout the balcony scene; Friar Lawrence uses 'thou' to Romeo and Juliet, presumably as marking his spiritual paternity and pastoral concern; throughout his cruel diatribe against Juliet for refusing to marry Paris, her father addresses her as 'thou', presumably not out of affection but marking her as an inferior, totally in his power. An example of the deliberate use of 'thou' as provocatively condescending is found in *Twelfth Night* when Sir Toby is instructing Sir Andrew on how to write a challenge to 'Cesario'; he remarks 'If thou "thou'st" him some thrice, it shall not be amiss' – that is, talk down to him, treat him as a social inferior, a mere fellow. At the end of Hamlet's 'To be or not to be' soliloquy he addresses Ophelia: 'Nymph, in *thy* orisons be all my sins remember'd' but he switches to 'you', even for the direct statement 'I did love you once', presumably establishing a formal distance between them and the previous state of affairs. In the subsequent dialogue he shuttles between the two usages, and it's worth considering why.

Interestingly, the distinction does not always work as one would expect (which is one reason for keeping an eye out for it). In the breathtaking moments in which Beatrice and Benedick at last confess their love for one another in *Much Ado*, they use language of the greatest simplicity, in contrast not only to their previous artful elaborations but also and more immediately to the impassioned and lengthy verse speeches that have preceded in the 'jilting' of Hero:

Benedick	Lady Beatrice, have you wept all this while?
Beatrice	Yea, and I will weep a little longer.
Benedick	I will not desire that.
Beatrice	You have no reason; I do it freely.
Benedick	Surely I do believe your fair cousin is wronged.
Beatrice	Ah, how much might the man deserve of me that would right her!
Benedick	Is there any way to show such friendship?
Beatrice	A very even way, but no such friend.
Benedick	May a man do it?
Beatrice	It is a man's office, but not yours.
Benedick	I do love nothing in the world so well as you. Is not that strange?

Is it not strange that this naked confession should be made using the equable 'you', one equal to another, with no marking of affection? Yet after Beatrice's convoluted response, which uses 'you', Benedick's exclamation is the presumably more intimate: 'By my sword, Beatrice, *thou* lovest me.' But then he reverts to 'you'; then says 'I protest I love *thee*'. Beatrice echoes his phrase but for the one word: 'I was about to protest I loved *you*.' For the rest of the scene Benedick uses the intimate form and Beatrice does not. Even in their final, public admission in Act 5 Scene 4, Benedick uses 'thou' and 'thee', and Beatrice does not. Both Claudio and Hero in their marriage use 'you'. Why? How much should be made of all this is a question for debate.

Another commonly occurring feature of both Early Modern and present-day English that pupils might consider as primarily lexical is contraction. This can be considered quite apart from any particular passage of Shakespeare. We might do a 'starter', pointing out that contraction is a common practice among us; we do it all the time (*will not, can not, it is, you are, fish and chips*). The pupils will have no difficulty in providing further examples. This can lead on to a discussion of *reasons* for contractions – such as laziness, informality, variety of pace and emphasis (compare 'I *didn't*, I *didn't*, I *didn't*!' with 'I *did not*').

Having highlighted this well-known but perhaps not much considered language feature, we can go on to point out that it was common in Shakespeare's day too, for similar reasons, and to consider some examples. An obvious starting place is *'tis*, which for us has been replaced by *it's*. Some fun might be had with trying to use *'tis* for a whole lesson where we would normally use *it's*. This could be followed by looking at some other common contractions in Shakespeare. For instance *i'* for *in* (as in 'the fire i'' the blood') often gives pupils trouble. This could also be played with like *'tis*; by an analogy with *fish 'n' chips* we might argue for *toad i' th' hole*, for example.

A number of contractions can be found in the first act of *Macbeth*, on one occasion clustering together in one line: 'In viewing o'er the rest o' th' selfsame day'. In Act 5 Scene 5, when Macbeth ''gins to be aweary of the sun', we find another crowded line: 'And wish th' estate o' th' world were now undone'. If pupils reading *Macbeth* have already considered the phenomenon of contraction, reading such lines should be less difficult.

Another reason for contraction in Shakespeare is the need to fit the sense to the iambic pentameter. (I think it's best to have introduced iambs to pupils quite apart from Shakespeare and before any close engagement with his plays. The anonymous verse 'A man of words and not of deeds' is admirable for this purpose, although in tetrameter rather than pentameter, and it's well worth puzzling over in its own right.) We should at some stage consider the distinction between pronouncing the suffix *ed* as a syllable and not doing so. Modern editions deal with the distinction in one of two ways, either marking the sounded syllable with an accent:

A *blessèd* labour, my most sovereign lord!

or (following the usage of the Folio) using a contraction to mark the elided syllable:

But nature never *fram'd* a woman's heart
Of prouder stuff than that of Beatrice.

Knowing about this distinction and how it is represented can help pupils with reading aloud and getting the feel of the pentameter line. An exercise that might be useful is to give some lines and ask the pupils to decide in which cases the final *ed* should be pronounced – preferably by trying the lines out loud rather than by counting syllables, although the latter is never to be despised and for some is necessary.

If a discussion of contraction has led to a look at verse, or if consideration of verse has led to a discussion of contractions, then two related features could also be included: adaptations of pronunciation to fit the stress pattern (Hamlet will wipe from his memory 'all trivial fond re*cords*'; Romeo asks 'What says my *con*cealed lady to our cancelled love?', thus bringing out an affinity as well as a contrast between the words) and elision, the deliberate swallowing of syllables to ensure a regularity of metre, even where no contraction is graphically represented. For instance in Anne's outburst to Gloucester 'In thy foul throat thou liest. Queen Margaret saw' 'liest' has to be one syllable, not two. Some pupils are scandalized to discover these features; they consider them to be cheating.

Popular culture can come to our aid in discussing such matters; hit songs sometimes afford examples of elision of syllables, slightly forced pronunciation or re-ordering of words to fit a metrical pattern. For example, I found Sandi Thom's curious 'I Wish I Was a Punk Rocker' useful for discussing with a Year 7 class how words may be stretched to fit an iambic metre. It's best to work with current examples, readily known – perhaps even introduced – by pupils.

As intimated above, a discussion of this sort need not be part of a 'Shakespeare' lesson at all, but one on verse writing, with examples bought in to show some of the ways in which writers, Shakespeare among them, have tackled it; nonetheless, the work may help remove, by anticipating, some obstacles in the later reading of Shakespeare.

This excursion demonstrates how quickly we are led away from consideration of mere lexis when we are thinking about ways in which reading Shakespeare might be difficult for our pupils and students. It is actually quite hard to isolate lexis for particular consideration.

There are some individual words that crop up often and may well be worth simply teaching in advance if they occur in a passage to be worked on: 'You'll come across these a lot so you need to know about them'. They can be learned for homework with some exercises as follow-up. Examples might be *want* in the sense of 'lack, be without', *yea* and *aye* for 'yes', *wherefore* ('why'?), *whither* and *thither* ('where' and 'there') and so forth. Pupils can be told that *ere* is pronounced 'air' and means 'before' and that *fie* rhymes with 'high' (for some reasons pupils often want to read it as 'fee') and is an expression of disgust or disapproval. Mild oaths (*marry*) and less mild (*zounds*) can similarly be explained, as can the more frequently encountered interjections. Barber usefully remarks:

> Interjections are common in dramatic dialogue. The attitude conveyed … no doubt varied according to the intonation with which it was spoken, and also the particular context. The following usages, however, are common ones in the Early Modern period: *Alack!* (deprecation, regret), *Ay me* (sorrow, pity), *Fie!* (disgust, reproach), *Ha!* (triumph, indication, surprise), *Helas!* (grief, sorrow), *Heyday!* (surprise, wonder), *Out!* (indignation, reproach), *Pish!* (impatience, contempt), *Welladay!* (sorrow, lamentation).[4]

It's worth bearing in mind that pupils are not always aware of the distinction between the obsolete and the unfamiliar, and may get the confident impression that certain words belong to Early Modern English simply because they haven't previously encountered them. It's worth making this distinction explicit (and perhaps also worth pointing out, at least to the gifted and talented, that *very* occasionally obsolete words re-enter usage). Unfamiliar but still current words that might form a useful part of a growing vocabulary can be highlighted in passing, or investigated in occasional vocabulary homeworks. That the words in question can be found in a modern dictionary will help reinforce the distinction.

When reading Shakespeare with a class there is in one sense no serious problem with words that we *know* we don't know, that jump out at us as strange: we know we're either going to skip over them, make a guess or look them up, and a good schools' edition will provide an uncomplicated gloss. Trickier are words that we *think* we know. We need to be aware of the possibility – even at times the probability – of anachronistic reading. C. S. Lewis's excellent *Studies in Words* introduces this topic with an anecdote:

> In the days of the old School Certificate we once set as a gobbet from *Julius Caesar*
>
> > Is Brutus sick and is it physical
> > To walk unbraced and suck up the humours
> > Of the dank morning
>
> and one boy explained *physical* as 'sensible, sane; the opposite of "mental" or mad'.

Lewis comments:

> if so much linguistic history were lost that we did not and could not know the sense 'mad' for *mental* and the antithesis *mental-physical* to be far later than Shakespeare's time, then his suggestion would deserve to be hailed as highly intelligent.[5]

Lewis describes this kind of anachronism as a word's 'dangerous sense'[6] – the sense of a word dominant in the time of the reader but not so in the time of the text. Another example he gives, without elaboration, is 'security'. So a pupil or student reading in *Macbeth* that 'security/Is mortals' chiefest enemy' might read it as a brilliant paradox (rather than an old-fashioned moral truism), unless informed that here 'security' means 'over-confidence' or 'lack of caution'. There is considerable scope for misunderstandings of this kind. Here are just two examples that our pupils may encounter:

1. Claudio claims in Act 4 Scene 1 of *Much Ado* that Hero 'knows the heat of a luxurious bed'. Pupils may not understand why he is so upset, since a luxurious bed actually sound quite attractive. The connection with 'lecherous' and the accompanying disgust at unlawful sexual activity is largely lost, at least at the public level, in our culture. (I may be exaggerating about this; the work done by the word 'slag' is worth considering.) Roma Gill glosses *luxurious* as 'lustful'.
2. 'Sad' in our pupils' English means either 'unhappy' or 'pathetic', so there is a strong possibility of them misreading Olivia's greeting to the cross-gartered and smiling Malvolio: 'Smilst thou? I sent for thee on a sad occasion.' Olivia means 'a serious occasion', but by no means an unhappy one; she is tremblingly in love and full of happy anticipation, after all. (The editors of the Oxford edition further point out that Malvolio understands 'sad' to mean 'melancholy'.)[7]

Forewarned of the possibility of anachronism, we can be on the lookout for instances in which it might crop up, and prepare accordingly. Also, I think, we need to be aware of the possibility of missing opportunities over words/meanings that are common to ourselves and Shakespeare. Relieved at what looks like an easy passage, we might hurry on, glad to have nothing to explain. Here, for instance:

> And all our yesterdays, have lighted fools
> The way to dusty death.

No hard words there. But might not there be advantage, for us and for our pupils and students, in pausing to ask: Who are the fools? And why is death 'dusty'?

The awareness that some problems with reading Shakespeare are not primarily lexical, and that there are different kinds of problems with lexis, should inform our teaching of Shakespeare. There are clearly questions raised here about what – and how much – as teachers of Shakespeare we need to know, and about the kind and quality of the editions that we use in the classroom. (Teachers may not need the same editions as their pupils.) As ever, there are questions of judgement; what degree of knowledge and understanding is going to count as sufficient for this particular class in these particular circumstances? How much do we need to think things out in advance, and how much can we manage 'on the wing'? How much can we depend on the apparatus in the editions that we use?

This last question is an important one. While I can't pursue a full investigation here, I offer a few considerations. The notes in schools' (and other) editions, whether at the back of the book, the margins or the facing page, offer different kinds of aid: glossing single words, explaining phrases or sentences (by explicating metaphors, clarifying cultural references, offering paraphrase). Some take up a more active teaching role, asking questions, promoting thoughtful responses, suggesting alternatives, giving activities. This range of aims can lead to the *clutter* familiar in some schools' editions, and affords a design problem for the makers of such editions. We are best off with editions that clearly separate these functions, so that glosses can perform their main function of locally assisting reading. In the immediate context of this section we are just concerned with the glossing of single old and unfamiliar words, although of course this will in some cases involve some explication of phrases.

An occasional problem is that words that need explanation don't get any. I'm not just thinking of words with improper meanings, which are often enthusiastically glossed in schools' edition – it was in the Macmillan School Shakespeare, not the scholarly Arden, that I first found unembarrassed explanation of 'dildoes' and 'fadings' in *The Winter's Tale*.

Conversely, sometimes explanations are given where it is not obvious that they are needed. Roma Gill's notes in the Oxford School Editions are thorough and accurate, often clarifying the sense in ways that are very useful. However, the very thoroughness begs questions of how many and what notes are needed, what particular pupils might need for particular purposes. Pupils don't need to understand *everything* (unless saddled with an examination system that absurdly expects them to do so). Why for Prince Escalus' phrase 'a glooming peace', do we need a gloss on 'glooming'? Isn't the sense *roughly speaking* clear enough? The gloss given is 'gloomy'. That doesn't strike me as meaning quite the same. 'Gloomy' is closer to the comfort of cliché (and may have a suggestion of 'sulky', a hint of self-indulgence?); it lacks the threat of 'glooming'. My youngest daughter (ten at the time) said that it made her think of something getting darker. Isn't that a suitably dramatic understanding of the line? Even if it could be shown to be in some sense 'wrong', why would that wrongness matter? Or, to take another example: Portia's question in the trial scene to Bassanio: 'You stand within his danger, do you not?' Any reader who has come this far in the play will have no difficulty with the general sense. The gloss is 'in danger from him'. What is gained? (What is lost?) Occasionally the explanations themselves stand in need of explanation: '*comply with his dug*: pay formal courtesies to his wet-nurse's breast'.[8]

The question of what glosses, and how many, are needed is worth practical investigation; there's a research opportunity here for someone with the time and inclination. There are clear implications again for our knowledge, being able to gloss on the spot, knowing when to enlarge, connect or skip over.

We will at times in our teaching encounter words whose significance seems to be larger than can be accounted for by a merely local explanation, words whose meanings need to be grasped more deeply and extensively (involving questions of context, culture, ideology and belief) than can be accomplished in a brief gloss. Such words might include 'nature' in *Hamlet*, 'man' in *Macbeth*, 'honest' in *Othello*, 'human(e)' in *The Tempest*, or – an example that I more or less stumbled on when teaching a Year 9 class, and which I consider in the next chapter – 'virtue' in *Much Ado about Nothing*.

Chapter 3

Case study: 'virtue'

It is hard for inexperienced readers of Shakespeare when a number of unfamiliar words cluster together – harder still when the words are played with through punning and complex syntax. These are the kind of problems that are most likely to foreground themselves both in preparation and in the classroom. But maybe we need to develop a more alert sense of which words matter *most* for an initial understanding. I suggest that these are not necessarily the words that will most readily occur to us, and I do so because of a classroom experience. There are words that, although they might strike the teacher as straightforward enough, stand for complex or (to pupils, anyway) unfamiliar ideas, and initial consideration of these words before reading them in context might help open up a scene, making it, for comparative newcomers to Shakespeare, more readable. Take, for instance, 'virtue' and 'virtuous' in *Much Ado about Nothing*.

'Virtue' first appears in the plural, applied to Benedick, who the Messenger describes as 'stuffed with all honourable virtues'. This is immediately deflated by Beatrice: 'It is so, indeed. He is no less than a stuffed man'. In this light-hearted context we may not bother to attend too closely to the word. In his soliloquy at the beginning of Act 2 Scene 3 Benedick rehearses privately – that is (probably) to the audience – what he requires in any woman he could conceivably be interested in. She must have 'all graces':

> Rich, she shall be, that's certain. Wise, or I'll none. Virtuous, or I'll never cheapen her. Fair, or I'll never look on her. Mild, or come not near me. Noble, or not I for an angel. Of good discourse, an excellent musician, and her hair shall be of what colour it please God.

Later in the scene his friends carefully place in his hearing the remark that Beatrice is '(out of all suspicion) virtuous', and in Benedick's succeeding soliloquy he rehearses the view again – Beatrice is 'virtuous', tis so, I cannot reprove it'.

What does the teacher say when, reading these lines for the first time, a Year 9 class of middle ability, showing real bafflement, asks what 'virtuous' means, what 'virtue' is? I was momentarily thrown, not having thought about it, and came up with feeble remarks about 'not sleeping around'. (In a society where being faithful means not sleeping with someone other than the person you happen to be currently with, and being single means not being with anybody *at the moment*, this first shot may not be utterly mistaken, but its inadequacy is all too obvious.) I didn't, as far as I can remember, mention 'virginity', perhaps because it would probably have had a merely physical meaning (and caused amusement – theirs, probably – and embarrassment – mine almost certainly). 'Goodness' and 'good' might be too insipid or empty – meaning, perhaps, not much more than 'nice' and not necessarily carrying any notion of a *moral* content. (While *evil* may have been restored to our vocabularies since 9/11, our day-to-day discourse tends to eschew an ethical dimension: we are far more likely in a school context to talk about *inappropriate* than *wicked* behaviour.) Given the pupils' puzzlement and the condition of our public language, it seems the word and idea of 'virtue' are not particularly current with us, especially our younger people. (However, Roma Gill's Oxford School Shakespeare edition sees no need to explain either 'virtue' or 'virtuous'.)

This is what Melvyn Bragg has to say about the word:

> A word like 'virtue' ... part of the theme of chivalry now woven into our thinking, brought a secular sense of moral attainment into a land where the church had provided all the words and thought for any elevated morality. The word then took off and metamorphosed into several other meanings: it allied itself with honour and courage, for example, embellishing both; it became a boast, it became a weakness to be satirized; from rare and aristocratic it became common and earnest. It came to mean reason or merit or worth.

He further comments that 'virtue'

> began to dip below the horizon of well-used words. Soon it may be obsolete. Yet in its life, for eight hundred years, virtue alone, that one word, has illuminated and explained something of what we think we are, it has enriched our description of ourselves, uncovered yet more of the human condition which seems to crave infinite description. It is not just a word but a little history of our thoughts and actions.[1]

So is the word now of merely historical interest? To our pupils, of no real interest or importance at all?

After the SATs were out of the way, and feeling that I'd missed an opportunity, I returned to the question of virtue by approaching the play's central scene, Claudio's rejection of Hero in the presence of all those who have assembled for their marriage (Act 4 Scene 1). The class collaborated on a spider diagram of 'virtue':

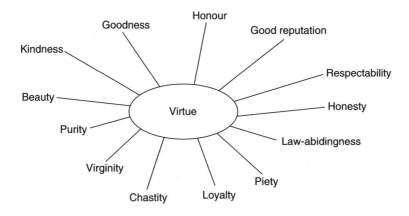

Figure 3.1 Mapping the meaning of 'virtue'.

'Piety' and 'chastity' were only my contributions *lexically* – it was the pupils who, with only a little prompting, raised the concepts. Of course such a collection is historically and philologically something of a mess, but it stakes out the ground in a rough and ready manner. I suggested that this set of qualities hung together in one concept; the word 'virtue' called them all up, so to speak. It might be that of our contemporary expressions 'integrity' comes closest to 'virtue'; but the adjective 'integral' will hardly serve for 'virtuous'. (I've come across the splendid 'integrity-ridden' somewhere.) More seriously, 'integrity' might be too close to a sense of *individual* wholeness rather than a wholeness that is not only an intimate quality (a quality of the self) but affirmed by and conformable to public standards (public because experienced as, believed to be, transcendent). Needless to say, I didn't raise this with the Year 9 class. What I did do was add that, for long historical periods, it has been felt (by men, at least) that for the woman – though not for the man – once the sexual integrity is gone, all is gone: she has lost her virtue.

It's worth asking 'What's the opposite of virtue?' before introducing the idea's historical opposite (or, as Sir Philip Sidney has it, 'her enemy'), vice. 'Vice' to most probably means at first thought a group of particularly nasty crimes. We brainstormed this concept and I introduced the adjective 'vicious' to pair with 'virtuous': it can come as something of a surprise.

I then introduced for discussion two more pairs of opposites: first, appearance and reality. We talked about how the seemingly virtuous may be inwardly vicious. Pupils are familiar with the notion of 'not judging a book by its cover' and are fortunate if they have no personal experience of duplicity. Since this is intrinsically important and interesting, and such a large theme in Shakespeare, it might be worth the teacher enlarging on it, if only briefly, perhaps introducing Lady Macbeth's instruction to 'Look like th'innocent flower,/But be the serpent under't', especially if the class is going on to study *Macbeth* at GCSE (and, in the far distance for a few, perhaps *Othello* at A Level). The other pair we looked at (like virtue and vice, alliteratively linked) was fair and foul, in both their physical and moral senses. There is opportunity in these pairings for individual exploratory and creative writing, as well as fertile ground for discussion.

We were by now set up to read the first part of Scene 4 Act 1. The charting of opposites provided a framework in which the pupils' spontaneous questions could be intelligent, enabling them to develop their understanding. Approaching the scene, we considered such questions as: As the characters enter, what is Hero expecting? What is Claudio thinking? What are the expectations of a first-night audience? We looked at the build-up to the moment of Claudio's rejection. When he asks if Hero knows of any impediment, is he making an opportunity for her to declare herself, or indulging in a private sarcasm before he springs his trap? Some glosses were needed: 'maid' makes pupils think of servants/hotel workers, but this can be explained quickly in passing, and its importance is immediately clear; similarly 'stale' and 'wanton' were quickly picked up and related to (one hopes, not adopted), and pupils are well aware of the importance of 'name', although that is not what they call it. Claudio's image of Hero as a 'rotten orange' was quickly grasped. Claudio's 'guiltiness not modesty' gave us another binary pair, as did the reference to Dian and Venus. Explanation can be sketched in, and as much or as little made of it as is deemed appropriate. Pupils were quick to see the apparent contradiction of appearance and reality:

> Comes not that blood as modest evidence
> To witness simple virtue? Would you not swear –
> All you that see her – that she were a maid
> By these exterior shows?

and

> Out on thy seeming! I will write against it.
> You seem to me as Dian in her orb,
> As chaste as in the bud ere it be blown.
> But you are more intemperate in your blood
> Than Venus or those pamper'd animals
> That rage in savage sensuality.

Having considered opposing qualities, pupils were ready to consider the force of Claudio's oxymorons:

> But fare thee well, most foul, most fair; farewell;
> Thou pure impiety and impious purity.

and Leonato's development of 'foul', with its identification of moral and physical filthiness:

> O she is fallen
> Into a pit of ink, that the wide sea
> Hath drops too few to wash her clean again,
> And salt too little which may season give
> To her foul, tainted flesh.

To reinforce the point, I compared this with Macbeth's 'Will all great Neptune's Ocean wash this blood/Clean from my hand?' Actually in the text I used with the class I had edited out much of Leonato's speech; if I had not done so, the pupils would have been able to relate Leonato's obsessive repetition of 'mine' to Claudio's going on so much about sex, which strikes them as hyperbolic (and plainly is so in 'the vile encounters they have had/A thousand times in secret'). This inflamed male imagination is something that we encounter a great deal in Shakespeare. We might dig into this further, and consider how the odious Claudio's obsessed and self-righteous moral disapproval coexists with his laddish insensitivity elsewhere in the play. And how is it that he and his friends can use other moral words – *fair*, *wise*, *mild*, *noble* – and yet at times show little of those qualities, to our modern eyes at least?

To most of my class his horror seemed incomprehensible – they could see why Claudio might be upset, but to *this* degree …? They considered his behaviour 'awful', 'stubborn and selfish', and commented that he 'didn't take into consideration other people's feelings'. One girl made the interesting observation that 'His behaviour completely drowns out the war hero image that he has become' (this is of course exactly *not* how his behaviour is seen by the other men in the play); another wrote that 'If he really loved Hero he should have gone up to her and asked her instead of humiliating her in front of everyone. This tells me that he can't have been that serious about her if he doesn't listen and believe a word she says.'

In some degree all of this appeared graspable to a class of middle ability. The glosses, observations and explorations have a context, a field of concepts and feelings, based on the enlargement and consideration of a single word, in which their consonance was apparent. The vice/virtue, appearance/reality, fair/foul opposition, far from being an imposed framework, are an essential part of the dynamic of the scene: isolating it for emphasis helps make the scene both manageable and fruitful for discussion.

Two further points emerge from this account of 'virtue' in *Much Ado*: first, the importance of contexts, in this case the context of a tradition of moral understanding and feeling; second, a recurrent question in this book, taken up most explicitly in the epilogue: what is it that we are we teaching, on any given occasion, when we are teaching Shakespeare? Are we, in this instance, introducing our pupils to a concept of profound and lasting value, or to a notion to be identified and resisted (or quietly forgotten) as intrinsically bound up in a discredited and abandoned patriarchal order's conceptualizing of 'woman'? (The inescapable involvement of the teacher's own values must be remarked on here.) Are we giving a history lesson? Or are we just explaining an old idea so that pupils have a better chance of passing an exam? Or making it possible for them to enjoy the play more? Something of several of these things? And what is our *intention*?

Once again, this excursion demonstrates how one thing in Shakespeare can lead to another – that consideration of even a single lexical item/word can carry us into deep waters involving unavoidable elements of judgement and choice (and, in anticipation of my final chapter, of value).

Chapter 4

Grammar

I suspect that lexis on the whole presents the *least* difficulty to young readers of Shakespeare, once their panic has to some degree subsided or their curiosity is piqued (or they've been persuaded to make the best of a bad job). While lexis inevitably presents some difficulties, it's probable that more difficulties in reading Shakespeare come from the grammar, particularly of more sustained passages. I put this to the test once by asking two GCSE pupils to look at an alphabetically arranged vocabulary list of a scene. One found no hard words; the other, less well read, quite a few. They then looked at the scene itself, and found it harder to follow than they had anticipated from the vocabulary. It may be suspected that these difficulties are not felt by younger readers alone.

The account of grammatical problems which follows is necessarily somewhat simplified. A much fuller account of ways in which Early Modern English grammar differs from our own and of the consequent potential misunderstandings may be found in Blake's *Shakespeare's Language: An Introduction*.[1] Particularly useful are his chapters on the noun phrase and the verb phrase; Blake brings out very clearly how a sense of 'blurring' can occur in inexperienced readings of Early Modern English. Barber's *Early Modern English*[2] is also very helpful. I'm assuming, though, that as classroom teachers of literature we can afford a less than linguistically adequate view of grammatical matters, as long as (i) our comments are sufficiently correct to help our pupils with learning to read Shakespeare, and (ii) they aren't howlingly *wrong*.

Most readers unfamiliar with Early Modern English will find that their grasp of it comes and goes, that at times they are altogether confused and can see no units of meaning, while at others they have at least the impression that something is making sense. The normal experience will be of things coming into and going out of focus. This will be not just a matter of identifying familiar words but also of spotting syntactical runs, partial coherences. Unfortunately sometimes what is identified is a product of misreading, a failure to see the full grammar.

For instance, in the first scene of *Twelfth Night* we read:

O spirit of Love, how quick and fresh art thou,

That nonwithstanding thy capacity,

Receiveth as the sea, naught enters there,

Of what validity and pitch soe'er,

But falls into abatement and low price

Even in a minute.

Even if the young reader is not tripped by 'how quick and fresh art thou', which looks to modern eyes like a question, s/he is likely to get lost quite soon: the clause most likely to stand out is 'naught enters there', which seems to make sense, as long as we don't reflect that it's odd to say that nothing enters the sea (but then maybe we're not expecting all that much sense). And the rest ... we pass over it, looking for the next bit that appears to make some kind of sense.

To take a non-Shakespearean example: an inexperienced reader, encountering Milton's 'I cannot praise a fugitive and cloistered virtue' might read 'fugitive' as a noun and so understand the first part of the sentence to mean 'I cannot praise a fugitive', with the consequence that 'and cloistered virtue' has to be read as a co-ordinating conjunction followed by a new subject rather than as the ending of a clause. The bit left over is what A. P. Rossiter calls a 'gagagram' – a floating bit of language that makes no apparent sense, because it is not seen as part of a grammatical whole in which it makes sense.[3] I suspect our pupils are baffled by a fair number of these.

Where lexis and grammar are closest to our normal reading experience we will experience the least difficulty. So much is obvious. Less able readers will often experience a considerable degree of bewilderment and helplessness at times if they simply *can't see the sentences* – and therefore the sense. They might even fall back on taking words in isolation (with a minimal grasp of their immediate context) as clues and guessing. This is presumably what had happened in the case of a Year 9 pupil reading (failing to read) Leonato's speech 'O my lord, wisdom and blood combating in so little a body, we have ten proofs to one that blood hath the victory' (*Much Ado* Act 2 Scene 2). Leonato and the others are talking about Beatrice in the hearing of Benedick and the reference is to the likely victory of passion ('blood') over reason ('wisdom'). The pupil, having understood that at the beginning of the play Don Pedro and his friends have returned from victorious battle, responded to the line as follows:

Leonato and Don Pedro, Claudio have fighting cloths on like example, armour shields on the arm ... Leonato should lift his sword saying line 160 'O my lord, wisdom and blood combating.' When he says that he should put his blade up in the air say BLOOD really loud.

It makes a kind of sense – 'combating' does, after all mean 'making war'. The failure of reading is at several levels – contextual (Leonato didn't go to war, Don Pedro and Claudio are unlikely to be still in battle gear); metaphorical (reading 'blood' and 'combat' literally) and grammatical – not reading the whole sentence. In this case the grammatical problem is presumably the relative clause 'wisdom and blood combating in so tender a body' and its relation to the main clause 'we have ten proofs'. How can we help our pupils to grasp this? What do they need to know? Probably the simplest thing to do is to substitute a 'when' clause for the one based on a participle ('combating'), along these lines:

> When reason and desire are at war in so tender a body (as a woman's, more specifically, as Beatrice's) ... then experience ('ten proofs') tells us that desire will win.

That is to say, this might be an occasion on which paraphrase is our best tool.

The participial construction is not unknown in present-day English, but it will certainly be unfamiliar to many of our pupils. Just as there's a distinction between *words* that are merely unfamiliar, although still in current use, and those that are genuinely obsolete, so there is a distinction between mere unfamiliarity with more complex grammatical structures and lack of knowledge about the grammar that is particular to Early Modern English. Either of these may lead to failure to see the sentence and so get the drift of a particular passage. There's a further distinction to be observed, between those features of Early Modern English that, while of interest from the point of view of the historical linguist, are not likely to be apparent to our pupils and students or to interfere with their comprehending at an appropriate level, and those that are potential sources of misunderstanding and confusion. Furthermore, some of what our classes think of as lexical difficulties may actually be matters of grammar, and some which appear as grammatical may for the linguistically trained be matters of morphology. I'm assuming that for classroom practice the last two distinctions are not at all helpful to our pupils, and that we shouldn't mention them explicitly. None of these distinctions will in every case be clear-cut in practice, but an awareness of them can help us anticipate some of the problems that we can meet by introducing our classes explicitly to some features of Early Modern English grammar.

This should be kept fairly simple and will vary in detail and timing from class to class. In some cases a lesson or two explaining, exemplifying and experimenting with some grammatical features may be the best approach, while on other occasions we might prefer to bring some of this knowledge to bear on a particular passage as it is encountered in the course of reading.

Verb endings

We might begin with verbs. Young readers of Shakespeare need to get used to earlier verb forms, particularly in the present tense with endings such as –*eth* and –*est*. They will frequently encounter *doth* for 'does' (and *dost* for 'do') – it crops up frequently enough to make it worth introducing in advance. It's a good idea to take examples from the text that the pupils will actually encounter. So, for a class shortly to embark on *Richard III*, they might be:

hath = has	*hast* = have	*hadst* = had	*canst* = can
mad'st = made	*drink'st* = drinks	*didst* = did	*dost* = does
shalt = shall	*liest* = lie	*wast* = was	*loveth* = loves

Once pupils have overcome the unfamiliarity, there's nothing inherently difficult about this; as Barber points out, 'The past-tense and past-participle forms of the verb functioned very much as today'.[4] There are a few exceptions, as he goes on to say: 'Quite often, however, the actual forms for any given verb are different from the ones we use today'. When these (e.g. 'holpen' for 'helped') occur they're probably best tackled in the course of reading.

Form of the negative and interrogative

Pupils can also be told explicitly that the negative in Early Modern English was often formed by placing 'not' after the verb instead of, as in present-day English, placing it with an auxiliary before the verb:

- 'I blame you not' rather than 'I don't blame you'
- 'Give not this rotten orange to your friend' rather than 'do not give'
- 'I found not Cassio's kisses on her lips' rather than 'I didn't find'.

We will also encounter negatives formed in the familiar fashion – but as these cause no difficulty there will be no occasion to comment.

Also, interrogatives are sometimes formed by inversion rather than by using the auxiliary 'do':

- 'Know you any, my lord?'
- 'What means this armed guard?'
- 'Heard you not …?'

These two features can be practised by 'translating' some selected examples both ways and then looking at, say, a suitably chosen double-page spread of Shakespeare and finding examples. Such exercises should help towards becoming more fluent in reading the text.

Inversion

Other occurrences of inversion are perhaps less immediately accessible. As more experienced readers of Shakespeare, I think teachers can overlook just how common these are. Again, it may help to introduce inversion as a topic, keeping it simple and using examples from the text that is to be read. We might broach the topic in relation to *Richard III* in this way:

> Quite often the words in a sentence are not in the order that we would put them. Here are some examples from a speech that you'll be reading soon:
>
> - *Plots have I laid.*
> - *Here Clarence comes.*
>
> See if you can rearrange these sentences into a more modern word order.

A useful working question at times when encountering unusual word order is 'What would *we* say (or write)?' This brings us again into the region of paraphrase, which is discussed further on pages 46–52. And we will sometimes want to discuss the question of emphasis – what *expressive* difference is made by this order of words?

For our (rather than our pupils') understanding of inversion, there are two useful comments from Barber. He comments that inversion 'is particularly likely to occur when the sentence begins with an adverb or adverbial phrase'. An example from *Much Ado* can be used to illustrate this observation. Speaking of Claudio's new-found love and its alteration of his behaviour, Benedick says 'now had he rather hear the tabor and the pipe'; this can sound to us like a question (and is further complicated for beginning readers of Shakespeare by 'had rather' meaning 'would rather'). Or from *Romeo and Juliet*: 'There stays a husband to make you a wife'. Barber also points out that 'If the object of the sentence is placed at the beginning, either for emphasis or to provide a link with what has gone before, this too can cause inversion'.[5]

Subordinate clauses

Confusion can also be caused, even in quite experienced readers, by 'floating' subordinate phrases and clauses that would be more firmly anchored in present-day English (that is, potential gagagrams). This can be illustrated by some examples of potential misconstruing from *Richard III*:

His Majesty hath straitly given in charge
That no man shall have private conference,
Of what degree soever, with your brother.

The adjectival phrase 'Of what degree soever' is so placed that it is likely to be read as describing 'conference' (and so 'degree' might be understood as something like 'significance, importance' – i.e. there's to be no chat even on trivial matters, *or* even if the matter is of the utmost importance) and not as describing 'no man', in which case 'degree' means 'rank' (which is the gloss given by the Longman School edition). Here grammar influences our reading of lexis. A second example from *Richard III*:

> Fellows in arms and my most loving friends,
> Bruised underneath the yoke of tyranny,
> Thus far into the bowels of the land
> Have we marched on without impediment.

Grammatically the adjectival phrase 'Bruised ...' refers to 'we', and clearly Richmond's 'fellows in arms' might regard themselves in that light, but the phrase arguably attaches with more depth of meaning to 'the land'.

However, examples such as these may be beyond most of our pupils, and we need to remember that our working questions are: How much does this misunderstanding matter? Will the gist (assuming for the moment that this is sufficiently apparent, or can be made to appear so) be enough?

Small words

While we are preoccupied with the larger and more obviously troubling factors in (mis)understanding Shakespeare, we may be inclined to overlook the important functions of small everyday words – words that establish relations between units of meaning (e.g. *if* and *and* – which sometimes means *if*), that move the argument on (*thus, so*) and which have shifted slightly in their use and significance (*but* meaning 'only', *yet* meaning 'still', *still* meaning 'continuously, always'). We can often clarify meanings by asking who or what demonstrative pronouns refer to. The excellent essay on short words by Sylvia Adamson, already mentioned on page 7, is especially helpful.

Ellipsis

At times young readers might be confused by ellipsis, a feature which, Blake remarks, 'helped to bring about the compression and pithiness which was so beloved of Elizabethans'.[6] A quick skip through *Romeo and Juliet* turns up the following:

> I have a soul of lead/[which] So stakes me to the ground I cannot move.
> Here are the beetle brows [which] shall blush for me.
> The day is hot, the Capulets [are] abroad.

In such (and in more complex) cases we need to be ready to expand the grammar – to supply the missing parts – if there appears to be a possibility of misunderstanding.

A more physical approach

A lively exercise used by the late Rex Gibson[7] can be used to highlight key elements of the grammar and, therefore, the meaning of a passage. After an initial reading, the teacher fires a series of questions that can serve to bring out, without being terminologically explicit about it, the grammatical structure (the what or who does what to what or who, how, why, where and when). The questions can be used to highlight noun phrases, verbs, adjectives and adverbial phrases – or more particularly their function within the given sentence – as seems appropriate:

Pupils   Is this a dagger that I see before me?
Teacher   Is this a WHAT?
Pupils   A DAGGER!
Teacher   That you see WHERE?
Pupils   BEFORE ME!

There's still, I suppose, the potential problem that some pupils might understand 'before me' as temporal rather than spatial (which is the kind of thing that we can easily not notice). With careful selection this exercise can point the relation between words in a passage, giving pupils a firmer grasp of the syntax and therefore the situation.

This approach may even be used to make clear the meaning of more grammatically complex passages:

Teacher   WHO is worthy to be a rebel?
Pupils   The merciless Macdonwald.
Teacher   WHY?
Pupils   For that the multiplying villainies of nature swarm upon him.
Teacher   WHAT swarm upon him?
Pupils   The multiplying villainies of nature
Teacher   WHAT do they do?
Pupils   Swarm upon him.
Teacher   Upon WHOM?
Pupils   The merciless Macdonwald.
Teacher   WHAT is he worthy to be?
Pupils   A rebel.

Another favourite of Rex Gibson's was drawing attention to deixis, any words that refer to (and can only be understood in) the immediate spatial set-up – *here, there, you, me, that, this* – and can therefore be accompanied by a pointing gesture. With the deictic element, this approach to grammar can become very physical and move imperceptibly into staging (see pages 92–3).

Kinds of sentence

We shouldn't just consider grammar as a source of difficulty, however. Even through quite an elementary approach it can help us to show our pupils how some of Shakespeare's dramatic power is achieved. A useful tool when looking at some scenes is to draw attention to Shakespeare's deployment of different kinds of sentence – declarative (statement), interrogative (question), imperative (command), exclamative. Sometimes we see a sustained build-up of questions, as in Hamlet's first speech to the ghost, which culminates on the line 'Say, why is this? wherefore? and what should we do?' At times we might note a variety of sentence types in play in even a quite short passage:

Hamlet	The air bites shrewdly: it is very cold.
Horatio	It is a nipping and an eager air.
Hamlet	What hour now?
Horatio	I think it lacks of twelve.
Marcellus	No, it is struck.
Horatio	Indeed I heard it not.

(This is how it appears in the Folio; modern editions tend to have the sharper 'Indeed? I heard it not'. Quite a different emphasis.) The switch between supportive and contradictory statements and a question help build up the air of nervous anticipation.

In the scene of Banquo's ghost, a study of Macbeth's rapid shifts between the four kinds of sentence – and, for more sophisticated pupils, through declarations, boasts, challenges, lies – can lead to an enhanced grasp of the drama (and of Macbeth's psychology).

Note the sequence of imperatives in Romeo's speech to Balthazar at the tomb:

> *Give* me that mattock and the wrenching iron,
> *Hold take* this letter, early in the morning
> *See* thou deliver it to my Lord and father
> *Give* me the light; upon thy life I charge thee
> Whate'er thou hear'st or see'st, *stand* all aloof,
> And *do not interrupt* me in my course.

And too soon marr'd are those so early made:	– *inversion ('Those so early made are too soon marr'd')*
The earth hath swallowed all my hopes but she,	– *single line main clause, no inversion*
She is the hopeful Lady of my earth:	– *single line main clause, no inversion***
But woo her gentle Paris, get her* heart,	– *two imperatives (each a half line)*
My* will to her consent, is but a part.	– *single line main clause (noun phrase/subject 'My will to her consent')*
And she agreed,	– *elliptical adverbial ('she being agreed', 'when she is agreed', 'if she is agreed')*
within her scope of choice	– *inversion ('My consent lies within her scope of choice')*
Lies my consent, and fair according voice:	– *does 'fair according voice' attach to 'choice' or 'consent'?*
This night I hold an old accustom'd feast ...	– *adverbial + single line main clause, no inversion*

* Emphasis here can help us to get the grammar and the sense right: 'get *her* heart' (rather than 'her *heart*', which is probably the most likely stress on a first reading) i.e. never mind mine, that's not what comes first – '*my* will to her consent is only part of what you need'. Some will argue, however, that this disruption of the pentameter should be avoided.
** The lines are effectively bound together by the rhetorical figure of antimetabole: 'earth ... she/she .... earth'.

Figure 4.1 Example of grammatical analysis.

This helps us to focus on the note of urgency. Only the performative 'upon thy life I charge thee' (which hardly lessens the intensity) interrupts the sequence. Romeo moves on from this to a declarative sequence, explaining his purpose to Balthasar, and then returns via a further imperative ('therefore hence be gone') and through a conditional ('if') moves on to a sequence of threats. (After which, doesn't Balthasar's plain statement 'I will be gone sir, and not trouble ye' have a comic effect?)

With some classes in Key Stage 3 and Key Stage 4 we can extend this kind of account into a fuller analysis, preparatory to the kind of work that will be expected of them at A Level. In Figure 4.1, an annotated passage from Act 1 Scene 2 of *Romeo and Juliet*, Capulet is talking to Paris, a suitor for Juliet's hand. Unlike his wife, Capulet is in no hurry to see his daughter married, and suggests that Paris waits for two years as Juliet is 'yet a stranger to the world'. To Paris' objection that 'Younger than she are happy mothers made', Capulet replies 'And too soon marred'.

The grammatical analysis can help us see the dramatic curve, through opinion/admonition, sad reflection, restrained encouragement, explanation and information. Notes of this kind might be prepared by the teacher for use with the class, or more able pupils might be encouraged to prepare them for themselves.

Chapter 5

Metaphor

By the time that pupils have to read Shakespeare in any depth or detail they are expected to know what similes and metaphors are. The former are almost invariably easy to spot, but the latter may provide some difficulties, especially if they are, as often in Shakespeare, not decorative, not easily detachable from their contexts, but intrinsic to thought and feeling, constitutive rather than illustrative of what is said. Sometimes the metaphors are touched on so lightly they may be hardly noticed, at others they are developed at length, in language of great complexity which makes grasp of the metaphor difficult.

Three other caveats are also in order. First, there is a danger that in explaining ('translating') metaphors for our pupils we may end up with something *less* than the metaphor, and that we may prevent the metaphor from working in the pupils' imaginations. Sometimes we should explore rather than explain. Second, we must beware of overdoing the common impression that metaphors are primarily visual (which we reinforce by speaking of 'images' or 'word pictures'). Where a metaphor *is* primarily visual, the 'illustration' approach – asking pupils to draw the meaning – can be productive; where they are not, it can be misleading. Some metaphors are as much to do with touch and bodily sense as with vision ('*endart* mine eye', 'Our fears in Banquo *stick deep*'). Some have almost a narrative import: 'Now old desire doth on his death-bed lie,/And young affection gapes to be his heir'. While 'gapes' has an undoubted visual element, it is not confined to it. Finally, we must always remain aware that the metaphor does not work in isolation from other qualities of language (rhythm and sound – 'creeps in this petty pace') that are also constitutive of its meaning.

Exploration of Shakespearean metaphor needn't wait to begin until we are 'doing' Shakespeare. When we're working on recognizing and understanding metaphor with, say, a Year 8 class, or extending GCSE pupils' awareness of metaphor's potential, there's no reason why at least some of our examples shouldn't come from Shakespeare. There are plenty of passages that can be taken in isolation as poems or as brief narratives and

studied for their use of language. We might choose to take what is in effect
a complete poem – the song from *Cymbeline*, or just its first verse:

> Fear no more the heat o' th' sun,
> > Nor the furious winter's rages,
> Thou thy worldly task hath done,
> > Home art gone and tae'n thy wages.
> Golden lads and girls all must,
> As chimney-sweepers, come to dust.

This could be treated as a riddle: what, from this verse, do we know
about the person being sung to? Or, to make it easier: 'The person they're
singing to is dead, but I think we know that from the song anyway.
What are the clues?' Why are lads and girls 'golden'? What's the significance of 'dust'?

Or – probably with an older class – we might look at an excerpt
of blank verse that can be fairly free-standing, such as Romeo's lines
on love:

> Here's much to do with hate, but more with love:
> Why then, O brawling love, O loving hate,
> O any thing, of nothing first created:
> O heavy lightness, serious vanity,
> Misshapen chaos of well-seeming forms,   5
> Feather of lead, bright smoke, cold fire, sick health,
> Still waking sleep, that is not what it is:
> This love feel I, that feel no love in this.
> Love is a smile made with a fume of sighs,
> Being purged, a fire sparkling in lovers' eyes,   10
> Being vex'd, a sea nourished with loving tears,
> What is it else? a madness, most discreet,
> A choking gall, and a preserving sweet.

Each phrase can be looked at independently; once we've seen that basically
this is an accumulating list (that the syntax is about as simple as can be)
then it doesn't matter too much if we don't pay them equal attention. We
can pick out, according to the nature of the class and our present purposes, phrases that can quite easily be grasped ('madness'), those that are
more complex ('serious vanity') and those that are, on the face of it, down-
right baffling ('feather of lead'). We might consider how important the
visual elements are in lines 10 and 11, and the appeals to other senses and
to the mind in other phrases. After some initial work on one or two chosen

phrases, pairs could work on a phrase each, leading to plenary discussion. Then they might write their own poems developing one of Romeo's phrases. (Here's a crazy thought: why not do this in a PHSE lesson?)

More syntactically and metaphorically complex is Macbeth's speech after he learns of the death of his wife (which might be used in a selection of pieces on life and death). Here we have metaphors within metaphors, a development through the senses of life as a journey, a manuscript, a stage play, a narration, with an inset apostrophe to life as a candle:

> To-morrow, and to-morrow, and to-morrow,
> Creeps in this petty pace from day to day,
> To the last syllable of recorded time:
> And all our yesterdays have lighted fools
> The way to dusty death. Out, out brief candle,
> Life's but a walking shadow, a poor player,
> That struts and frets his hour upon the stage,
> And then is heard no more. It is a tale
> Told by an idiot, full of sound and fury
> Signifying nothing.

To anticipate a discussion in my epilogue, this use of language enables so much more to be said than can be done by, for instance, saying 'life is shit'. (Which, by the by, it isn't: we mustn't forget the dramatic context of Macbeth's utterance, although commentators often do.)

When, reading Shakespeare in class, we encounter metaphors *in situ* we may or may not choose to dwell on them. Sometimes it's interesting to see how a metaphor develops out of what precedes it. Here Queen Elizabeth counters Richard's disingenuous claim not to have killed the Prince in the Tower:

> Whose hand soever lanced their tender hearts,
> Thy head, all indirectly, gave direction:
> No doubt the murderous knife was dull and blunt
> Till it was whetted on thy stone-hard heart,
> To revel in the entrails of my lambs.   5
> But that* still use of grief makes wild grief tame,
> My tongue should to thy ears not name my boys
> Till that my nails were anchor'd in thine eyes;
> And I, in such a desperate bay of death,
> Like a poor bark, of sails and tackling reft,   10
> Rush all to pieces on thy rocky bosom.

* *But that*: 'If it wasn't for the fact that'

The anatomical sequence 'hand–head–heart–entrails–tongue–nails–eyes–bosom' keeps the speech intensely physical. The pause at the end of line 5 leaves us focusing on the appalling significance of 'revels' before Elizabeth leaves her first metaphor behind. Via the verbal violence of 'anchor'd' (which surely is kinetic rather than visual) she proceeds to the sustained metaphor of shipwreck that concludes the speech. This metaphor contains the simile 'like a poor bark' (so *where* is the 'desperate bay of death'?); and the speech ends with her (imagined) physical contact with Richard, in which 'stony' refers both to the rocks of the bay (literal within the metaphorical picture) and the obduracy of Richard's heart (metaphorical within the imagined literal picture) – on which the knife that killed her boys was whetted. Are we here seeing emotional and metaphorical development going hand in hand? Or have the metaphors remained, to some extent, emblematic, even decorative? With older students, and with gifted and talented pupils, there's no reason why some of our investigations may not go this deep. Given that much of metaphor works by ratio and analogy, there are forms of thought that may well appeal to logically minded pupils (who may not necessarily feel they have an affinity with 'English').

Sometimes we will decide that a particular metaphor is not to be focused on in a study of a scene that contains a great deal besides. Other metaphors, we might decide, are so important within the meaning of the play as a whole that we must, after careful preparation, dwell on them. These might include Romeo's apostrophe to death in the final act of *Romeo and Juliet* – the association between love and death having been so insistent throughout the play, or the metaphor of monstrous conception and birth that underlies so much of *Othello*, or the metaphors of disease that run through *Hamlet*.

Examples could (obviously) be multiplied. If one of our aims in teaching Shakespeare is to help young readers to grasp something of the variety, depth and power of Shakespearean metaphor, we will have to select our occasion and the metaphors that we are going to give full attention to carefully, and – as ever – know when to hurry on with minimal comment.

Chapter 6

Allusion

Everybody makes allusions, it's just that we often fail to notice them as such. It's worth introducing as a topic in its own right: Why *do* we quote and refer? Why don't we have to explain our allusions? What about private allusions which other people won't 'get'? This could lead to an exercise in historical imagination: what might have to be explained in four hundred year's time (Jade Goody, hip-hop, 'wicked'). With older students this could be developed in some detail: they could be given an early twenty-first-century text and some examples of scholarly editions of old texts which use different conventions for the explanatory apparatus. Their task would be to produce an edition of the text with scholarly annotations for readers in – say – two hundred years' time. However briefly we raise the issue, we can go on to refer to the allusions in Shakespeare as something quite straightforward in principle; while they present us with immediate difficulties, most of them can be cleared up by brief explanations (usually a marginal note). We do, however, need to consider what weight to give to particular allusions at particular times in our teaching.

The main areas of allusion in Shakespeare are of course classical and Christian. Our education system guarantees no particular knowledge of either. (Ian Robinson once argued that the first year of an undergraduate course in English Literature should consist entirely of the study of 'Shakespeare, the English Bible, and three different English versions of Homer'.)[1] The Christian references in some cases will be specifically doctrinal. They may be either explicit, as in Henry IV's allusion to Christ:

> Over whose acres walked those blessed feet
> Which fourteen hundred years ago were nail'd
> For our advantage on the bitter Cross.

They can also be less so, as in Isabella's appeal to Angelo:

> Why, all the souls that were, were forfeit once,
> And He that might the vantage best have took
> Found out the remedy.

These both require an understanding of the doctrine of the Atonement, which (for non-Christian members of the class) will require more than a footnote. We touch here on a subject of enormous importance. If we're studying *Measure for Measure* at A level, doubtless this element must be explored in relation to the play. In the case of *Henry IV*, say at GCSE, it may be thought less integral – unless it is seen as framing the significance of the whole play. Further, we may consider, regardless of belief, that the doctrine is of such importance in the history of Europe that we must give time to it to enhance our students' historical understanding. Or, believing, we may wish our students to know of it for their souls' sake. In no other case does – can – the question of allusion touch on such a serious matter.

The range of classical allusions is arguably bittier, more miscellaneous, and it requires a lot of glosses in the margin. The question is how much and what kind of attention we need to pay to them on any given occasion – pausing to explain or draw attention to a note, or inviting a fuller consideration.

Sometimes how easy allusions are to understand will depend on the relation they bear to the speeches in which they occur – whether they are illustrative and therefore detachable, or whether they are more deeply related to the thought being expressed. The former can be illustrated from the soliloquy in Act 3 Scene 2 of *Henry VI Part 3* in which Richard, Duke of Gloucester, enlarges on his powers of deception and destruction:

> Why, I can smile, and murder whiles I smile,
> And cry 'Content' to that which grieves my heart,
> And wet my cheeks with artificial tears,
> And frame my face to all occasions.

So far the going is plain enough. However, in the lines that follow there are eight references (one per line) to mythology and folklore, only two of which are likely to be in the knowledge of a secondary school pupil:

> I'll drown more sailors than a mermaid shall,
> I'll slay more gazers than the basilisk,
> I'll play the orator as well as Nestor,
> Deceive more slily than Ulysses could,
> And like a Sinon, take another Troy.
> I can add colours to the chameleon,
> Change shapes with Proteus, for advantages,
> And set the murderous Machiavel to school.

In one sense this is still plain sailing in that each reference stands in the same relation to the main point, each being just another example, so it's straightforward enough, if tiresome, to explain each in turn. Furthermore, each line could be removed without obvious damage to the overall sense – we could provide an edited version that reduced these lines, or removed them altogether, so that comprehension is not slowed down over references that on face value are merely illustrative. (However, in some contexts it might be worth considering whether or not the *sequence* of examples is in any way significant, what composite picture they create, how closely or loosely put together the lines really are.) This kind of cultural reference presents no real difficulties.

More deftly managed, but not dissimilar in principle, are the references in Hamlet's first soliloquy when he speaks of his mother being 'like Niobe, all tears' and Claudius as being 'no more like my father,/Than I to Hercules'. (Thanks to television, some of our pupils may have some sort of idea about Hercules.) The references can't be excised without real damage to the speech, but once they are explained the meaning is quite clear. Hamlet's speech to his mother about his father is, like Gloucester's, a list, but more subtle and varied in its syntax and rhythms:

> See what a grace was seated on this brow,
> Hyperion's curls, the front of Jove himself,
> An eye like Mars, to threaten or command,
> A station like the herald Mercury,
> New-lighted on a heaven-kissing hill:
> A combination, and a form indeed
> Where every god did seem to set his seal,
> To give the world assurance of a man.

Sometimes such allusions will recur throughout a play, having obviously a more than occasional significance; for instance the appearance of Hercules and Cupid throughout *Much Ado*. In such a case we might decide to spend longer on it rather than just glossing briefly as we read, perhaps along these lines:

1　Pupils research Adam, Cupid and Hercules. What are the essentials of each figure? Why are they important?

2　In pairs or threes find all the references to Adam, Cupid and Hercules in specified scenes. For each reference: quote, give line numbers, identify who makes the reference, provide an explanation for what is said.

3　Plenary discussion: what important aspect of the three figures is stressed? Which of the three is most significant? Is it significant who makes the references? What other points arise from this investigation?

4　Pupils write about the importance of these mythical figures, explaining why they are mentioned so often, supporting their points by quotations and detailed commentary.

5   Final question for class discussion: would it be better to cut these references in a performance for a modern audience?

A more 'embedded' use of allusion can be illustrated from the first scene of *Twelfth Night*:

Curio   Will you go hunt my Lord?

Orsino   What Curio?

Curio   The hart.

Orsino   Why so I do, the Noblest that I have:

O when mine eyes did see Olivia first,

Me thought she purg'd the air of pestilence;

That instant was I turn'd into a Hart,

And my desires like fell and cruel hounds,

Ere since pursue me.

Here the reference to the story of Actaeon and Diana is not fully explicit, as neither name appears, nor is it merely illustrative. The metaphor renders the intensity and the self-division that Orsino's love has instantaneously brought about (*'my* desires ... pursue *me'*). The h(e)art that he hunts is (part of) himself. This suggests an element of pain and perplexity which might make it a little harder to condemn him for being in love with being in love – unless we pursue the unsympathetic reading and see it as *display* (and point out that he is muddling his metaphors a bit).

Is it enough to consider the lines at this level with a class? There is, after all, plenty to consider, whether at Key Stage 3 or 4. Or do we – so to speak – exhume the allusion and also look at the implied equation of Olivia and Diana? (Since it does not appear to be sustained throughout the play, I suspect not – although the opposition between the appreciative surge of admiration and the thrust of anger at inferred cruelty appears again in the final scene when Orsino confronts Olivia.) Do we need to tell our class what happened to Actaeon, and ask them if they think that has a bearing on the situation here?

Practice in schools editions varies. Roma Gill explains the reference and suggests something of the application: 'Orsino compares himself with Actaeon'.[2] (This raises a question about levels of consciousness within a scripted character.) The edition produced by Coordination Group Publications (CGP) (of which more on page 47) goes the way of paraphrase, offering 'It was love at first sight. Since then thoughts of her have followed me everywhere'.[3] Is this level of understanding good enough even for Key Stage 3? If we think the Actaeon story is of deep importance to *Twelfth Night*, maybe it's worth dealing with it in its own right *before* beginning work on the play. Year 9 pupils who have researched the story and written their own modern variants have produced some work that is worthwhile in its own right. (One began, stunningly: 'The stars are wise. They believe in absolute justice. The true story must be known.')

In the next scene of *Twelfth Night* the Captain describes seeing Sebastian clinging to a piece of wood after the shipwreck:

> Where like Orion on the dolphin's back,
> I saw him hold acquaintance with the waves,
> So long as I could see.

In this case the simile seems merely illustrative – except of course that it might be said to ennoble or romanticize the vision of Sebastian and so encourages Viola, who gives the Captain gold for it, in a gesture that can seem to modern audiences comical. (I suggest that Olivia pays the kindness she sees in his gilding a not very promising lily. It would be in line with the poised and affectionate intelligence that she shows elsewhere in the play, and it is actable.) We might consider that Orion is not to be dwelt on, and there may be many such references that we decide to pass over quickly.

There are passages in which it might not be obvious that – or it might be arguable whether – an allusion is being made. When in *Richard III* Act 1 Scene 2 Anne, presumably taking (or being made to take) the ring that Richard offers her, says 'To take is not to give', some commentators argue that she refers specifically to the marriage service's 'giving and taking of a ring', and that recognition of this is essential to grasping her meaning. In such cases schools' editions probably won't supply a note. Would we?

A further thought: when we are looking at the programme of work for a year or a Key Stage, it's worth considering how various units in it might relate to the study of the chosen Shakespeare play (or scenes). For instance, should the presence of key allusions in the Year 9 Shakespeare play influence our choice of the myths and legends we tackle in the previous years?

Chapter 7

Rhetoric

In Shakespeare's time training in uses of language was not linguistics (a modern enterprise which got under way, after a few bumpy starts, in the early twentieth century), but rhetoric.[1] Schoolboys at the time learned the various figures of sound, grammar and meaning. Particularly in Shakespeare's earlier plays, these occur in abundance. Therefore it may be that a (necessarily sketchy) introduction to some of them may be helpful to our pupils and students. A few notes are offered here together with some suggested activities.

While we are studying a play with a class we might notice that a particular rhetorical figure crops up fairly frequently, and decide that it is worth giving it a lesson or two's attention in its own right. For instance, when studying *Much Ado* pupils might be asked to hunt the antithesis. The teacher introduces pupils to the rhetorical figure of antithesis by showing and discussing this example:

she hath often dreamt of unhappiness and waked with laughing

Note that it's based on a pair of opposites built into two phrases of the same construction:

dreamt – waked   unhappiness – laughing
            dreamt of unhappiness – waked with laughing

Then she moves on to another, more complex example:

doing in the figure of a lamb the feats of a lion

Again, the antithesis is built on a pair of opposites and the linking is of two grammatically parallel phrases, but now the figures are metaphorical (or emblematic) and enhanced by cross-alliteration:

figure – feats   lamb – lion

With this example there is more scope for discussion in drawing out the second of the pairs at some length, considering the qualities of 'lamb' and 'lion' that come into play.

Sometimes the antithesis is much simpler, not elaborated at all:

> neither sad, nor sick

(Once again, note the alliteration.) Sometimes the antithesis doesn't work out quite as expected:

> I had rather be a canker in a hedge than a rose in his –

We might expect 'garden', but even that doesn't quite stand in direct antithesis to 'hedge' (unless we are to imagine a wild hedge). How does the actual word – 'grace' – stand in relation to 'hedge'? 'Canker'–'rose' is much more straightforward.

After this introduction, pupils can work in pairs to find and analyse more examples. When some have been collected and discussed, a plenary session can consider: Are some characters more given to antithesis than others? How is antithesis used in the service of wit, anger, explanation, cleverness, etc? In each case, what's the *effect*? Finally, pupils can experiment with antithesis in their own writing.

Similarly students studying *Hamlet* can be asked to hunt the hendiadys (in which the idea is presented in two expression – e.g. 'rank and gross', 'morn and liquid dew') – as long as we don't just stop at noting their occurrence and frequency. What are they *doing*? Simon Palfrey has some interesting things to say about hendiadys – among other things.[2]

Sometimes we might stop in our reading to note, comment on and even play with a particular structure that occurs just once – for instance in this exchange from *Twelfth Night*:

> Olivia   What's a drunken man like, fool?
>
> Feste   Like a drown'd man, a fool, and a mad man: one draught above heat, makes him a fool, the second mads him, and a third drowns him.

I once tried this out with a Year 9 class. They found it hard to stick quite to the pattern – not getting the sense of a process through three stages – but I still think it was worth doing, because it's brief and concentrated and asks them to think about analogies, structures and processes. Some of the more successful examples include an interesting try by Natalie:

> What's a young man like, fool?
> Like an unripe fruit, like a sour grape, or even like a sour orange. The fruit unable to be eaten, the grape to be left to age, and the orange impatient to be sweet.

(This might take us on to Malvolio's attempt at wit when introducing Cesario.) More aware of the idea of process was Janina:

> What's a vengeful man like, fool?
> Like a sly fox, a precise executor and a lost sheep. He prepares his plan carefully and secretively, he follows it out properly and efficiently, but ends up lost when he realizes revenge does not taste as sweet as he first thought.

And Lisa subverted the whole exercise nicely with:

> What's a fool like, fool?
> Like me, like me and like me. He is asked a philosophical question, gives a silly answer, and is laughed at.

The use of a certain figure, such as oxymoron, may lead us to consider questions of characterization in relation to the expression of emotion. Romeo's parade of contradictions in Act 1 Scene 1 – 'heavy lightness, serious vanity … bright smoke, cold fire, sick health' – may strike us as on the one hand self-indulgent and tricksy-clever, the adornments of fashionable passion, or on the other as explorations of a complex emotional state – or possibly as both. (That is, if we don't take them as poetic experiments of the youthful Shakespeare.) If we decide they are self-indulgent, do we decide the same for Juliet's 'beautiful tyrant, fiend angelical … A damnèd saint, an honourable villain'? We could move on further here to consider Othello's attempt at self-evaluation: 'an honourable murderer, if you will'. Arguably here the oxymoron is an attempt to express what Othello at least feels to be a genuinely paradoxical condition, although some might consider it self-deception. Othello, who comes to regard his chaste wife as 'the fair devil', could be said to occupy the ground mapped out by the oxymoron – less paradoxically stated here: 'O thou weed:/Who art so lovely fair, and smell'st so sweet,/That the sense aches at thee,/Wouldst thou had'st never been born'. We should feel the full force of that 'aches'. I think we feel more agony in Claudio's lines to Hero – 'But fare thee well, most foul, most fair; farewell/Thou pure impiety and impious purity' – than we do with Romeo.

On occasions, we might introduce a selection of rhetorical figures, showing the class definitions of a select dozen or so. For instance:

Anadiplosis	repetition of the last words of a clause at the beginning of the next
Anaphora	repetition of a word at the beginning of each of a sequence of clauses or phrases
Antanacasis	repetition of a word with variation of its meaning
Antimetabole	repetition of words in reverse order
Anexis	words arranged in ascending order of importance

Chiasmus	repetition of ideas in inverted order
Climax	like anadiplosis, but continuing through further stages
Epanalepsis	repetition of a word at the beginning and end of a line or sentence
Epistrophe[3]	repetition of the same words at the end of each of a sequence of words or phrases
Hyperbole	exaggeration
Isocolon	clauses of identical length and structure
Parison	symmetrical syntactical structures
Polyptoton	repetition of a word in a different grammatical form.

(As many of these terms describe some kind of repetition, with some classes 'repetition' might be sufficient as a technical term.) They could then go on to experiment with them in their own writing. Here's a piece by Emma produced after I had asked her Year 9 class to write a speech for Viola to woo Olivia with, using as many rhetorical figures as they could (I'd previously also mentioned the 'rule of three'):

> I have a message from the great Count Orsino whose generosity, handsomeness and power are nothing compared to his love for you, good Lady Olivia.
>
> He loves you in so many ways, countless, endless ways.
>
> He loves you more than bronze, silver, gold or any other precious material.
>
> He loves you like the first glimpse of hopeful sunshine after a lifetime of stormy misery.
>
> He loves you like the first flower appearing on a warm spring day after a long bare winter.
>
> His love for you is deeper than caverns, canyons or the endless oceans and stronger than man, beast or God above.
>
> He says your beauty is as radiant as the sun and as wondrous as Heaven.
>
> Your lips are as red as the reddest rose, your eyes as blue as a bright summer's sky. Your tumbling ringlets are like flaxen gold and your womanly figure like that of an angel.
>
> You are his sun, moon and Earth, his light at the end of the tunnel; his one, his true, his only love. Without you his life would cease to be joyous, happy and gay. Instead it would be tiresome, lonely and heart-breakingly sad.
>
> Please say that you, great, wise and beautiful Lady Olivia, feel even a little of these feelings as will return the love that Orsino gives, so openly, to you.

Of course this is highly artificial, and such techniques incorporated too consciously into a pupil's own writing might well produce insincerity; but as an isolated exercise it has its uses.

Without using specific rhetorical expressions, analysis of a passage can still go quite deep if we work in terms of what for the last twenty years or so we've been calling 'persuasive language'. (As if all language is not in some degree persuasive.) We can catalogue a number of persuasive techniques that are in the play and ask the class to go in search of them, or we can ask the class to prepare a list starting from scratch: 'What persuasive devices can you see at work in this scene?' A worked example follows, a set of teacher's notes on the two scenes set for the 2008 SAT on *Richard III* – work that could easily transfer to GCSE. The scenes are both two-handers: Richard's wooing of Lady Anne (Act 1 Scene 2) and his approach to Elizabeth for the hand of her daughter (Act 4 Scene 4).

1   *Insults*: Plentiful! Note that those directed at Richard use imagery of animals and devils. Are there more insults in the first SAT scene or the second? Advise pupils to look out particularly for the effect of *adjectives*.

2   *Compliments/flattery*: Note that Richard's compliments to Anne play on the heavenly and angelic. How does he flatter Elizabeth?

3   *Direct counter-insult*: In a head-to-head you'd expect a lot of these, as they are very common in real-life arguments (and in plays). But are there any in these scenes? And if not, why not?

4   *Returning a compliment for an insult*: 'Devils ... angels ...' [Which of these techniques is most frequent? Why?

5   *Returning an insult for a compliment*: 'Sweet saint ... Foul devil ...'

6   *Changing the subject/starting a new line of argument*:

   i   'But, gentle Lady Anne,/To leave this keen encounter of our wits/And fall something into a slower method ...'
   ii 'You speak as if that I had slain my cousins.'

   In the first case Richard is comfortably in control; in the second he is escaping from being wrong-footed. Are there any more examples?

7   *Twisting meaning of words, including puns/wordplay*: More common in 4.4, where Elizabeth does it a lot. 'Cousins, indeed! And by their uncle cozened.'

8   *Repeating the form of a sentence but twisting or reversing its meaning*: 'O wonderful, when devils tell the truth!'/'More wonderful, when angels are so angry.' 'at their birth good stars were opposite ... to their lives ill friends were contrary.'

9   *Antithesis*: Loads of examples – angel/devil, fairer/fouler, heaven/hell, death/life, sweeter/fouler, destiny/grace, head/hand ... Also the rhetorical figure of antithesis is found in whole lines –

   i   *Your* children *were* a *vexation* to your *youth*,
   ii But *mine shall be* a *comfort* to your *age*.

10 *Denial*: 'I did not kill your husband.'

11 *Evasion*: 'I will not be thy executioner.'

12 *Sarcasm*: Elizabeth's suggestion for wooing her daughter. Plenty of other examples in this scene. Any in 1.2?

13 *Rhetorical questions*: 'What were I best to say?' and the rest of the speech. Elizabeth often combines rhetorical questions and sarcasm. A point to raise with able pupils and sixth-formers: Can we be sure that her questions are rhetorical in every case? Might she be exploring the possibility of successful wooing?

14 *Simile*: Sun/beauty – arguably analogy rather than simile; 'like trees bedashed with rain'. Why is metaphor more common than simile in these scenes?

15 *Metaphor*: Drenched in it! Most of the insults are figurative in one way or another. Elizabeth's sustained use of metaphor is worth close study with an able group.

16 *Insinuation*: 'Never came poison from so sweet a place' – suggesting softness, intimacy, sex.

17 *Shock tactics*: 'Your bedchamber.' Did she see that coming?

18 *Accumulation – building-up of details, ideas (including lists)*: e.g. 'Of comfort, kingdom, kindred, life.'

19 *Appeals to feelings/exploitation of weakness*: Richard's offering of his breast for Anne to stab; Richard's appeal to Elizabeth's isolated position and loss of family.

20 *Developed argument/explanation/reasoning*: Attention needed here to the long speeches.

An analysis might also spread over a whole play, for instance in an exploration of styles in *Romeo and Juliet*, investigating the uses of: stichomythia; exchange of shorter units; puns and other wordplay; oxymoron; balances/ pairs/contrasts/parallel syntax; mere repetition; image chains or clusters. The class can consider:

- Where in the play are these styles to be found?
- What dramatic effect do they have in context?
- Are particular styles associated with particular characters?
- Where in the play do you find the strongest contrasts of style?
- Do you respond differently to the different styles?

An interesting passage to look at in this respect is the responses to Juliet's apparent death:

Nurse	She's dead: deceased, she's dead, alack the day.
Lady Capulet	Alack the day, she's dead, she's dead, she's dead.

Is this bad writing? Is the intent, as well as the effect, to be comical? Can the lines be saved in performance? During such a discussion the teacher might bring in Lear's terrible 'Never, never, never, never, never'. Why is that so unmistakably the expression of an intolerable grief?

There's nothing automatic or guaranteed about rhetorical devices. Identifying them is only a start. We need to consider what is *made* with them in the particular dramatic context. And why do some work so well that we may not even particularly notice them?

Chapter 8

Paraphrase

When I took A Level English the exam required us to put a passage from the set Shakespeare play into our own words, so we had to practise doing so. There was no pretence that what we produced was in any way to be preferred to the original, or even that we learned much from the process; the aim was simply to find out whether we understood what we'd been reading. This form of examining has largely disappeared, perhaps because of arguments like this from Michael Pafford:

> With Shakespeare, as with other poets, we will frequently have to paraphrase for children because the paraphrasable part of the sense of the language is often obscured for them by poetic compression or convention or archaism. We will, however, *never* ask them to paraphrase for us: as a testing device we do not need it because we can sense whether they have understood it or not: as a teaching exercise it is toxic to poetry in giving the impression that when you have said what it is saying in other words you have said all that it is saying.[1]

I'm not quite so sanguine about our ability to tell if they've understood or not. I was dumbfounded on one occasion by very able GCSE pupils who read sustained passages of Shakespeare fluently, with every appearance of understanding, and yet insisted they had no idea of what they meant. Pafford also begs the question (which should be in the background of all our thinking) of what *counts* as understanding Shakespeare. However, his warning is otherwise well made, especially with the insistence that we should not abet the feeling that paraphrase provides the 'real' meaning, something that Shakespeare either wilfully obscured or was only, as we so often gather from our GCSE pupils considering poetry, *trying* to say.

But paraphrase is among the teacher's – and editor's and critic's – necessary tools, as Pafford makes clear. It's often to be encountered in the explanatory notes offered on facing pages or in foot- or side-notes in many of the editions that are used in the classroom. At their best these are brief, deft and only used to clear up meanings that are obscured by grammatical or lexical obscurity or ellipsis.[2] But some offer to do more. For instance, Coordination Group Publications (CGP) publish versions of the SAT texts with gaily coloured cartoon illustrations. The strapline reads: 'The complete play together with handy hints and notes.' These notes are a combination of glossed words and phrases and loose paraphrases of whole sentences. Looking at their notes on the opening of *Twelfth Night* Act 1 Scene 3 can illustrate some pitfalls of this approach. The text reads:

> *Sir Toby*   What a plague means my niece to take the death of her brother thus? I am sure care's an enemy to life.
>
> *Maria*   By my troth Sir Toby, you must come in earlier a' nights: your cousin, my Lady, takes great exceptions to your ill hours.
>
> *Sir Toby*   Why, let her except, before excepted.

This is Sir Toby's first appearance in the play. Shakespeare brings him on with a resounding declaration of his utterly insensitive selfishness, for which he has the nerve to give philosophic justification. CGP renders his first speech 'Olivia's mourning spoils all our fun'. The advantage of this is that it moves us on, enables a quick 'reading'. The disadvantage is a palpable loss of expressive force by offering a single declarative sentence in the place of an indignant question and a hearty avowal. Lurking somewhere here is the notion that language is for making statements, giving information – although it may be information about how we're feeling. This notion narrows the immense range of what language is used for in Shakespeare. Sir Toby's character note is not sounded. (If we *must* give a written paraphrase, 'Why the bloody hell is Olivia still moping about the place? Taking life too seriously just spoils it' might be more like it.) The immediate identification of Sir Toby as Olivia's uncle is also delayed. I suspect that this is a case in which the paraphrase is lexically and grammatically so far removed from the original that children may have difficulty seeing it *as* a paraphrase.

Maria's 'Your cousin, my lady, takes great exceptions to your ill hours' becomes 'Olivia doesn't like you coming in late at night'. 'Ill hours' of course means far more than that, and anyway Maria has already referred to his late nights. We lose 'your cousin, my lady', which explains with swift economy who Maria and (again) Sir Toby are and are perhaps needed to get Toby's attention. Also by these substitutions the 'let her except, before excepted' joke isn't properly set up.[3]

At least the CGP glosses don't pretend equivalence to Shakespeare's text, unlike the *Shakespeare Made Easy* series which, despite its quite proper disclaimers, can have the appearance of offering its full facing-page 'translations' as somehow equivalent to the play. Perhaps because of the wholesale approach, almost *everything* is rephrased, whether it needs to be or not. Some early reviews of the series showed beyond doubt that the language of the translations is barely English and often unwittingly hilarious. These reviews established what should have been obvious, yet the series remains in print, so it must continue to be popular with pupils and teachers. There is a place here for a reminder of its shortcomings.

Take the first scene of *Macbeth*. Firstly, the opening couplet is altered by a single word:

(Shakespeare)	*(Made Easy)*
When shall we three meet again?	When shall we three meet again?
In thunder, lightning or in rain?	In thunder, lightning and in rain?

The 'and' may be better meteorology but it has the unfortunate effect of turning the lines into an enquiry about the weather. In the Folio the lines are made up of *two* questions, the second raising for the alert audience the question: For what kinds of creatures are thunder and lightning *alternatives*? In *Made Easy* a certain trivializing has taken place; the lines are less mysterious.

In the second witch's reply, 'hurlyburly' stays intact. But surely that word will not be plain to a young audience? Shouldn't it, on the principle of the series, be glossed (after all, as we'll see in a moment, 'Greymalkin' didn't survive). Shakespeare's 'There to meet with Macbeth' allows the possibility of a slight pause before the name is uttered, whereas the awkwardly alliterative 'meet Macbeth' garbles the rhythm and gives no proper prominence to a name being heard for the first time. (For those experiencing the play for the first time, 'Macbeth' is the name of someone who will be met with by witches.) It's hard to see any justification of the change. Then:

(Shakespeare)	*(Made Easy)*
– I come, Graymalkin.	– I'm coming, Cat!
– Paddock calls.	– The Toad calls!
– Anon.[4]	– Coming!

What's needed here at some point is an explanation about witches' familiars. These substitutions don't explain anything, they just raise another question. As for 'Coming!' – it sounds like hide and seek.

Finally, an extra and altogether unnecessary 'we' is added to the final couplet:

Fair is foul, and foul is fair.
We hover through the fog and filthy air.[5]

Two statements are given in place of an incantation and an imperative; the full stop neatly separates them where the Folio gives a comma. The first statement, bereft of its rhythmic setting, becomes plainly false rather than mysterious; the second invites the response 'Go on then; I'd like to see that'. 'They disappear', says the stage direction. And well they might.

The first thing to do with this scene in the classroom is to get the children to *say* it – again and again until they know it. Explore the rhythms. Let 'Graymalkin', 'Paddock' and 'hurlyburly' (great words to get your tongue round) remain for a while as part of the mystery of the scene. A footnote on each of these words can be given at some point, or we can tell the pupils if they ask, but let's not rush in to reduce this scene's dramatic import by explanation. Talk about what 'fair is foul' might mean, and how a battle can be 'lost and won'. Learn it. Perform it.

In the next scene, which is genuinely difficult in ways which the first is not, 'Except they meant to bathe in reeking wounds/Or memorise another Golgotha' becomes 'As if they meant to swim in blood or copy Calvary'.[6] 'Bathe' and 'swim' have quite different suggestions. 'Calvary' will probably need explanation as much as 'Golgotha', and explanation of the latter can include giving the translation – Golgotha: the place of the skull – that will enhance the sense of atmosphere. The skipping alliteration of 'copy Calvary' trivializes.

There are huge lapses in tone: Duncan's 'great happiness' becomes 'Splendid!'. And finally, the scene ends with 'Cawdor's loss is noble Macbeth's gain!',[7] so that we miss the chime with the sisters' 'lost and won' in 'What he hath lost noble Macbeth has won'. In neither of these cases is there any *need* for paraphrase.

This analysis could be protracted. The shortcomings of the kind highlighted here are probably inevitable when trying to provide a continuous version that can be read, without interruptions for explanation, as a dramatic script. But too often the paraphrases themselves are in need of explanation, or seriously distort Shakespeare's dramatic language. If we want to give our classes a dramatic experience first, it's probably best to use a carefully edited script (see page 56) rather than a continuous paraphrase.

A further disadvantage of using fixed paraphrases is that of encouraging the habit of looking for the meaning elsewhere than in Shakespeare's words, and increasing the pupils' suspicion that poetry is a matter of 'hidden meanings'. Further there is a danger that, rather than using the paraphrase to get them back into the text, they work with the paraphrase itself, sometimes even quoting it instead of the text in their essays (and so, possibly, in exams).

When trying to worry out the sense of some passages which at first look fairly straightforward a combination of explanation and paraphrase is essential. For instance, in *Richard III* Act 1 Scene 2, in which Richard is wooing the lady Anne, he responds to her exclamation that he is 'unfit for any place but hell' and the exchange develops as follows:

Richard Yes, one place else, if you will hear me* name it.
Anne Some dungeon.

Richard	Thy bedchamber.
Anne	Ill rest the chamber where thou liest.
Richard	So will it madam, till I lie with you.
Anne	I hope so.
Richard	I know so.

* hear me: permit me to?

Apart from 'Ill rest the chamber' this appears to presents few lexical or grammatical difficulties. The natural tendency to look for declarative sentences as the norm may lead some pupils to read 'Ill rest' as a noun phrase, which leaves a gagagram, so a note may be needed to make clear that the line is a performative. (The Longman School edition gives 'Bad sleep come to …'.) Some of my Year 10 class misread 'Ill rest' as 'I'll rest' and understood the line to mean 'I'll rest in the room that you're lying in'. Once these points were cleared up, what really bothered them was Anne's 'I hope so', a line apparently perfectly straightforward in its monosyllabic directness. Why should she, apparently, hope that her having sex with Richard will bring his ill rest to an end? The paraphrase that I made *with* the class (not *for* them) was:

- I hope that you'll never get a good night's sleep.
- I won't, madam, until I have sex with you.
     (Richard cunningly slips from one sense of 'lie' to another.)
- I hope that's true, because you'll never have sex with me and so you'll never enjoy rest.

Paraphrase is useful as a tool later in the scene when trying to come at the import of Anne's response here:

Richard	Vouchsafe to wear this ring.
Anne	To take is not to give.

Anne's expression is perfectly clear as a statement, but we might ask why she responds in such a gnomic fashion: why this near-proverbial utterance, without a trace of the first, second or third person? What might we take her to mean by it here? What is her underlying intention? Here are some possibilities, which are to do with *tone* as much as anything:

- Just because I'm taking this ring, don't think that you've won me over.
- Well all right, but don't expect anything.
- You do realize, don't you, that while I may have got this ring in my hand I have made no commitment whatsoever, nor will I.
- I'm beginning to come round, but don't get your hopes up just yet.

• You've put me in a very awkward position, but you should understand that thrusting a ring into my hand achieves nothing.

Are we seeing and hearing equivocation, self-deception, firm resistance, dignified rejection or a last half-hearted attempt to hold out? (Should the possible allusion mentioned on page 38 be taken to decide the question?) Of course performance here will also raise the question of *how* Richard offers the ring, and how Anne takes it. This is discussed further on page 99.

As this example suggests, paraphrase is useful in trying to explicate not only passages that are on the face of it obscure, but also passages in which, although the plain sense presents no particular difficulty, the context makes likely undertones that render the sense less apparently straightforward. That is, when we feel that there is sub-text to deal with. Before the duel Hamlet asks, 'Have all these swords a length?' Is he consciously saying, and will he be understood to be saying 'Am I to expect cheating and treachery? Is the fight rigged?' At times we will be able to bring such possibilities of meaning out through (leading?) questions, encouraging consideration of emphasis, implication, undertones, hints and suggestions.

The upshot of these considerations is that such resources should be used, if at all, sparingly and with circumspection – certainly not *instead* of what we as teachers can offer our classes. When we use a schools' edition that offers facing-page glosses, we must look at them and see how well they do their job, and be prepared to supplement them appropriately. We need to be aware that the glosses do not always mention some of the things that bother our pupils, and we must develop our own ability to explain on the spot. In whole class work, paraphrase is most usefully done orally. It's a good idea not to offer a fixed paraphrase but to shoot around the target a bit, suggesting a range of possibilities, particularly with regard, where appropriate, to tone/nuance (see the discussion on the passage from *Richard III* above), asking some questions. What we offer shouldn't always be at the level of the proposition ('He's saying that ...'); we need at times to make it clear what is exclamation, threat, promise, curse, quip, retort, etc. As there's no doubt that explanatory paraphrase breaks the flow of reading, we need to develop the skill of weaving in and out of the text, always coming back to the main dramatic import. Once there's been explication, read the passage again, letting the increased understanding inform the dramatic sense. Generally speaking, we should observe these guidelines:

• Don't just use, or refer children to, printed explanations.
• Use paraphrase tactically, combining it with other forms of explication.
• Paraphrase in more than one way/offer more than one paraphrase.
• Let it be clear that paraphrase is only a temporary tool: always go back to the text.

- Use paraphrase to explore tone and sub-text.
- Use paraphrase orally for the most part.

There is some place for written paraphrase, though. First, as already mentioned, it's used effectively in some of the better editions, usually only indicating the meaning of a phrase, especially where the grammatical construction is unfamiliar or unclear. Second, orally or in writing, we can give a paraphrase of some parts of a speech with the challenge 'Find me the bit that means something like ...' I've found that even some of the less able pupils are pretty quick with this. A more refined exercise is to offer two or three paraphrases of a section and ask which is the closest, and why. Finally, written paraphrase can be useful for familiarizing pupils with the basic argument of some long speeches, for instance the Friar's in *Much Ado* Act 4 Scene 1 (see page 60).

Chapter 9

Some strategies

This chapter outlines four techniques that can, used appropriately, enable close attention to Shakespeare's language.

Key lines

One way of easing pupils into the language is, after going through a summary of the plot, to invite them to relate selected lines to the plot summary: Which characters are likely to have said these things, in what circumstances? The aim is not to be right, but to make sense. The lines must be carefully selected in relation to the abilities of the class, keeping a balance between the obvious, so that they can succeed to some degree straight away, and the really quite difficult. The lines can also be chosen to focus on those aspects of the play that the teacher wants to focus on, whether it's the nature of love in *A Midsummer Night's Dream*, servanthood and slavery, or magic and power, in *The Tempest*, or passion and destiny in *Romeo and Juliet*. After the pupils have discussed and attempted justification of their answers, they will have an enhanced sense of the plot and will have begun to get the feel of some limited samples of the language. It may be best not to finish this discussion by giving the 'right' answers; instead leave the class to notice the lines as they come up in the reading of the play.

Sometimes a single line might be chosen to introduce work on a scene. Caesar's 'Such men are dangerous' is an interesting one to take out of context: Who might say this? What kind of men might be considered dangerous, and why? (A colleague and I once began work on *Julius Caesar* by strewing the classroom with copies of the line in various presentations and photographs and pictures of a variety of men who might or might not be considered dangerous.) Later the line is read in context. One advantage of doing this is that with no special stress being placed on doing so, pupils *learn* the line.

Eventually pupils should be invited to elect their own sentences/phrases: Which are the three most important lines in this scene? Why? (Or simply: which line do you like best? Practise saying it out loud.)

Find the responses

Another method is to give pupils slips, each containing a fragment of text, and inform them that another pupil has a fragment that goes with it. Their task is to go round reading each others' fragments until they have paired up and can give reasons for the pairing. The pairs of lines are then read out loud to the class and what makes them pairs is discussed. Pairs of various kinds can be prepared: question and answer, statement and response, echoed words and phrases, rhyme, syntactical parallels, development of metaphor, etc. A few examples from *A Midsummer Night's Dream*:

- The more I hate, the more he follows me.
- The more I love, the more he hateth me.

-                      You may perhaps think
  Because she is something lower than myself
  That I can match her.
-                      Lower? Hark, again!

- Your hands than mine are quicker for a fray
- My legs are longer, though, to run away!

- I would my father look'd but with my eyes.
- Rather your eyes must with his judgment look.

The method can work particularly well with a scene such as *Richard III* Act 1 Scene 2, which is almost entirely based on such exchanges and full of different forms of patterning. Pupils might be asked to diagram the connections they see, along these lines:

- *Never* came *poison* from *so* SWEET* *a* place.   } sentences have
- *Never* hung *poison* on *so* FOUL* *a* toad.   } the same shape

*OPPOSITES   *italics*: exactly the same (key words 'Never' and 'poison')

This can lead to a fuller consideration of the use of rhetorical devices in that scene.

Exercises can be devised at varying levels of challenge. Trios of lines can also be prepared, or lines that develop a metaphor or a train of thought.

Spot the difference

During revision, once pupils have a working knowledge of the play, one way of focusing attention on particular uses of words is to present lines that have had small alterations made in them. The changes from the original text can be made to provide potential discussion of the following points:

- *lexis*: Has the meaning of individual words been successfully preserved, substituting the more familiar substituted for the less familiar?
- *scansion*: Does the new word *fit*? (Has it the right number of syllables and does the stress fall in the right place?)
- *expressive force*: Is the new word *emotionally* right? (Is it too strong/not strong enough?)
- *sound*: Does the new word sound right in this context? Does it lose some feature of the original? Consider alliteration in particular.
- *period*: Is the substituted word too modern, sticking out like a sore thumb, just plain wrong?

A few examples from *Richard III*:

Altered line	*Original word*
Avaunt, thou *vile* minister of hell.	*dreadful*
Lady, you know no rules of charity, Which renders good for bad, *kindness* for curses …	*blessing*
If I thought that, I tell thee, *murderer*, These nails should *tear* that beauty from my cheeks.	*homicide* *rend*
Never hung poison on a fouler *frog*.	*toad*
Lo here I lend thee this sharp-pointed sword – Which if thou please to *stick* in this true breast …	*hide*
You have a daughter called Elizabeth, Virtuous and *foxy*, royal and *good-looking*.	*fair, gracious*
Cousins, indeed! And by their uncle *conned* …	*cozened*
Then know that from my *heart* I love thy daughter.	*soul*

And a couple from *The Tempest*:

… they all do hate him As *much* as I do.	*rootedly*
Monster, I do smell all *urine*, at which my nose is in great indignation.	*horse-piss*

The aim isn't necessarily to argue for the superiority of Shakespeare's choices – pupils may well prefer the substitutions and be able to give reasons for doing so – but to get them thinking about specific uses of language.

Editing

As texts of Shakespeare's plays are readily available on the internet (e.g. at http://shakespeare.mit.edu) it is feasible for the teacher to edit scenes down, shortening the more sustained speeches and removing, for instance, cultural references or complex metaphors that will slow down comprehension and so inhibit the immediate sense of drama. The occasional substitution of words for ease of comprehension may be defensible (for instance printing 'wedding day' instead of 'nuptial hour' in the first line of *A Midsummer Night's Dream*).

It's as well to keep blank verse lines intact, although we may have to put up with the occasional half-line. Using an edited text can be a means of giving a class a lively if attenuated experience of Shakespeare. It can also be used as an interim measure: the class get used to the action and the main feelings as represented by the edited version, and then read the fuller version (for which they sometimes state a preference). At some point it should probably be made clear to the class when an edited version is being used.

It can be very interesting to get pupils to consider what might be suitable in editing Shakespeare, especially for a younger audience. They can be challenged to remove ten lines from a passage (they needn't all be consecutive) that they consider surplus to requirements, and justify their choice. For more sustained and detailed work, small groups might each be given a portion of a scene and instructions along these lines:

> Prepare a text from this passage to be used as a script for an intelligent Year 6 class.
> Edit in this way:
>
> 1 Cut anything that you think (a) will be too difficult to understand, (b) is not essential to the scene. Remember that the main aim is to preserve as much of Shakespeare as possible in an enjoyable and accessible form.
> 2 Make small changes – a word here and there – that you think will make understanding and enjoyment of the scene easier for your audience.
> 3 Add stage directions – moves, gestures, expressions – that you think will clarify meaning.
>
> Discuss your changes before recording them on your copy of the text.

Chapter 10

Long speeches

As already noted, difficulties with Shakespeare's language rarely come singly, but in whole battalions, and nowhere is this more likely than in long speeches. For our pupils the very appearance on the page of a long speech may well be off-putting, especially for those who suddenly find that, sight blind, they are required to read one out loud (this is best avoided, but it often happens). For this reason it may be hard for them to experience such speeches as dramatic. Often they talk about the pace slowing down in longer passages. Further, as Pamela Mason writes:

> Since the eye tends to anticipate, the reader always knows (until just before the page turn) how much more a particular character has to say. There is, therefore, a temptation to impose a sense of structure that is essentially non-dramatic. However, when a character starts to speak on stage, an audience cannot know whether it will be a short speech or an extended utterance. Theatre works moment-by-moment and long speeches are built – they do not appear on stage ready assembled.[1]

Our work on long speeches must both assist comprehension and encourage a sense of the dramatic development. When we see a long speech coming up we need to decide if, on a first encounter, we are going to take the speech slowly and explore it in detail, or if we are just going to give (or invite the class to work out) the gist. It might be possible with some speeches to find key phrases or sentences that we choose to dwell on. Obviously our practice will vary according to our class, time and purpose, and any requirements imposed by forms of public assessment. However, in the remainder of this section it's assumed that we're dealing with whole speeches.

One way of approaching a long speech for the first time is to play a good audio recording. Audio is better than video for this purpose because there are no visual distractions from the sound of the words. Also film versions often cut – and even in some cases rearrange – long speeches; in Zeffirelli's *Romeo and Juliet*, Juliet's long soliloquy in Act 4 Scene 3 leading to her drinking of the potion is reduced to 'Ay, me'! The class hear the passage leading up to the speech, the speech and the passage leading away, *listening* rather than following in their books. They can then follow the impetus of the speech and feel it reaching its ending, rather than knowing that it still has so many lines to go, and can experience it as a response that is in turn responded to (in some cases long speeches following long speeches). The actor's pace and tone will encourage a more dramatic conception of the scene and will to some extent assist comprehension. The difficulty remains, however, that much of the speech may not be understood, so some form of detailed follow-up may well be necessary. Pupils are unlikely to 'get it' on one hearing, but having listened to it they will begin with some sense of the speech as drama.

The speech might then be presented on OHP or PowerPoint, revealed line by line or (better) clause by clause until it's all there. The teacher leads a class reading. Pupils join in at first with the bits that they feel confident reading, until a whole class reading has been built up. The dramatic element will be pointed by the varied pace, intonation and volume of the teacher's lead reading. This can then be extended by inviting pupils to thump their desks for emphasis on particular passages (repeated words for instance – 'banished' in Romeo's speech to the Friar in Act 3 Scene 3 – or lines with pronounced iambic emphasis), to *point* on deictic lines ('Thou, thou, Lysander'), or to devise a particular gesture for specific phrases, as here:

> Our revels now are ended. *These our actors,*
> As I foretold you, were all spirits and
> Are melted *into air*, into *thin air.*
> And, like the baseless fabric of *this vision,*
> *The cloud-capp'd towers, the gorgeous palaces,*
> *The solemn temples, the great globe itself,*
> Ye all which it inherit, *shall dissolve*
> And, like *this insubstantial pageant* faded,
> *Leave not a rack behind. We* are such stuff
> As dreams are made on, and our little life
> Is *rounded with a sleep.*

Further familiarization with the sound and progress of the speech can be established by getting the pupils to take it for a walk: each with a copy of the speech, they walk around the room, carefully avoiding each other but consciously trying to cover all the available ground and changing direction often (perhaps at the ends of sentences). As they do this, they read through the speech to themselves aloud, twice. This reading may be slow and considered or as quick as possible – or the teacher may vary the pace by calling out instructions. An additional feature might be that on the second reading the pupils direct lines to each passer-by.

Another well-established classroom method of reading a long speech, which has the advantage of relieving any one pupil of the burden of sustained public delivery, is to read it round the class, each pupil stopping at the next punctuation mark, like this:

Pupil 1	If it were done
Pupil 2	when 'tis done
Pupil 3	then 'twere well
Pupil 4	it were done quickly
Pupil 5	if th' assassination could trammel up the consequence
Pupil 6	and catch with his surcease
Pupil 7	success
Pupil 8	but that this blow might be the be-all and the end-all
Pupil 9	here
Pupil 10	but here
Pupil 11	upon this bank and school of time
Pupil 12	we'ld jump the life to come

The pupils can read from their copies of the play; alternatively, the teacher might choose to give the pupils cards with only their individual 'bits', which has the advantage of them not being distracted by what's on either side, or reading the wrong bit, or not stopping at the punctuation mark; and the even greater advantage that they have to *listen* to the speech as it develops.

This exercise can be fun (but then, should we find this dreadful speech 'fun'?) and, if the sequence is practised until it runs without inappropriate jerkiness, it can highlight such repetitions as 'here, but here', the chime of 'surcease/success' and, if we are lucky, something of the nervous, driven nature of Macbeth's thought. And the *sound* of it is well in their ears before they look more closely at the speech's meaning. (Of course with this method it may be difficult, depending on the speech and the relation of lines and clauses, to highlight the verse. On some occasions we may decide this is good enough reason for not using it.)

In relation to meaning it's vital to establish the context of the speech. What has prompted/provoked it? Is it a response to what has gone before, or does it start a new movement? Who is it directed to? Does the addressee change during the course of the speech? What is the speaker *doing* in this speech? (Arguing? Expressing feeling? Thinking? Buying time? Entertaining?) How is the speaker physically related to others on the stage? To the audience?

A useful approach is to divide the speech into paragraphs. We can either do this for our pupils, or invite them to do it and then discuss their suggestions. Where does the speaker change subject/tack? Why? What is the main point made in each paragraph? In relation to this it's helpful to emphasize key little words – connectives, prepositions and pronouns in

> 1. When people think Hero's dead, they will all mourn her. We always value what we've lost more than when we had it.

1 *She* dying, as it must so be maintain'd,
Upon the instant that she was accused,
Shall be lamented, pitied and excused
Of every hearer: for it so falls out
That what *we* have we prize not to the worth
Whiles *we* enjoy it, but being lack'd and lost,
Why, then *we* rack the value, then *we* find
The virtue that possession would not show us
Whiles it was ours.

2 *So* will it fare with Claudio:
When *he* shall hear *she* died upon his words,
The idea of her life shall sweetly creep
Into his study of imagination,
And every lovely organ of her life
Shall come apparell'd in more precious habit,
More moving-delicate and full of life,
Into the eye and prospect of his soul,
Than when she lived indeed.

> 2. So Claudio will remember how beautiful she was in every way. He'll even think she was more beautiful than she was.

> 3. So if he ever really loved her, he'll feel sorry, even if he thinks she's still guilty.

3 *Then* shall he mourn,
If ever love had interest in *his* liver,
And wish *he* had not so accused her,
No, though *he* thought his accusation true.

4 Let *this* be so, and doubt not but success
Will fashion *the event* in better shape
Than I can lay it down in likelihood.

> 4. You can be sure that if this plan works, it will turn out even better than I can say.

> 5. But even if it doesn't turn out as I hope, they'll still think she is dead and she can become a nun, out of harm's way.

5. But if all aim but *this* be levell'd false,
The supposition of *the lady's* death
Will quench the wonder of her infamy:
And if it sort not well, *you* may conceal her,
As best befits her wounded reputation,
In some reclusive and religious life,
Out of all eyes, tongues, minds and injuries.

Figure 10.1 Presenting the main argument of a speech – *Much Ado about Nothing* Act 4 Scene 1 lines 207–236.

particular – that keep the speech located in relation to its subject, speaker, addressees and help articulate its argument. Figure 10.1 gives an example of how the Friar's speech from Act 4 Scene 1 of *Much Ado* might be presented to a class to bring out clearly its argumentative sequence. As well as the paragraph divisions the pupils are given a paraphrase summary of each section. Some words are printed in italics; the pupils can be asked what they refer to (Who is 'he'? When is 'then'?). The answers should help clarify the speech's meaning. Able pupils can be invited to develop a presentation of a later speech in the play along the same lines.

On some occasions we will want to set, formally or informally, specific detailed questions to test or develop comprehension of a whole speech. In setting such questions we should consider not only the paraphrasable meaning but the emotional weighting and dramatic import, asking why words or phrases are repeated, why there are so many adjectives, what the effect is of active verbs, what is suggested about character and motivation, and so forth. Some questions should emphasize stage location, or we will be in danger of losing the embodied nature of the drama. For instance, there's a lot to follow in the Friar's speech, and we might be inclined to stop once the class has grasped the main points of his argument. It's clear that he has room to develop his argument/make his case, and he does so through an orderly exposition (*so ... then ...* (implicitly) *if ... but ... and ...*) which enables comprehension. However, *dramatically* the speech is best considered in relation to the tensions that are present on the stage, in particular those that stem from Leonato's rage and sorrow – there is something for the Friar to *hold off*, and he might fail. It's also necessary for Benedick to add his voice in support before Leonato acquiesces. To develop a sense of this tension the speech could be tackled in pairs. With less confident pupils, this could be done using the paraphrases at first, and then moving on to Shakespeare's lines. One pupil reads the speech section by section. The other plays Leonato attempting interruption. At what points might he do so? How might the Friar prevent him through tone and gesture? Then this could be put into the larger picture: Who else might respond visibly during the speech? This exercise might go some way to answering why the Friar's speech is, to the eyes and ears of modern children, so very long. It has work to do.

Pamela Mason touches on a valuable point when she writes:

> A lengthy speech can be delivered by a character who has a lot to say and is determined to say it. Alternatively, a character can keep speaking because others are unwilling to speak or have nothing to say.[2]

In light of this comment on silent listeners, King John's speech inviting Hubert to kill the young prince (*King John* Act 3 Scene 3) is particularly fascinating. Does Hubert's silence draw John deeper into the development of his thought; is there (for John, that is) something *seductive* about Hubert's silence? This speech is well worth practical exploration.

Mason's observation also suggests that a useful question to ask our classes is 'Why is this speech so long?' A more finely tuned question could be 'Why doesn't it stop *here*?' – with 'here' being carefully selected (there might be several such points in a particular speech). What prompts the speech's continuance? This question is rather a blunt instrument but it's well worth using in relation to soliloquies, where there are no on-stage characters to influence the development of the speech (other than in the speaker's imagination of course – as in Lady Macbeth's first soliloquy), where the speech has somehow its own impetus. Asking the same question in relation to different speeches will yield very different answers, but consider, for example, Macbeth's dagger soliloquy. Macbeth dismisses his servant with an instruction: 'Go bid thy mistress, when my drink is ready,/ She strike upon the bell. Get thee to bed.' He is alone on the stage. Banquo's earlier conversation has established the darkness of the night. Why does Macbeth begin to speak? Because he sees, or believes he sees, a dagger:

Is this a dagger which I see before me,
The handle toward my hand? Come, let me clutch thee.
I have thee not, and yet I see thee still.
                                   Why doesn't he stop here?

Art thou not, fatal vision, sensible
To feeling as to sight? or art thou but
A dagger of the mind, a false creation,
Proceeding from the heat-oppressed brain?
                                   ... or here?

I see thee yet, in form as palpable
As this which now I draw.
Thou marshall'st me the way that I was going;
And such an instrument I was to use.   *... or here?*

Mine eyes are made the fools o' the other senses,
Or else worth all the rest; I see thee still,
And on thy blade and dudgeon gouts of blood,
Which was not so before.
                                   ... or here?

          There's no such thing:
It is the bloody business which informs
Thus to mine eyes.   *... or here?*

          Now o'er the one half world
Nature seems dead, and wicked dreams abuse
The curtain'd sleep; witchcraft celebrates
Pale Hecate's offerings, and wither'd murder,
Alarum'd by his sentinel, the wolf,
Whose howl's his watch, thus with his stealthy pace.
With Tarquin's ravishing strides, towards his design
Moves like a ghost.
                                   ... or here?

Thou sure and firm-set earth,
Hear not my steps, which way they walk, for fear
Thy very stones prate of my whereabout,
And take the present horror from the time,
Which now suits with it. Whiles I threat, he lives:
Words to the heat of deeds too cold breath gives.

... or here?

I go, and it is done; the bell invites me.
Hear it not, Duncan; for it is a knell
That summons thee to heaven or to hell.

Why doesn't he go on?

To a certain extent the sections are responses to things (apparently) per-
ceived externally – the dagger, the dagger's acquisition of blood, the
dagger's disappearance, the firm-set earth, the bell. In each case the perception initiates the speech (or the two are intimately connected) and a physical response is required of the actor, not just a delivery of the lines. That
gets us so far – but why doesn't he stop after 'It is the bloody business
which informs/Thus to mine eyes'? That's pretty conclusive, after all. The
dagger has gone, if it was ever there. He is left alone, starkly aware of 'the
bloody business'. Why doesn't he just get on with it? Because – we might
suggest – an intense awareness of the night crowds in on him as he articulates it further in the following lines (we might point out how the sentence
elongates in comparison with the abrupt questions and statements of the
first part of the speech): the scene-painting, the mood-setting is Shakespeare's for the audience and Macbeth's for himself, perhaps a kind of self-
hypnosis needed to overcome a still-felt reluctance, a deep sense, shown in
his previous soliloquy, of the undeniable *wrongness* of the deed ('the deep
damnation of his taking-off'). Nothing breaks into this mood, and he can't
stop at 'Moves like a ghost' because at '*thus* with his stealthy pace' he
must have started walking – it's that which makes him aware of the 'sure
and firm-set earth' over which he moves like, in his imagination, a ghost.
Just possibly, this might take him off the stage – but at this point the bell
rings – the one that just before the soliloquy he had ordered to be rung
when his drink was ready (a wonderfully harmless domestic detail) – and
he interprets it as an external call to what he has intended all along to do:

I go, and it is done: the bells invites me.

The final couplet clinches things for him, and he leaves the stage. The
couplet is also a conventional scene-ender, signalling closure to the audience. So the speech ends here.

Such considerations encourage our pupils to consider what structures the speech, what gives it the form and sequence that it has. At times we will also want to ask them to consider how the speech is structured, to look at it more analytically in terms of language and style. The one consideration can sometimes lead on very naturally to the other. For instance, a lively activity that can be used as a lesson starter focuses on a speech from *Much Ado* (it needn't be part of a study of the whole play). Beatrice is about to enter and Benedick appeals to Don Pedro to be instantly given a task – *any* task – so that he does not have to converse with her (Act 2 Scene 1). The dramatic situation being clear, the class stand round in a circle with a copy of Benedick's speech. The teacher explains that they are going to share the speech round the class, with each person saying one of the impossible things that Benedick is willing to do. Each reader is to stop at the next punctuation point, emphasizing the active verbs as in the division below.

Pupil 1   Will your grace command me any service to the world's end?
Pupil 2   I will *go* on the slightest errand now to the Antipodes that you can devise to send me on;
Pupil 3   I will *fetch* you a tooth-picker now from the furthest inch of Asia,
Pupil 4   *bring* you the length of Prester John's foot,
Pupil 5   *fetch* you a hair off the great Cham's beard,
Pupil 6   *do* you any embassage to the Pigmies,
Pupil 7   rather than hold three words' conference with this harpy.

It will quickly appear there aren't enough to go round. So everyone will have to think of an impossible or absurd task that Benedick can promise to do. They can have a minute or two to think of something, or go straight for it. Go round the class again, but this time distribute cards with each element from Benedick's lines at random round the class. (These can be swapped round after each attempt, to keep them all on their toes.) Pupils without cards have to invent. The sequence doesn't matter as long as someone always kicks off with 'Will your grace' and someone else ends with 'rather than hold'. Once they've managed a good run, round off with a great communal cry of 'You have no employment for me?'

Alternatively – or subsequently – pupils could work in pairs. One has a copy of Claudio's speech in numbered sections. The other (Don Pedro) has no sheet. Claudio delivers the first line to Don Pedro, who says 'no', 'sorry', shrugs, or some such. Claudio stomps off discontentedly, then comes back with the second line, and so on until he's run out of ideas. This can build up quite a head of steam, and pupils can be quite varied in their delivery. Follow-up discussion points might be: Why has Shakespeare concocted this sequence of lines for this point in the play? Should the actor play these lines humorously or desperately? Does their order matter?

What makes Benedick's speech suitable for this treatment is that it is mainly a list, one of the simpler forms of organization in that there are few grammatical restraints: what distinguishes lists from other forms of writing is that each item is discrete and grammatically equal with the others, so that there are no *grammatical* rules for their ordering. A list may be a sequence of noun phrases, verb phrases (as with Benedick above), adjectival phrases, adverbial phrases and so on. What orders them may be a matter of chronology, of gradation of some kind, of spatial arrangement (deixis), of association, and so on. An advantage for the classroom is that parts of the speech can be given to groups to work on individually, as they are detachable units, only related to the rest of the speech by parataxis. With lists with a high visual content, small groups might produce a tableau of each item, to be displayed as the speech is read so the class can see the sequence of images.

Other examples of speeches which are largely organized as lists include: Prospero's renunciation of his magic (*The Tempest* Act 5 Scene 1); Kent's accumulation of insults directed at Oswald in *Lear* Act 2 Scene 2 – 'A knave, a rascal, an eater of broken meats, a base, proud, shallow, beggarly, three-suites hundred pound, filthy worsted-stocking knave ...' – and he's only just got started! Rex Gibson is good on lists in Shakespeare: he gives a useful brief anthology with comments in his *Teaching Shakespeare*.[3]

Other structures which are basically simple in grammatical/syntactical terms (however complex some sub-units may be) can be found in some of Shakespeare's long speeches. The large structures can be highlighted aurally and/or visually. This can be done most easily with speeches that are based on contrasts/dualities – for instance this extract from the sequence from *Romeo and Juliet* Act 3 Scene 1 in which Mercutio accuses the irenic Benvolio of being a troublemaker. This can be read antiphonally if we want the pupils to hear the pattern, displayed on OHP or whiteboard if we want them to see it, or (probably best) both:

Thou wilt quarrel with a man
> that hath a hair more or a hair less in his beard than thou hast

Thou wilt quarrel with a man
> for cracking nuts, having no other reason but because thou hast hazel eyes

Thou hast quarrelled with a man
> for coughing in the street, because he hath wakened thy dog that hast lain asleep in the sun

Didst thou not fall out with a tailor
> for wearing his new doublet before Easter?

> Didst thou not fall out with another
>
> for tying his new shoes with an old riband?

Once again, this is a kind of list in that there is no *grammatical* reason for the order of discrete items, so pupils might consider if there are *any* reasons for the order. And obviously, as with Benedick's speech, this pattern can be imitated, with pupils inventing their own versions.

Taking the visual approach a step further, PowerPoint enables us to take a slow-motion look at a passage based on antithesis, seeing how the meaning of a speech develops and beginning to anticipate Shakespeare's patterning. For instance, we might take Benedick's exasperated musings on the change wrought in his friend Claudio by love. First on the screen the pupils read:

> *I have known* when there was no music in him but the drum and the fife,

They discuss its meaning briefly before, whether fading in, shooting in smartly from the right or left, with accompanying sound effect, or after whatsoever flourish your nature will, they see the next clause:

> *and now* had he rather hear the tabor and the pipe.

Working in this way it is easy for the class to see the two-part structure of the sentence with its contrast of past and present (key phrases highlighted in colour) and the parallelism of 'the drum and the fife' and 'the tabor and the pipe', and time to dwell on it without being distracted by surrounding text. With the appearance of the next clause –

> *I have known* when he would have walked ten mile afoot to see a good armour,

– the pupils can be asked to anticipate what follows; they will probably have no problem guessing 'and now', and may enjoy thinking what the lovelorn substitute for 'a good armour' might be before seeing:

> *and now* will he lie ten nights wake carving the fashion of a new doublet.

They will now be anticipating 'I have known' as the beginning of the next clause, so on seeing

> He was wont to speak plain and to the purpose, like an honest man and a soldier,

they may consider why Shakespeare didn't continue the verbal pattern, even though keeping to the 'before/after' comparison with:

> *and now* is he turned orthography.

Again this can lead to antiphonal reading and pupils writing their own brief compositions using such a pattern. Another way of developing this approach is to give pupils a speech on a file and get them in pairs to arrange it to bring out the structure(s).

Passages of this kind may be considered in one sense as static – a similar figure is repeated with variations, and while there is development (and maybe considerable emotional impetus) it is largely through accumulation. Speeches which have an argument – a developing chain of reasoning or feeling – may present more difficulties, but even with some of these it is not too hard to find some kind of antithetical or other organizing pattern, or a sequence of key linking words (which may well be the 'small words' discussed on page 26). Both may be found in a splendid speech in Act 3 Scene 5 of *As You Like It* in which the shepherdess Phoebe has fallen in love with the youth Ganymede (i.e. Rosalind in disguise) but is at pains to conceal it both from herself and her dejected lover, Sylvius. As she sashays between denial and affirmation it's easy enough to identify the pros and cons and to see the function of the linking word 'yet', and the speech can accordingly be set out on the page:

Against Ganymede	*For Ganymede*
Think not I love him,	though I ask for him:
'Tis but a peevish boy;	yet he talks well;
But what care I for words?	yet words do well
	When he that speaks them pleases those that hear.
	It is a pretty youth:
not very pretty:	
But, sure, he's proud,	and yet his pride becomes him.

As the speech proceeds, the tug towards affirmation becomes more pronounced, so she has to pull herself back to denial; the conclusion is nicely poised, so perhaps needs a central position:

I'll write to him a very taunting letter,
And thou shalt bear it: wilt thou, Silvius?

The play on 'shalt' and 'wilt' is beautifully turned but may be missed by modern readers who are uncertain of the distinction between 'shall' and 'will'. 'Shalt' implies certainty ('you are going to deliver my letter'), 'wilt thou …?' is a request. How does Phoebe manage the transition? It's a wonderful moment for an actress to make something of.[4]

Phoebe's speech can be taken in isolation – the class need no more of the context than a light sketch, as above. They can explore the speech in a variety of ways, perhaps ending in a performance, or watching an actress (preferably two actresses) on video. In their own writing they might see if they can make something of the to-and-fro with the underlying one-way current by writing a monologue halting between two opinions, or only partially resisting an emotional tug. This of course is not an instruction to 'write like Shakespeare' or produce pastiche, but to explore an imagined state of emotional tension or duplicity in the pupils' own terms – although we will hope that their understanding will have been enlarged through the experience of Shakespeare.

There are a number of long speeches which, like Phoebe's, can be made the basis of a lesson separate from the reading of the whole play or even the whole scene from which the speech comes, the teacher indicating as much of the context as s/he deems necessary. Such lessons, suitably tailored, can occur at any stage throughout Key Stage 3, and might be part of an overall strategy of 'creeping up' on Shakespeare, so that he doesn't arrive in the sudden slab (or two shorter slabs) of the play set for the Key Stage. I'm not advocating a 'beauties of Shakespeare' approach in which pupils are invited to admire set pieces of Shakespeare's best writing (although such an approach is not altogether beyond the pale)[5] but a set of occasional lessons, each with specific aims and objectives that may or may not be primarily to do with Shakespeare. These might concern: verse form; an introduction to Early Modern English; stimulus to individual writing; investigation of metaphor; using rhetorical figures; a group of texts exploring a particular theme – love, death, friendship, qualities of description, etc. This strategy of course depends on the opinion that Shakespeare is worth the trouble of regular or at least occasional attention throughout both Key Stages, and the additional (and pragmatic) view that a number of things can be taught with passages from Shakespeare as the vehicle and that Shakespeare can be a stimulus to the pupils' own writing. (Should you doubt this, read Fred Sedgwick's brief and stimulating *Shakespeare and the Young Writer*.[6] The book is concerned with primary school children, but the secondary school teacher can learn a great deal from it, including perhaps a healthy dose of humility.)

Useful passages abound – Mercutio's 'Queen Mab' speech from *Romeo and Juliet*, Juliet's soliloquy before taking the potion that will render her to all appearances dead, Richard II's self-deposing, for instance. Some speeches from the plays are complete inset narratives (discussed in Barbara Hardy's very interesting book *Shakespeare's Storytellers*);[7] one that can go well in the classroom is Clarence's vision of drowning from *Richard III*. All the class need to know is that Clarence is in prison in the Tower of London because of the machinations of his brother, Richard, Duke of Gloucester, who Clarence believes is his friend. Gloucester has plotted his death, which occurs later in the scene. The speech is the narrative of Clarence's dream of drowning, a straightforward chronological sequence, with the frequent linking word 'methought(s)' and containing lists of rich imagery (which might stimulate a visual response), building up to this climax:

> Methought I saw a thousand fearful wrecks;
> Ten thousand men that fishes gnaw'd upon;
> Wedges of gold, great anchors, heaps of pearl,
> Inestimable stones, unvalued jewels,
> All scatter'd in the bottom of the sea:
> Some lay in dead men's skulls; and, in those holes
> Where eyes did once inhabit, there were crept,
> As 'twere in scorn of eyes, reflecting gems,
> Which woo'd the slimy bottom of the deep,
> And mock'd the dead bones that lay scatter'd by.

The dream doesn't end here. In a subsequent speech Clarence tells us the dream 'was lengthened after life' and builds to further horror without the mitigating beauty. Pupils might look at that speech also. And they might compare these speeches with Ariel's song 'Full fathom five' from *The Tempest*.

Not all speeches have a structure, whether emotional, rhetorical, narrative or logical, that can easily be displayed or explored. For instance if we try to set out Benedick's speech outlining his attitude to women (*Much Ado* Act 1 Scene 1 lines 177–182) to highlight its structure, we end up with something like this:

> That a woman conceived me,
>> I thank her;
> that she brought me up,
>> I likewise give her most humble thanks
> but that
>> I will
>>> have a recheat winded in my forehead,
>> or (*that*
>>> *I will*)
>>> hang my bugle in an invisible baldrick,
>>>> all women shall pardon me.
> Because
>> I will not do them the wrong to mistrust any,
>> I will do myself the right to trust none;
> and the fine is,
>> for the which I may go the finer,
>>> I will live a bachelor.

While it may help the teacher (and perhaps some pupils and students) to diagram the speech in this way, I am not convinced that it will prove particularly useful to younger (Key Stage 3) or less able (Key Stage 4) pupils. It's obvious that the difficulty is in the grammar and syntax, the artful periodic structure, rather than in the lexis, although 'recheat' and 'baldrick' are tricky. (The trickiness belongs to allusion rather than vocabulary, which may be easily enough glossed.) Roma Gill uses paraphrase: ' "I will wear in my forehead a horn for summoning hounds, or hang my hunting-horn in an invisible belt" – i.e. "risk being known as a cuckold, or try to hide the fact that I have been a cuckold".'[8] I think this is one of those cases where pupils will find it hard to see how the paraphrase relates to the lines it explains. It's further complicated by the likelihood of the pupils not going back to the speech and seeing that the paraphrase's 'I will' has to be inserted back into the 'but that' clause in order to grasp Benedick's meaning (rather than its opposite). The teacher has a specific problem here, which admits no easy solution. There are some sequences of Shakespeare that *will* be too difficult for our classes, and we need to consider what to do at these points – which may well, as with Benedick's speech, occur in scenes set for Year 9.

However, there are various ways of dealing with the complicated, other than by passing it completely by offering a rapid paraphrase. It depends on the source of the difficulty. For instance, in Hamlet's first soliloquy, expressive of his reaction to the death of his father and remarriage of his mother (events that have poisoned the world for him), the intensity of the emotion leads to continuous crowding in of interjections and exclamations as phrases are elaborated and reacted to. In spite of the intensity of emotion, Hamlet keeps control of the grammar and syntax of his speech, always regaining his main sentence and bringing it to a conclusion – so that the speech can be regarded as having both centrifugal energies and a forward-moving purpose. This struggle, these restless energies are intrinsic to the meaning of the speech, and are precisely what a prose paraphrase will remove. However, we can strategically approach this confusingly difficult speech by editing it down to its main statements and first introducing it in this form:

O, that this too too solid flesh would melt
Thaw and resolve itself into a dew!
Or that the Everlasting had not fix'd
His canon 'gainst self-slaughter! O God! God!   *canon*: law
How weary, stale, flat and unprofitable,
Seem to me all the uses of this world!

That it should come to this!

She would hang on him,   *would*: used to

As if increase of appetite had grown
By what it fed on: and yet, within a month
(She) married with my uncle,
It is not nor it cannot come to good:
But break, my heart; for I must hold my tongue.

Once this is grasped, students can go on to look at the full speech, perhaps with one reader reading the main sentences and others the interjections, and then considering why the latter occur where they do.

Most of the examples discussed above are all highly specific, with approaches designed only with the given speech in mind. More (as we say) generic approaches to the meaning of longer speeches can also be used, selected as they are seen to be appropriate to particular passages. A number of these were developed in the 1980s by Bob Cunningham working for the Derbyshire Advisory Service, and I am indebted to him for permission to give an account of some here, with a few additional comments and suggestions of my own. The methods are sequencing, chaining, matching and charting Information Units and they work as follows.

Sequencing

Choose a speech. Cut it up in two different ways. Working in pairs, some pupils attempt to sequence one version, some the other, and then they compare notes. The cuts should be made in places where there are sufficient clues. This exercise can lead naturally into the next, which invites the pupils to become explicit about the elements that give the speech the cohesion that has enabled them to do the sequencing.

Chaining

Pupils annotate excerpts of text, indicating all the elements that give the passage cohesion, such as: linking words; discourse markers; sound patterns; grammar; related ideas; metaphors/images; rhetorical patterns. Instructions can indicate explicitly the type of connections to look for. For instance, pupils might highlight in different colours all the words associated with the seasons, wealth, illness and Nature in Titania's long speech on the disturbance of the seasons in *A Midsummer Night's Dream* or words related to night in Juliet's pre-consummation soliloquy.

Matching

A sequence of text is given with modern 'equivalents' of some of the expressions in it printed at the bottom of the page; pupils, individually or in pairs, find the equivalents in the speech. The focus may be on lexis, looking for individual words ('slain' for 'killed', 'nice' for 'trivial', 'martial' for 'warlike') or on larger units, sentences or phrases ('As she is mine, I may dispose of her' for 'Since I'm her father I can do what I like with her'). This method can be developed into a study of the syntax of units of 'information', as in the next exercise.

Charting information units

A speech is presented together with a 'flow chart' analysis of its argument. The aim is to give the 'backbone' of the argument in paraphrase, inviting pupils to find the 'information units' in the speech itself and seen how they are related. Having seen the method at work, they can go on to develop it themselves, taking another speech and producing an analysis along the same lines. Of course the speech must have an argument sufficiently sequential and structured for the analysis to work and to be illuminating, but there are plenty of speeches to which it is particularly well suited. Examples include Egeus' complaint to Theseus and Brutus' attempt to convince himself that the assassination of Caesar is necessary.

Part II

Aspects

Chapter 11

Narrative

Because Shakespeare's language is difficult, sometimes prohibitively so, teachers commonly begin with an introduction to the story of the play before, if at all, moving in to a closer engagement with the text. (I sometimes wonder just what experiences Year 7 pupils who tell me that they have read *Macbeth* or *The Tempest* have had.) The stories of the plays are of course important; Shakespeare was a dramatic poet, and that involved making plots from stories, and plots into scenes. But it's this very dramatic shaping as well as the language (ultimately they can't be divorced) that can easily be lost or distorted in a narrative retelling for children.

Many teachers will opt for something ready made, perhaps sharing with the class a reading of a published prose version (more likely nowadays to be Garfield than Lamb) or using the summaries provided in various schools' editions. The advantages of working in these ways are obvious: our first wish is for pupils to grasp the basics of character and plot, the narrative line – we want then to get the gist, and their difficulties with (even their hostility to) the language can prevent them getting it. Although I'm certainly not saying we shouldn't do it, there are potential disadvantages that I think we should be aware of and guard against. I want to (1) discuss briefly some of these disadvantages before going on to consider (2) introductory uses of narrative that may prepare pupils more specifically for an engagement with dramatic writing and (3) how pupils' own retellings of Shakespeare's stories can grow out of and benefit from their own close reading of the plays.

Caveats

The tendency of a prose version for young readers may be to *un*dramatize, to produce a block of exposition at the beginning which tells young readers what they are deemed to need to know. This is invariably the case in the Charles and Mary Lamb's *Tales from Shakespeare*. Here is the opening paragraph of *Macbeth*:

> When Duncan the meek reigned King of Scotland, there lived a great thane, or
> lord, called Macbeth. This Macbeth was a near kinsman to the king, and in great

esteem with the court for his valour and conduct in the wars; an example of which he had lately given, in defeating a rebel army assisted by the troops of Norway in terrible numbers.[1]

Shakespeare, however, begins his play with the riddling witches before moving rapidly on to a scene that is so knotty and in places ambiguous that some editorial tidying up has been thought necessary and in the course of which an image develops of a terrifyingly bloody Macbeth ('his brandished steel/Which smoked with bloody execution' … 'carved out his passage' … 'unseamed him from the nave to th' chops'). This image is what is hidden by Lamb's decorous phrase 'valour and conduct in the wars'. Where Shakespeare's (adult) audience struggles to keep up, Lamb's readers are informed.[2]

Such 'putting the pupil in the picture' is entirely sensible, up to a point, but it does put readers at a remove from the narrative and excuses them from a more closely engaged construction of the action. They won't ask such questions as 'Who are these people? What is happening here? What will happen next?' precisely because they are being told.

An example which can easily go unnoticed is Viola's name in *Twelfth Night*. Prose retellings introduce her by name, as does the playscript: '*Enter Viola, a Captain and Sailors*'. These practices conceal from us that *in the theatre* Shakespeare does not give her name (or much about her station) at this point. The name he insists on the audience getting, making sure that we hear it three times in only a few lines (beginning of Act 1 Scene 4) is her assumed name, Cesario. Drawing our class's attention to this can prompt closer reading of what Shakespeare actually did write – poetry and drama, not just narrative.

Viola's name is not heard by the audience until the moment of her reunion with her brother, the moment at which, restored to him, she can be Viola once more (and the moment in the play in which Shakespeare is for the first time explicit about Viola's status/background). And even here the approach to the name is slow and roundabout. Sebastian, amazed to see himself divided, apparently doesn't jump to the conclusion that his sister is alive, but approaches tentatively. He asks:

> Of charity, what kin are you to me?
> What countryman? What name? What parentage?

Viola answers directly only to his second and third questions; the name which comes into play is not hers but his own, their father's; and she speaks of her brother in the past tense:

> *Viola*   Of Messaline: Sebastian was my father,
>   Such a Sebastian was my brother too:

> So went he suited to his watery tomb:
> If spirits can assume both form and suit,
> You come to fright us.

Sebastian   A spirit I am indeed,
> But am in that dimension clad,
> Which from the womb I did participate.
> Were you a woman, as the rest goes even,
> I should my tears let fall upon your cheek,
> And say, Thrice welcome drowned Viola.

Although Sebastian's speech appears to culminate in welcoming recognition, it both does and doesn't; the subjunctive mood of the preceding lines holds a note of reserve. And there are unresolved depths in 'drowned Viola'; to what extent does 'drowned' negate 'Viola' (and on the name's very first appearance)? The lines can be played with humour, if the actors have decided that the pair have recognized each other and are already secure in the knowledge, even if there is a kind of reserve, a process to be played through/out in order to secure a true arrival. The slow, oddly formal dance of the dialogue continues, Viola talks of 'my father', but of 'Viola' in the third person, as if perhaps still not quite herself (maybe she needs time to recognize herself as Viola) and Sebastian says 'my sister', not 'you':

Viola   My father had a mole upon his brow.
Sebastian   And so had mine.
Viola   And died that day when Viola from her birth
> Had numbered thirteen years.
Sebastian   O that record is lively in my soul,
> He finishes indeed his mortal act
> That day that made my sister thirteen years.
Viola   If nothing lets to make us happy both,
> But this my masculine usurp'd attire:
> Do not embrace me, till each circumstance,
> Of place, time, fortune, do cohere and jump
> That I am Viola, which to conform,
> I'll bring you to a captain in this town,
> Where lie my maiden weeds.

Even here, grammatically Viola does not simply say 'I am Viola', although that sense is contained and an actress's warmth and a strong stress on 'I am' will make the affirmation apparent. There is no difficulty in recognizing this sequence as a movement towards revelation and completion, but the degree to which it is so can be masked for us simply by our already knowing Viola's name.

How much of this we go into with any class is, as ever, a matter of judgement, but at some level something of these subtleties can be grasped by most classes. It's worthwhile looking at Shakespeare's exposition in specific cases. Sometimes he introduces characters immediately, without introduction (Iago, Petruchio, Viola); sometimes he has them referred to several times before they appear (Olivia, Othello, Macbeth). His introduction of setting is also worth considering (for instance, the careful placing of 'This is Venice: my house is not a Grange'.)

A further problem of prose retellings is that interpretation, especially of character, is sometimes made part of the narrative. Here, for instance, in Jennifer Mulherin's *Twelfth Night*:

> The Duke is young but rather moody. He is in love with being in love. His love for Olivia is unlike the real affection he feels for Viola. He is a cultured man and loves music. Everyone, including Olivia, has a good opinion of him. When he proposes to Viola we feel sure that they will make a happy couple.[3]

Leaving aside the splendid 'but' of the first sentence, the problems arise with the second sentence. That Orsino is 'in love with being in love' is a judgement, not a fact, yet it is presented here as information. Many, many pupils have been told this in one way or another. But how many have arrived at that judgement themselves, or been equipped to do so? How do competent readers arrive at such a judgement? The paragraph's third sentence might be the beginning of an answer, but once again it begs questions (why *should* one's love for a beautiful and inaccessible woman be like the affection that one feels for a male companion?). And what of 'He is a cultured man and loves music'? Can't his love for music be seen as part of his propensity for emotional indulgence? ('Enough, no more ...' – do lovers of music cut it off in mid-cadence? But then maybe he doesn't; maybe the musician has just concluded a piece and after a brief pause begins the next.) Just like Sir Toby and Sir Andrew he craves a love song and cares not for good life. We might say he enjoys the aesthetics of being in love. The critical question bypassed is: what enables our pupils to hear the notes of self-indulgence in *Twelfth Night's* opening scene?

Mulherin's character notes on *Macbeth* are rather different – longer, more analytical (perhaps because 'Macbeth is one of the most complicated of Shakespeare's characters') – they give an account of his moral progress from 'a brave soldier and a good man' to 'a butcher and a tyrant without any feeling of remorse' who nonetheless 'dies bravely'.[4] It's hard to object to this, given the young audience; although it does bypass some of the play's deeper questions, rendering *Macbeth* more of a cautionary tale and less horrifying than it arguably is, it is probably the right level at which younger minds should grasp the play. This is the kind of thing that we have to make decisions about.

Of course not all prose narratives are undramatic, far from it; story-tellers have their own devices of delay, involvement, surprise. So far I've been considering a particular genre, the introductory or explanatory narrative, which does not presume to stand in its own right so much as to serve another text by preparing for a fuller engagement with it. Less modest are the *Shakespeare Stories* of Leon Garfield.[5] Garfield is a highly dramatic writer with a feeling for concealment, contrast and large gestures, for climax and reversal. Garfield narrates his Shakespeare with sustained art and with attitude; the reader is to be gripped by his stories in their own right, whatever their relation to Shakespeare (a relationship that varies). His versions are very much interpretations, in some cases interpretations that a more informed reader might find contentious. They certainly aren't 'just telling the story'. Indeed his version could be argued to be too distinctive and highly wrought to be particularly useful as introductory material in the classroom (quite apart from anything else, a number of them are quite long). They are, however, well worth reading both for enjoyment and for study in their own right, with pupils realizing that the story is not the play and that they may encounter the latter later in their education, or in the theatre, or both.

It may be best for teachers to stick to briefer summaries. Several schools' editions give, in addition to a full summary, a brief account of the action at the head of each scene. Similarly, some teachers give their summaries serially before engaging with each scene in turn (perhaps together with a recap), with the needs of their particular class in mind. Of course it's hard to 'just tell the story'. Stories are drenched in value, and their values alter with their proportions and perspectives. Any retelling involves choice, emphasis and a sense of purpose in relation to an audience. It's helpful for us to have clear in our own minds, whatever preparatory method we are going to use, what view of the play we want to begin with, so that we can get our opening pitch right.

Exploring plot elements

The narrative materials that Shakespeare drew on and shaped into his plays are worth some attention in their own right, as long as we don't confuse work on them with work on – much less reading – Shakespeare. There is plenty of scope for using narrative elements with our classes, as there is a wide variety of stories and story types to be found in the plays, as only a brief selection can make clear: a king bargains power for love; children from feuding families secretly marry; an isolated girl gains by a trick a husband who despises her; a man is hired to kill a child; a girl is born in a storm at sea; a man is sworn to vengeance by a ghost; a despised monster sees a drunkard as a god; an older black man marries a younger white woman. Any of these or the many others available could serve as the kernel for a wide variety of work across a range of age and ability: What is the potential of the story? In what ways might the story be told? What does the story remind you of? Can we find similar stories in what we read and watch today? Why do people tell these kinds of story? What seem to be the values implicit in the story? Which of the stories might make a good play?

Each pupil in a Year 7 or 8 class can be given a card bearing a name and a sentence (e.g. 'PERDITA When I was a baby I was abandoned on a sea-coast by the order of my father'). Mingling and reading each other's cards, they find the other characters that belong to their story. Groups could then investigate the possibilities of their story, analysing it, testing its potential, re-presenting it in drama or writing, before the class goes on to discuss the various types of story, if the initial selection has been made to demonstrate variety, or look at a group of similar stories, if the selection has been made to explore variety within similarity.

While this kind of work might be done without any mention of Shakespeare (nonetheless paving the way for later recognitions), if our eye is more immediately on reading a particular Shakespeare play or scene, we can angle it towards a consideration of the story's potential for specifically dramatic realization, beginning to invite the class to think like dramatists. We might start by bringing the story elements into relation with bits of text (see page 53). More ambitiously, pupils can work on clusters of characters, exploring some of the possible relations and tensions (and therefore their dramatic potential) between them. For instance, a group of four pupils from a class that is going to work on all or part of *Twelfth Night* might be given the following:

Your group contains these characters:

CESARIO
A young woman dressed as a young man. Cesario isn't her real name. None of the others know she's really a young woman. She serves a Duke, Orsino. She is in love with him, but obviously she can't tell him. Orsino is in love with Olivia. He sends Cesario, who he trusts, to woo Olivia for him.

OLIVIA
A lady of a great household. Her brother has died and she has said that she will have nothing to do with men for seven years. When she sees Cesario she is attracted to 'him'.

MARIA
Olivia's waiting gentlewoman. Witty, mischievous.

The fourth member of your group acts as director/audience.

THE TASK
Cesario arrives at Olivia's house. Improvise the scene that takes place. Try to make it last for five minutes.

Arguably this will make the pupils aware of some of the potential tensions in the situation. Other groups could be given similar instructions concerning a pair of Viola and Orsino (improvising a conversation about love and women and ending with 'Cesario' being sent to woo Olivia), a quartet of Sir Toby, Sir Andrew, Feste and Maria – and so on. It would also be possible to stir some selected lines into this mix also.

The emphasis here is on group oral work. Alternatively teachers might set individual written work exploring some plot and character possibilities. This is an approach I tried one year with a Year 9 class in an exercise entitled 'Characters and conversations from a land of the imagination':

In an imaginary land, there are the following people (among others): a lonely young woman; a love-sick lord; a foolish suitor; a drunken uncle; a grieving sister; a proud lord; a lost brother; a young woman disguised as a man; a bitter comedian; a servant with a sense of humour.
And there has been a shipwreck and a death.

- Choose four of the characters.
- Write at least a paragraph about each of them: who they are, what they're like, how they behave, how they feel, what their history is, etc.
- Combine the four characters into two pairs.
- Write a dialogue for each pair (at least a page for each dialogue).
- In pairs, read and perform the dialogues.

In their different ways, these exercises give opportunities for pupils to think their way round/into some of the dramatic possibilities provided by the narrative material, and they can produce much that is enjoyable and valuable in its own right. However, a sound objection – a fair indication of the limits and pitfalls – of this way of working is that it might well only lead to inert remakings according to our own habitual clichés for understanding relationships, our assumptions about attitudes. Rather than countering the pull into a story-book world that does not involve us, it might work *against* reading the plays, although it might please. This danger might be overcome, or at least resisted to some degree, if we build into the exercises something of the values implicit in the stories (or realized by Shakespeare's treatment of them). While continuing along similar lines, it's possible, especially with older pupils, to probe deeper, exploring the tensions, which may not be the ones that we would anticipate, in more extended speeches and soliloquies as well as in quick exchanges

For instance, an approach to *The Winter's Tale* that builds in a belief in the absolute inviolability and indissolubility of marriage (something which, as Ian Robinson has pointed out somewhere, for some of our young people involves an effort of the historical imagination). The following exercise was designed for GCSE and A Level students with no previous knowledge of the play, preparatory for a visit to Stratford where they saw the whole play before proceeding to further study.

The students work in trios to begin with. Each trio is made up of one character (Hermione, Polixenes, Camillo, Antigonus or Paulina) with two advisers, one positive and one negative. Each is given a card containing instructions. The information common to all participants is this:

> You are in the royal court of Sicilia, a Mediterranean country, many years before the birth of Christ. The imagined period is a time when kings had power of life and death over their subjects. It was a time in which marriage was taken with absolute seriousness by all, as it still is by some.
>
> The king of the country is Leontes, and his queen is Hermione. Both are respected and popular. They have one young son, of whom they are very fond.
>
> Leontes' childhood friend, Polixenes, the King of Bohemia, has been staying with the family for nine months.
>
> Hermione is nine months pregnant.

Hermione's card reads like this:

> Your husband Leontes accuses you in front of other people in your court of adultery with his best friend Polixenes, who has been staying at the court as an honoured guest for nine months. You are heavily pregnant, and Leontes says that Polixenes is the father of your child.
>
> In the envelope is a card telling you whether you are innocent or guilty. Only you and Polixenes have absolute knowledge of this. Do not show the card to anyone else, even your advisers.
>
> What do you *feel*?
> What do you *think*?
> What will you *do*?

Her positive adviser's instructions read:

> Hermione should stand up for her innocence. Tell her that eventually Leontes will come to realize his mistake. But she should also appreciate her husband's feelings.

And the negative:

> It's useless for Hermione to claim that she's innocent, even if she is. It will only make things worse. If she owns up, things might not go so badly for her. He's only a stupid man, after all. Men deserve to be cheated.

The other trio members have similar cards tailored to their character.

The first task is to prepare the characters for their part in a sequence of improvised scenes. The advisers can only advise; the choice of action is left to the character. Pupils can ask for additional background information and clarification of the task, but not for information about the plot. After the period of preparation, the trios are recalled and sit in a large circle. A teacher (or student who has been prepared in advance) role-plays Leontes. The scenes follow the sequence given below as far as possible, although some characters' choice might re-shape the plot as the exercise unfolds. Advisers and observers may comment and make suggestions, but they cannot actually join the action. The sequence is that found in the play:

1   Leontes and Camillo.
2   Camillo and Polixenes.
3   Leontes and Hermione – this key scene requires some pre-preparation of students working as 'extras'. A tableau can quickly be set up with Hermione, Mamilius by her side telling her a story ('A sad tale's best for winter') and waiting-women. Leontes instructs two guards to take the child from Hermione. The scene is improvised from this point. At the appropriate point the guards take Hermione away to prison.
4   Paulina – in soliloquy to the circle: what she proposes to do – followed by discussion, followed by action.

What comes next is not easy to predict, as there are a number of possibilities. Somehow, it should come round to:

5   Leontes, Antigonus, Paulina.

There are a number of possible moves from here – into the trial scene, for instance (another group could have been set up in relation to the oracle). Or the class might be asked how a playwright could get a happy ending out of this – and what stands in the way of a happy ending. Students who have worked through this or similar exercises will come to the study of the text or to a performance with certain expectations and questions already in mind. This should enhance their response to what Shakespeare has made out of the narrative materials.

We can be even more explicit in prompting our pupils/students to consider a narrative from the perspective of a playwright, asking what plot can be developed from a particular narrative, and how its dramatic potential can be variously realized in playscript. How can it be effectively rendered in *scenes*? For example when teaching *Macbeth* we might begin by issuing a bare summary, as 'factual' in tone as possible (as already indicated, this is far from easy):

> Scotland, hundreds of years ago.
>
> Macbeth, Thane of Glamis, a mighty warrior in King Duncan's army, is greeted after his success in battle by three strange women, who tell him he will be Thane of Cawdor and king. They tell his fellow warrior Banquo that his descendants shall be kings. Almost immediately Macbeth learns that he now has the title that was taken away from the Thane of Cawdor, who has been discovered as a traitor. Banquo warns him that the message from the women might be a temptation from the powers of darkness. Duncan announces that his eldest son, Malcolm, will be the next king.
>
> Macbeth writes to his wife about what he has been told. She is determined that he will become king. When Duncan comes to Macbeth's castle as an honoured guest, she devises a plot to kill him and encourages Macbeth to carry out the murder. When the body of Duncan is discovered his sons run away. Macbeth is crowned king. He hires murderers to kill Banquo and his son. At a banquet Macbeth is unsettled by the appearance of Banquo's ghost. He visits the strange women again, and their masters give him riddling messages, telling him that he needn't be frightened of any man born of woman, and that he cannot be defeated until Birnam Wood comes to his castle at Dunsinane. Encouraged by this, Macbeth sends his men to kill another potential enemy, Macduff – but he has fled to join Malcolm in England. Macduff's family is killed.
>
> In England, Macduff tries to persuade Malcolm to come and fight to save his country, of which he is the rightful king, but Malcolm doesn't trust him. Once Malcolm is sure that Macduff is not a traitor, he reveals that an army is already organized and ready to fight against Macbeth.
>
> Lady Macbeth walks in her sleep, obsessively reliving the scene of the murder. Later she dies. A number of Macbeth's people run away to join Malcolm's army. The army gets nearer, closing in on Macbeth's castle. They cut down branches from Birnam Wood as camouflage and march on Dunsinane. Macbeth rushes out for one last desperate battle, and is killed in single combat by Macduff, who reveals that he was 'untimely ripped' from his mother's womb. Macbeth's severed head is presented to the new king, Malcolm.

The pupils then have to consider/discuss questions such as the following (this set was given to an able GCSE class to consider over the summer holiday):

> Before we read and study the play next term, work your way through the following questions. Make some notes as a basis for discussion. You might even try writing some scenes!

1 Think about the story and its potential for drama.

    a What features does it have that could make a good play?

    b Choose five events from the story that you think would make effective scenes. Consider their potential for surprise, climax, suspense, psychological interest, contrast of characters. How would you present the scenes on stage?

    c Which of the scenes, if any, would you set at night?

2 Think about different possible emphases that versions of the story might have. For instance, it could be made into:

> a horror story   a philosophical investigation of evil
> a whodunit   a psychological study of a murderer

    a What other possibilities are there?

    b In each case, where would be the best place to begin? What might make an effective scene to set the tone for the play that is to follow?

    c You may know Shakespeare's opening scene already. If so, think about why he began the play in that way. As you should have seen by now, he needn't have done.

3 If you wanted to explore the thoughts, feelings and motivations of the characters, how would you do it?

4 Think of two different ways in which a play based on this story might end. What might be the final impression given to the audience?

5 How would a play on this theme be different from a novel or a historical reconstruction? What might be the importance in the play of the following?

> male characters   female characters   children

6 Which elements of the story are still reflected in our world, and which are not? If you were going to modernize the story, which elements would be changed? Would the story be weaker or stronger?

This is a very full set of questions; clearly elements could be selected for use on particular occasions with particular classes. For instance, we can focus on the introduction of Lady Macbeth. How would you first introduce her into the play? After the rapidity of Act 1 Scenes 1–4, Shakespeare brings a solitary woman on to the stage. How would you proceed from here? Why does Shakespeare proceed as he does? This can lead into close reading of a sequence that moves through various phases: the reading of the letter, her responses as she – isolated but in interplay with her (imagined) husband and the (imagined?) spirits – works through to the dreadful conclusion that Macbeth may or may not overhear.

To take another example, while working on *Richard III* it could be worthwhile to pause and look at the treatment of the narrative in More's history or Hall's or Holinshed's chronicles and consider Shakespeare's expansions, contractions, alterations, omissions and inventions – his eye for the dramatic possibilities. Such an approach can tie in effectively with the GCSE requirements to look at dramatic structure and the significance of historical and cultural context.

Much of the work outlined here is time-consuming, and many teachers may feel that that is a sufficient objection to it. However, I discuss it in detail not to argue that all of it should be used on all occasions, but that work of this kind is among the possibilities that we may dip into from time to time, according to our present purposes – and to tease out further the implications of working in a variety of introductory ways. But of course the introductory and exploratory can only go so far, and many teachers will still feel that the handy summaries provided in schools' editions are quite sufficient. I would argue, though, that such a summary should make use of a walk-through element – that pupils should stand for the characters and move in relation to each other, perhaps speaking some selected lines, so that the story is already thought of as inhabiting theatrical space (see pages 92–6).

Retelling Shakespeare's stories

It may be that the best time – it's certainly a productive time – for considering Shakespeare's stories and how they may be told or dramatized is *after* reading/studying/looking at a play, whether in part or in whole. This can sharpen pupils' reading of Shakespeare considerably. They might begin by thinking about the task of retelling in general terms, for instance considering what problems rewriting the play for 7- to 9-year-olds will involve and what choices would have to be made about inclusion, exclusion, emphasis, sequence, how much of the original language to use and so forth. They can then go on to consider some specific examples – extracts from, say, four versions – and discuss such questions as: what assumptions – about Shakespeare, about children – are the re-writers making? What choices has each writer made? How would you describe the style of each version? How are characters introduced? What have the writers focused on and what have they omitted? (Of four versions of the imprisonment of Malvolio that one class looked at, one version simply left it out!) Which writer has done the best job, and why? This leads to some worthwhile discussion (particularly of the capacities of readers in the intended age range; pupils can too easily assume that young readers need very simple stuff, with no difficult words) and it can produce some quite alert critical writing.

Pupils can then go on to write their own versions. This may be set up in a number of ways. They can be given a free choice of what scenes to work on, scenes might be distributed throughout the class to cover the whole play (it can be interesting if some scenes are done in two versions – see below) or each pupil might be asked to produce a version that covers the whole play.

Something of the variety of outcomes from this exercise can be seen from two versions of Act 1 Scene 2 of *Twelfth Night* produced by Year 9 pupils. The first, by Emma, adopts a comic-book approach, in which the main appeal is pictorial, with each picture having a clear narrative caption. The dialogue in the speech bubbles makes some use of Shakespeare's lines ('What country, friends, is this?' – 'This is Illyria, lady' and 'For saying so, there's gold' – the latter being clearly explained by the picture and caption), the rest is paraphrase and invention ('It's this way'). Emma's' commentary on her work draws attention to the colour 'to catch the eye of the young reader' and her attempt 'to make it as simple as possible'. She was, however, dissatisfied with her effort: 'If I was to do it again, I would-n't be so patronizing. I think I have misunderstood how clever some chil-dren are today. It's a bit tedious.' She is perhaps a bit hard on herself.

By way of contrast, Lisa's version is a page of continuous prose, largely dialogue after an introductory paragraph of narrative ('A bedraggled young lady stumbled to the shore') and makes more demands on her intended audience, although she does say that the response of her younger sister was that it was 'a bit easy'. She adds 'She is quite smart for her age though, and I don't think that most children of her age would find this a problem'. Her only conscious concession to her audience is given in her commentary: 'To keep the piece more suitable for children, I added a picture behind the text.'

The scene is clearly realized in Lisa's retelling (although not as a scene in the theatrical sense), with clear indications of actions and response ('drop-ping down to her knees', 'a faint smile', etc.). It's noticeable that, unlike Emma ('One lady made it on to land. Her name was Viola.'), Lisa keeps Viola anonymous – as Shakespeare does. She is explicit about this in her commentary: 'I think I could have improved this piece of writing by devel-oping the characters slightly more, but instead, I decided to keep them more mysterious, because at that point in Shakespeare's play, not much is known about them. The characters are developed and explored in greater detail, later in the play.'

Also apparent in Lisa's page is a degree of subtlety in the adaptation of the dialogue. She keeps the initial exchange between Viola and the Captain, but feels free to simplify the antithesis 'And what should I do in Illyria?/My brother he is in Elysium'[6] to 'And what should I do in Illyria? My brother, – he is dead'. Of course the 'Illyria/ Elysium' pairing is a considerable loss, but the curious punctuation of the second sentence makes its own contribution to the power of the line as it enacts the catch in Viola's throat as she voices her fear (unlike Shakespeare's Viola, without a poetic/witty evasion).

Similar success in balancing exposition, characterization and dialogue – some adapted, some original – can be found in the work of Sameena in the opening of her version of Act 1 Scene 1. In the splendid opening phrases, she very nicely distances Illyria into a land of story and imagination; she then introduces Orsino in a way that avoids the whole 'in love with being in love' business, neatly linking the first and second scenes, and deftly incorporating the play's opening line in her exposition:

> Some time ago, I'm not quite sure when, when dukes were still around, a duke lived in an island known to man as Illyria. He was just like any other duke; he lived in a castle, had quite a few attendants and servants and had loads of money. But then just like any other duke he had problems – in this case the Duke Orsino had love problems ... when he thought about his love for the lady Olivia and heard the crashing of the waves that seemed to play a kind of music he thought to himself 'if music be the food of love, play on!'

Another example of adapting dialogue can be found in Rebecca's version of the shipwreck:

> She looked frantically round for her brother Sebastian, – where was he! The sickening feeling inside her grew worse, surely he wasn't in those roaring seas?
>
> 'Where is Sebastian, my brother?' she said.
>
> The Captain answered, – 'Madam, it was by good fortune that you yourself were saved from these angry, shark infested waters.'
>
> 'Then perhaps by good fortune my brother was saved as well ...'

And another in Sam's retelling of Act 1 Scene 3:

> 'He can play the cello and speak four different languages without looking at a book, these things just come naturally to him.'
>
> 'The only thing that comes "naturally" to that fool,' said Maria, 'is being a fool!' She pushed past Sir Toby and began dusting a vase.
>
> 'Be polite, Sir' whispered Sir Toby, as Maria's face turned as dark as thunder.

Now Sir Andrew being thick as two short planks took 'be polite' the wrong way, and thought it was Maria's name!!

'My name is *Maria*!' said Maria as she gritted her teeth with anger and pulled her hand away.

'Oh,' said Sir Andrew, 'I'm terribly sorry good mistress *Maria Polite*.'

This strikes me as very successful, and Sam is quite clear about the motivation for her deviations from the original: 'There was a lot of "sexual flirtation" between Maria and Sir Andrew and I felt this was not suitable.' She has, however, caught the air of unmistakable mockery.

A similar sense of purpose/strategy and awareness of questions of suitability, worked out more fully, is apparent in Natalie's commentary on her version of the same scene:

> I wanted to give an overall impression that Sir Andrew was just a man in an intricate game between Maria and Sir Toby. I wanted to put an emphasis on Maria treating Sir Andrew badly without using the adult phrase. Mainly about how Maria said 'It is Dry Sir'. I felt that for the target age group this would not be in a way innocent enough. So I believed that there would be other ways of making him feel bad. Even with the last part where Maria says she has more humour in her little finger than in his whole body I thought that made a complete idiot of him. Which served the task well. I also thought it would be hard for the younger reader to know that Sir Toby had the man there only for his own humour. And in a way I think he knew that. But because of his loneliness he was prevented from seeing that as being wrong.

The final comment here captures very sympathetically Sir Andrew's pathos.

Pupils were also particularly successful at times in the ways in which they introduced characters into their narratives; for instance Sam bringing in Sir Andrew after dialogue between Maria and Sir Toby:

> Then entered the man of the moment. Sir Andrew Aguecheek, a tall skinny man with a thin face and a big nose. His hair hung limply on his head and his breath smelt like sour milk.

A completely different approach, and much bolder, was adopted by Graham, who jumped in with the first person, again incorporating phrases from Shakespeare to good effect, but this time from quite elsewhere in the play:

> Greetings children, I am the all singing, all dancing, all drinking kick-ass kinsman known to my lady as Sir Toby Belch. I have been sent by

the wickedly, wild writer Sir Willy Shakespeare to tell how the nig-
gardly sheep biter Malvolio the mad was imprisoned as a looney due
to him being fooled black and blue as a trout is caught with tickling.

The class showed an awareness of the need to balance the nature of Shakespeare's play against the supposed need of the target audience. Perhaps
James' comment showed the most awareness of the pedagogical issues
involved:

> I have managed to keep the language slightly complex as the children
> will learn from this. I also contemplated with the idea of adding even
> more difficult words and having a sort of dictionary down the side so
> that if a child were to get stuck they could easily refer to it.
>
> I think in ideal circumstances this book should be read by a parent
> to a child but for the more adventurous readers they might like to
> build up their confidence and read alone. I feel that this is worth
> reading because I read it to my younger sister and she thought it was a
> good idea of trying to introduce Old English [sic] at an early age so
> that you can build up basic knowledge so work in later years is
> slightly simpler.

This final comment returns us nicely to my earlier reflections on published
versions, their nature, uses and value. The exercise also shows that more is
gained from the narratives that the children produce themselves than those
produced for them. The pupils quoted here have clearly read and thought
about Shakespeare in some depth, and have extended and tested their own
skills as story-writers. Unlike the awareness of the plays that comes from
being introduced to the stories in advance of a reading of the play, work of
this kind shows an awareness that clearly couldn't be acquired without
having, in some depth and with some attention to detail, *read* Shakespeare.

Chapter 12

Theatre

In most of the widely used Oxford School Shakespeare volumes, Roma Gill reminds us that 'Shakespeare's plays were written to be *performed*, not studied in a classroom'. She advises pupils to 'Act the play, or at least part of it. You don't need scenery or costumes – just space and people'.[1] However, two questions go unconsidered: what do pupils have to know in order to make something of this instruction? In what ways can their knowledge and understanding (and enjoyment) be developed by doing so? It often looks as if pupils 'acting out' bits of Shakespeare don't really grasp what they're reading. This may be apparent in a number of ways, including the failure to observe shifts of tone or meaning, even changes of addressee, especially in long speeches, and the tendency to 'add expression' through merely vigorous delivery of lines. A performance-based approach, therefore, needs to be complemented by an approach that will enable pupils to grasp the potential meanings of the text in a way that will inform their performances and their understanding and appreciation of others' performances. An emphasis on performance must go hand in hand with an emphasis on reading, and, rightly managed, will enhance reading, encouraging greater depth of understanding and attention to detail.

There needs to be specific recognition of Shakespeare as drama, as something that is quintessentially *watched*. Shakespeare wrote his plays to be acted in a performance space of a particular type, to be spoken out loud to a listening and watching audience, with actors taking up and changing positions on stage in varying combinations, in broad daylight. When we are sitting in a classroom reading Shakespeare it's easy to lose track – or even to be unaware – of this theatrical dimension, especially when we are struggling with the language. We can fail to be aware of who is on stage at a given time, of where they might be and in what physical relation to others, of who might be listening, of what silent characters might be doing.[2] Without us prompting them, our classes may neglect to consider the possibilities of the text in terms of stage picture and various possibilities of delivery.

There are some quite simple things we can do during class reading of Shakespeare in order to alert our classes to the importance of use of space.[3]

Pupils can be encouraged to hold their books up in order to be able to project their voices more clearly. We can think about the positions in the classroom of the pupils who are reading certain parts. Where there are moments of confrontation, pupils can be facing one another. Pupils can be prompted to turn in the direction of the character they are addressing. Where appropriate, they should establish eye contact, even if it interferes with their reading for a moment. After all, they can read an exchange a few times until they get used to it, and repetition will help establish it in the class's mind. (The teacher's art may show here in the choice of which lines are to be so emphasized.) If the classroom is spoken *across*, rather than merely *in*, it begins to become a theatrical space. As pupils become more confident, they might be prompted to move. (It's worth mentioning at this point a disadvantage shared by listening to recorded performance and watching film versions of Shakespeare – that is, in neither case do the actors and the audience share a common space.)

Beginning to develop a sense of space

At first an emphasis on physicality might just be a matter of gesture, using the elements that Rex Gibson[4] did so much to alert us to – the gestic element entailed by deixis, for instance. Readers can be encouraged at particular times to accompany words with a gesture, pointing at the words' referent (as remarked earlier, this can help clarify the grammar as well as the situation). In the first scene of *A Midsummer Night's Dream*, for instance, Egeus' animus can be strongly brought out with pointing:

> *Thou, thou, Lysander, thou* hast given her rhymes,
> And interchang'd love-token with *my child*:
> *Thou* hast by moonlight at *her* window sung

To complicate matters a little, we can observe that editorial punctuation can have a bearing on how these lines are delivered. The Folio punctuation is 'Thou, thou Lysander, thou hast given her ...', giving the line three thrusts at Lysander instead of four. (For a fuller discussion of editorial punctuation, see pages 175–7.)

A gesture accompanying Horatio's lines about the dawn helps with the sense of *locatedness* that it's important to establish:

> But *look*, the morn in russet mantle clad
> Walks o'er the dew on *yon* high eastern hill

Being alerted to this dimension through such questions as 'Who – and where – is *my child*?' 'Where is *there*?' may lead to a habit that can be fruitful in later work – for instance when considering a line such as Othello's 'I have a pain upon my forehead, *here*,' where the deixis invites (from Desdemona) recognition of an area not merely physical, but also the site of the cuckold's imagined horns. (The location of 'there' in Othello's later speech 'Had it pleased heaven …' – 'But there, where I have garnered up my heart,/Where either I must live or bear no life,/The fountain from the which my current runs' might also be worth consideration at A Level.)

So far, pupils needn't have left their desks. With growing confidence we can be more adventurous in our use of classroom space. For example in a first reading of Act 4 Scene 1 of *Macbeth* the three Weird Sisters can be positioned around the sides of the room, and Macbeth placed centrally. (There's no need to clear the central area, although it might help, and can certainly give a sense of occasion.) This makes it hard for Macbeth to address the sisters simultaneously; he has to break and re-establish eye contact repeatedly, and without eye-contact – eye-*command* – he's cut adrift. When they address him he has to turn, not necessarily being able to anticipate who will speak next. This makes for a combination of insecurity and aggression which works very well and can help illuminate a lot about the scene, including the comedy (isn't that what we encounter when, after the enormous piling up of Macbeth's world-destroying threats, the weird sisters simply reply 'We'll answer'?).

It can also help in this lesson to have large drawings or paintings (they might be commissioned from GCSE or A Level art students) of the three apparitions on the classroom walls. They can remain through subsequent lessons as a reminder of the predictions that Macbeth finally falls foul of.

Moving into the space

Initial exploration of the theatrical dimension is not best managed by sending pupils away in groups with a general instruction to 'act out a scene' – at least not without further supporting direction. While pupils undoubtedly enjoy such activity, they often don't know enough to do it with point and purpose, and as a result it does not reliably engage them in close reading, reading for dramatic and particular meanings. They will be able to make more of it if they have worked with some of the methods outlined above, and there needs to be, at least on some occasions, a framework of understanding, maybe even quite tightly structured questions, to help focus attention more closely and bring out more precisely the dramatic possibilities of the text.

At the very least they should be asked to think about the kind of playspace they are going to prepare their scene for. It's best at first to concentrate on the type Shakespeare wrote for: a large wooden platform stage with audience on three sides, open to the sky, with two doors at the back for entrance and exits, a trapdoor, a balcony and very little else: no curtains, no lighting, everything always in plain view, very little scenery. The De Witt drawing of the Swan Theatre (type 'De Witt Swan' into Google Images) is probably the best visual aid; it is the only contemporary drawing of the Elizabethan stage and it makes the likely performance conditions of the Shakespearean stage very clear. It doesn't, however, show an inner stage between the doors (as there is in the New Globe). I'm not sure whether the most up-to-date scholarship grants the existence of an inner stage (it comes and goes over the decades), so I usually just mention it as a possibility. Later they may be asked to consider other, more modern alternatives.

Once the stage has been introduced, three words much used in the play-texts but easily overlooked in the classroom may be highlighted: *enter*, *exit* and *exeunt*. At which door? How far on to the stage? In what manner? And, from the dramatist's and the character's point of view, why? These simple questions serve to get the pupils thinking further in the theatrical dimension.

When 'acting out' a passage from the play, pupils should be encouraged to consider such basic questions as these:

- Where are the characters on stage at the beginning of the sequence?
- When do the characters change position on stage?
- How do they move?
- When are they are close together and when far apart?
- Where should they be looking? When should they make eye contact?
- Are there any gestures that they should make?
- Are there any specific actions indicated, either directly or indirectly, by the text?
- Should they touch each other at any point?
- How should specific lines be spoken?
- How should they react to what is said?
- What should their relationship to the audience be at any given point?
- How they should exit?

Such questions can be very productive. They can be used ad lib by the teacher with a group working on a scene, or given in written form for pupils to consider while they annotate passages of text with their suggestions before trying them out. I have found it useful to set this as homework, so that each individual pupil has a contribution to make to class direction in the following lesson. If pupils are uneasy about acting, it can be very useful to have sixth-form drama students on call. They don't need to know the text by heart; it can be shown on the OHP for them to sight-read. An advantage of this is that the words are spoken into the air and to an audience, not into a book. Sixth-form students can respond to suggestions from the class – 'Try it with a bit more reluctance', 'I think she should sound more angry' – with the nuances of which more mature readers are capable. They can take suggestions and develop them. And, very usefully, they are not the teacher. The younger pupils are hearing and seeing new possibilities in the text.

On some occasions a more specific set of questions might be given. For instance on the sleepwalking scene from *Macbeth*:

First work out the size/shape of your stage and where the audience would be. Then *Up to the entrance of Lady Macbeth*:

- Try different ways of having the Doctor and Waiting Gentlewoman enter. Do they come in together? If not, who comes in first? Do they use the same entrance? Does the Doctor enter straight away? What sort of mood is he in? What is the relationship between them?
- What positions do they take up on stage? Try having them standing near each other, close together, far apart. Try one sitting and one standing. Try them close to and well away from the audience. Who has the dominant position?
- How will the different positions affect the way they speak their lines?
- Try out different positions for them to be in when Lady Macbeth enters.

From Lady Macbeth's entrance to the end:
- Try different entrances for Lady Macbeth, and different positions for her in relation to the other two and the audience.
- Does she take up a particular position, or move about? Who should be able to see her face?
- Are Lady Macbeth's movements natural or stylized? Try out both to see which works best in your opinion.
- At what point can the Doctor and the Waiting Gentlewoman respond explicitly to what Lady Macbeth says?
- Try different positions for the Doctor and Waiting Gentlewoman to speak their comments from. Who might they be speaking to?
- How do the Doctor and the Waiting Gentlewoman go out?

For the whole scene:
- After you have tried out all the possibilities that you can think of, decide on the combination of moves that you think works best for this scene and practise a presentation of it.

These questions have prompted excellent work from Year 9 and GCSE pupils, as well as A level students. For instance, the Year 9 pupils had some splendidly arrogant Doctors. A GCSE group played a naturalistic pair of watchers; Lady Macbeth's commanding entrance was on a line straight down to the audience, her face an impassive mask. As she spoke, the watchers were drawn closer and closer to her until at 'Who would have thought the old man to have had so much blood in him' they recoiled in horror almost the whole distance of the stage. Some A level students used the balcony to experiment with stylization and naturalism. One group showed the Doctor and Gentlewoman on the balcony as choric commentators speaking out directly to the audience and Lady Macbeth acting naturalistically on the forestage in furious communion with the audience; another showed the watching pair on the forestage gazing up at an erect, almost immobile stylized Lady who spoke in a trance.

Stage directions

This kind of experimental questioning of staging possibilities is of obvious value. However, the tendency of some editors is to do a lot of it for us by providing extra stage directions. (There are very few in the Folio.) The most notorious example of this is John Dover Wilson's *Hamlet*. He makes his theory that Hamlet has two entrances in Act 2 Scene 2, during the first of which he overhears the king plotting before withdrawing in order to make his second, into part of the text by adding several stage directions to that effect.[5]

Although this is extreme, the tendency is common in *The New Shakespeare*, of which Dover Wilson was general editor. The editions include not only descriptions of locations, suitable more to the nineteenth-century scenic stage than the unlocalized Elizabethan, but also directions as to how lines are to be delivered and clarifications of stage 'business' (for instance with the letter in Act 1 Scene 2 of the same play). The intention may well be to appeal to 'the theatre of the mind', but what we are given is something like 'Shakespeare Designed to Be Read as Literature'. I can't be alone in finding such editorial stage directions intrusive and irritating, even though some of them are undoubtedly interesting as *suggestions*. Such interpretations, which are only among the possibilities, belong in discussion and on the stage, not on the page. Where they occur in school texts, we should make it clear that they are editorial.

Schools' editions quite often introduce directions of this kind, with, arguably, more justification. They also often make explicit the directions that are implicit in the text. Young readers may well need help to visualize what is happening on the stage, but not always. For instance in Macbeth's 'dagger' soliloquy we read:

> I see thee yet, in form as palpable,
> As this which now I draw.

Quite clearly he draws his dagger here. An added direction might seem unnecessary. As here, in Pyramus's build up to his suicide:

Thus die I, thus, thus, thus, thus.

It's quite obvious what he's doing. Nonetheless, some editions add directions. Fair enough, we might feel; but they could forestall certain considerations. For instance, exactly *when* and *how* does Macbeth draw his dagger? Does Pyramus stab himself four times? If so, why? Or does Pyramus flunk it three times and only strike home on the last? Thinking about this kind of thing can enhance pupils' reading of Shakespeare's playtext in terms of stage action. The question is whether what is most suitable on any given occasion is (a) the ease that comes from having the direction, or (b) the discussion (that may develop the pupils' ability to read Shakespeare) that can come from not having the direction.

A method we might use from time to time while studying a scene is to offer a set of invented stage directions and ask pupils where they might be used in the text (and whether they would use them). These directions might include some that are arguably implied by the text as well as some that aren't, and it might be an idea to include one or two that are just plain wrong. The exercise involves close reading while foregrounding the performance element. For example, these directions might be considered for Act 2 Scene 2 of *The Tempest*:

Caliban lies down. Trinculo crawls under Caliban's cloak. Stephano grabs Trinculo delightedly, really pleased to see him. Stephano pulls at Trinculo's legs. Caliban looks round fearfully. Trinculo bends down for a closer look. Trinculo looks surprised. Caliban kneels. Caliban gets up. Stephano looks as if he might be sick. Caliban drinks from the bottle. Stephano takes the bottle and drinks. Stephano gives Trinculo the bottle to carry. Caliban dances. Caliban kisses the bottle. Caliban looks adoringly at Stephano. Trinculo looks at Caliban with contempt.

These are presented here in the order of the scene, but a set could be jumbled to make the exercise more interesting. Groups of pupils could also prepare their own sets for others to try out. Also pupils might consider which lines are spoken *boldly*, *insinuatingly*, *hesitantly*, *eventually* and so forth.

There are occasions on which concentration on stage directions, implied or given, can help focus and develop a reading of a whole scene. In *Richard III*, the extraordinary wooing by Richard of the Lady Anne (Act 1 Scene 2) is an excellent scene for classroom work. Interestingly, much of the sequence is omitted in Olivier's film version. Instead Claire Bloom has to imply the whole progress of her seduction through facial expressions, for which of course there are no directions. This gives a good occasion for class discussion, both as to why this has been done and what the gains and losses may be. Does Anne succumb because she is weak? Because there is a peculiar sexual attraction in Richard and that 'Thy bedchamber,' while – maybe even because – horrifying, *excites* her? The implication of the film version is that Richard's techniques of insinuation, beyond the bare statement of his sexual intent, are unnecessary. (Also relevant may be Samuel Johnson's remark, made in relation to *Measure for Measure*: 'I am afraid our varlet poet intended to inculcate, that women think ill of nothing that raises the credit of their beauty, and are ready, however virtuous, to pardon any act which they think incited by their own charms.')[6]

The intense physicality of this scene came out well when a group of Year 10 pupils working on the scene were put off by the thought that they might have to spit. They asked if Anne couldn't slap him instead. This sent some back to the text:

> Anne   Would it were mortal poison for thy sake.
>
> Richard   Never came poison from so sweet a place.
>
> Anne   Never hung poison on a fouler toad.

They pointed out the importance of it being spit, and noted that she spits *at* him (the stage direction, while not necessary, is given in the Folio), not on the floor at his feet (a traditional gesture of contempt – the opposite, one pupil suggested, of worshipping the ground he walks on), that the spit must be on his face, raising the question of whether he wipes it off.

Richard's seduction passes through various phases up to his master stroke of offering her his sword and his naked breast:

> Lo, here I lend thee this sharp-pointed sword;
> Which if thou please to hide in this true breast,
> And let the soul forth that adoreth thee,
> I lay it naked to the deadly stroke,
> And humbly beg the death upon my knee.

At this point we get as authentic a stage direction as we are likely to get in Shakespeare: *He layes his brest open. She offers at [it] with his sword.*

Beginning with the stage picture of the kneeling Richard and the armed Anne, pupils can go on to look closely at the ensuing action, perhaps being prompted by some questions as follows. When Richard says 'Nay, do not pause', *has* she paused? Or does Richard forestall a lunge by suggesting that she's paused? Richard continues:

> for I did kill King Henry,

Does Anne at this point begin (again) to press the sword forward? And is she again forestalled by Richard's next line?

> But 'twas thy beauty that provokèd me.

If there is a lunge-pause pattern it can continue with the next lines (might a tone of open sarcasm accompany 'Nay, now dispatch'?):

> Nay, now dispatch; 'twas I that stabbed young Edward,
> But 'twas thy heavenly face that set me on.

There could even be an element of comedy if the lines are played in a certain way. Or are the contradictory impulses in Anne just reflected in her facial expressions? However the lines are played, Anne's confusion is sufficient to motivate the next Folio direction: '*She fals the sword.*' This gives Richard the opportunity to offer an ultimatum:

> Take up the sword again, or take up me.

She tries to do neither – but in the terms that Richard has offered, she has already capitulated. From here on, Anne's speeches are tentative, evasive and equivocal. So Richard makes another offer – not of his life this time, but a ring:

> *Richard* Vouchsafe to wear this ring.
> *Anne* To take is not to give.

There is no direction in the Folio to indicate that Anne takes the ring (a direction like Dover Wilson's '*she puts on the ring*' begs the question), but it is clear from the following line that it arrives somehow on her hand:

> *Richard* Look how my ring encompasseth thy finger ...

How does Richard give her the ring, and how, and at exactly what point does she take it? Does he press it upon her in a way that would require her to force it away physically if she wished not to accept it? So that, will she, nill she, she is holding the ring? Does Richard then himself put the ring on her finger, holding her hand as he invites her attention to it? Or does Anne reach out for the ring, and put it on herself? (If so, 'To take is not to give' looks even more questionably evasive.) The physical movements here can interact intimately with the speaking of the lines, raising questions about *tone* that would be harder to explore without the physical dimension.

Stage picture and dramatic meaning

Another function of editorial stage directions is to indicate which lines are to be spoken 'aside'. This can be very helpful and remove no end of puzzlement (there is general editorial agreement about which lines are asides, and usually on perfectly sound grounds). To do that thinking for the young reader may be no insult but a genuine service. The directions can get them some way to an imagined performance of the play, a dramatic understanding. But they can also fix or limit the understanding. Showing them one possibility is just that, but the text suggests, by being a text, something more final. (There is a similar danger with showing pupils any one performance, whether on stage or screen. 'I didn't realize that Helena wore glasses' remarked a Year 9 pupil after watching a scene from the BBC *Dream*.) Of course the realization that there are other possibilities might well come in later, and a serious danger of what I'm going on to suggest is a continual jigging about and no settled, graspable dramatic experience. As ever, balance and particular judgement are needed, a sense of tact and the present purpose. However, this caveat aside, the working method I'm suggesting with editorial stage directions is: take them out.

Consider this passage from Act 5 Scene 5 of *Macbeth*:

Macbeth	Hang out our banners on the outward walls.	
	The cry is still, they come: our Castle's strength	
	Will laugh a siege to scorn: here let them lie,	
	Till famine and the ague eat them up:	
	Were they not forc'd with those that should be ours,	5
	We might have met them dareful, beard to beard,	
	And beat them backward home. What is that noise?	
	A cry within of women	
Seyton	It is the cry of women, my good Lord.	
Macbeth	I have almost forgot the taste of fears:	
	The time has been, my senses would have cool'd	10
	To hear a night-shriek; and my fell of hair	
	Would at a dismal treatise rouse, and stir	
	As life were in't. I have supp'd full with horrors,	
	Direness familiar to my slaughterous thoughts	
	Cannot once start me. Wherefore was that cry?	15
Seyton	The Queen, my Lord, is dead.	
Macbeth	She should have died hereafter;	
	There would have been a time for such a word;	
	To-morrow, and to-morrow, and to-morrow,	
	Creeps in this petty pace from day to day,	20

To the last syllable of recorded time;
And all our yesterdays, have lighted fools
The way to dusty death. Out, out, brief candle,
Life's but a walking shadow, a poor player
That struts and frets his hour upon the stage,   25
And then is heard no more. It is a tale
Told by an idiot, full of sound and fury,
Signifying nothing.

Enter a Messenger

Thou comest to use thy tongue; thy story quickly.

Most modern editions have stage directions '*Exit Seyton*' at line 8 and '*(Re-)enter Seyton*' at line 15, although the Folio gives no warrant for them. Presumably the thinking behind these directions is that this is the only way of making sense of the scene. Seyton knows what the sound is, but he does not know its cause until he goes off to find out; having found out, he is able to answer Macbeth's question, itself prompted by his re-entry. Indeed, that makes perfectly good sense. However, Alan C. Dessen points out,[7] it is not the only sense that can be made of the scene. Suppose, he suggests, we take the text as in the Folio; what do we find? If Seyton doesn't leave the stage, and yet can answer Macbeth's question, who or what is he? Dessen finds an unsettling, eldritch figure, capable of preternatural knowledge. (We might add to this the sense of contempt that seems, or can seem, to emanate from him – this is the servant that told his *King* in a previous scene, when Macbeth ordered his armour to be brought, that he didn't need it yet. Anyone who might show Macbeth any deference or respect is long gone. Whatever else he is, Seyton is what Macbeth has left.) Also, if Seyton does not leave the stage, we must consider the possibilities of his being an on-stage audience for Macbeth's speeches – a question particularly apt for practical investigation at both GCSE and A Level.

But first, in order to get the scene right we have to establish its opening dynamic. The choices we make at the beginning of the scene will affect the way the whole scene goes, and if we get that wrong the rhythm of the whole scene in performance might falter. (Textual choices have their influence here also, depending on whether we read, with most modern editions, 'The cry is still, "They come!"' or with the Folio 'The cry is still, they come,' which makes the last two-word clause not a record of what the others are saying, but Macbeth's own recognition of the meaning of the shouting having stopped; the punctuation proposed by Robert Nichols – 'The cry is still. They come.' – makes that recognition even bleaker.) We need to see how the scene has its place in a rhythm alternating between the scenes at Dunsinane and the near-choric scenes of the gathering and approaching army, during which we are told of Macbeth:

> Some say he's mad: others, that lesser hate him,
> Do call it valiant fury.

These lines raise the question of what we *see*. Our readings of Act 5 Scene 3 – do we see there courage, desperation, resignation or an unsettled combination of all three? – will also influence our sense of how Macbeth comes on here. We may decide that in the earlier scene his abrupt shifts from one hearer to another suggest a restless nervous energy perhaps best realized in physical movement, and that this can be picked up as a point of continuity in his entrance to Scene 5, unless we feel that a contrast would be both more effective and more appropriate.

With such considerations in mind we may ask: is Macbeth's opening speech spoken to Seyton? To himself? To the audience? Restlessly moving from one to the other? Is 'there let them lie' thrust out scornfully in defiance, or murmured resentfully? If defiance, is that defiance bold or reckless? ('Some say he's mad ...') Is there a pause after 'beat them backward home'? Is *that* where we hear the 'cry of women'? (The Folio positioning of the stage direction might strike us as odd and more a question of printing convenience than dramatic significance.) What should the cry sound like? Could it be a long, low howling of which we have – and Macbeth has – been dimly aware, and which becomes unignorable at this point? If so, Seyton could have been listening to it, interpreting it and known the answer before Macbeth asked the question – a choice which would reduce his 'eldritch' possibilities. (As does Nicholas Brooke's comment that 'it is possible that someone enters to tell him'.[8] But why would the message be given to Seyton and not directly to Macbeth, as other messages in this and other scenes are given? Perhaps because the putative messenger didn't have the nerve to do so.)

Is Seyton's 'It is the cry of women, good my Lord' derisive, sympathetic or matter-of-fact? These questions can best be answered by trying out the various possibilities, and no answer will be final, although some will strike us as irresistibly right.

If Seyton remains on stage, Macbeth's 'I had almost forgot the taste of fears' becomes no longer a soliloquy, and the range of questions concerning how it might be delivered increases. It might be treated as an aside, that is, in effect as a soliloquy, but offset in a stage picture with potentially more than one focus (compare Macbeth's speeches after the entrance of Ross and Angus in Act 1 Scene 3). The audience can focus on Macbeth as he makes his statement about his isolation, or shift its view to take in a *picture* of that isolation in the distance between him and Seyton or, if the staging permits, focus on the sardonic on-stage audience to Macbeth's words. These possible choices (which would be made for us by the camera in a film version) may be reduced or removed by letting Seyton recede so much that he becomes merely background, ignored by the audience (in which case he might as well have left). It's also possible that the lines might be delivered *to* Seyton. (It's been suggested that Hamlet's 'To be or not to be' could be spoken directly to Ophelia, making 'Nymph in thy orisons' some kind of conclusion.) The irony of Macbeth telling this contemptuous time-server – if that is what he is, if he is nothing more sinister – of his predicament as regards loyalty could be grimly comic. Teachers trying this out during an INSET session found that while it worked to speak the beginning of the speech directly to Seyton, it became necessary at some point during it to move away from him, so that 'Wherefore was that cry?' was delivered turning back to him, separating it from the main part of the speech. The text seemed to resist the attempt to speak the whole speech to Seyton. However, it was felt that to begin with Seyton as Macbeth's audience *was* effective. (A passage of related interest is in *Othello* Act 4 Scene 2 in which Othello's speech beginning 'Had it pleas'd Heaven,/To try me with Affliction' has something of the appearance of soliloquy. Students might experiment with playing the speech directly to Desdemona, and seeing if there is no point at which they feel they must pull away, and as a soliloquy either to himself or to the audience. If the latter, what is Desdemona doing?)

Even in current editions, Macbeth's most famous soliloquy, 'To-morrow and to-morrow', is technically no soliloquy but an aside. Now that we are alert to questions of the effect that stage picture and (potential) on-stage audiences can have on dramatic meaning, we must look at the possibilities of delivering this speech. We may find, as with the previous speech, that, even if we can begin it as something spoken to Seyton, or consciously in his hearing, it 'naturally' pulls away to the manner of a soliloquy, something with no sense of an audience. Or we decide that it is delivered *at* the audience, inviting recognition of its truth (if it is indeed true, and not just an outpouring of spite) before Macbeth turns back to the messenger who has entered upstage behind him. (What if the messenger comes in hearing what Macbeth is saying? Compare that possibility with Macbeth entering in Act 1 Scene 5 *before* the end of Lady Macbeth's soliloquy.)

Work with a Year 10 group suggested further possibilities of how the stage picture can create possibilities of meaning. I had set up work on the scene containing this instruction:

> Work out two settings (placing of actors, moves) for the scene: (a) with just Macbeth and Seyton; (b) with Lady Macbeth and her women visible to the audience.

I had no more in mind than the possibility of a background tableau of death and mourning, giving a visual representation of what might be involved in 'the cry of women'. But the pupils took it a step further, having the women actually bring the corpse of Lady Macbeth into the area of the stage occupied by Macbeth. While 'To-morrow and to-morrow …' was shouted directly at the audience, 'Out, out brief candle' was spoken quietly to the dead body of his wife.

Does this go beyond what Shakespeare intended? Who can say? Who can say whether it matters, or in what way it matters? This might be fertile ground for discussion with classes. (Pupils and students can be very conservative about what is and is not proper to do with Shakespeare.) Practical discussion of this kind can take us deep into the dramatic possibilities, the potential range and meaning of the drama.

Before moving on from this short scene, I should mention the stage direction from the Folio, which I suppressed at the beginning of my long quotation. The scene actually begins '*Enter Macbeth, Seyton and Soldiers, with drum and colours*'. At what point in the scene, if any, do the soldiers exit? (No direction is given in the Folio before the end-of-scene '*Exeunt*'.) If they don't, what difference does their presence make? Are they just scenery? The previous Dunsinane scene had no soldiers. It began with a partly domestic emphasis: '*Enter Macbeth, Doctor, and Attendants*'. By the end of that scene the Doctor has gone, the opposing troops are nearer. The whole process has gone further by the opening of Scene 5. If set up rightly, these things may be grasped instinctively by a theatrical audience. In the classroom they need to be brought out in discussion and commentary.

Several general points emerge from this account: the importance of establishing the opening dynamic of a scene; the potential effect of on-stage listeners; how a stage picture with more than one focus can increase tension and the range of potential dramatic meaning. To these may be added the importance of not taking soliloquies in isolation, but considering how the character got to the point of that utterance, and how the speeches belong in the larger dramatic rhythm.

A distinction that is useful in investigating passages of dramatic text in this way is that between the *locus* and the *platea*. The locus is the area in which the acting is either naturalistic or ritualistic, played not to but for the audience, that is, without a direct acknowledgement of the audience by the actors. Roughly speaking it will be the upstage area, away from the audience. The action there is beheld by the audience, but not participated in (which is not to say that we may not be intensely involved). The *platea* occupies the space between the locus and the audience, and is ground from which the actors, or rather the characters which they play, may relate more directly to the audience, through aside and sustained direct address; it is the region of clowns and commentators, from which these figures can remark on what is happening in the *locus*. A modern equivalent would be comments direct to the camera on film or television. If Macbeth addresses

Seyton directly, the action remains in the *locus*: if he delivers his nihilistic pronouncement to the audience, it shifts into the *platea* (perhaps privileging the utterance as supra-dramatic). Clearly these distinctions may be thought of in a hard and fast or in a quite fluid manner – and may most profitably be considered as distinctions of style rather than physical location. The terms can be taught straightforwardly to A Level and GCSE classes, and can be used in the investigation of soliloquies in relation to whether a given soliloquy is to be conceived as direct self-explanation to the audience or a kind of self-communing which the audience happens to overhear. This can help students to distinguish between different kinds of soliloquy (for instance, Richard's 'Now is the winter of our discontent' and Macbeth's 'Is this a dagger …?').

The *locus/platea* distinction, questions of stage picture and the productive question 'who's listening?' can be particularly useful in devising work on more sustained passages, looking at the structure and potential dynamics of whole scenes from, for example, *Measure for Measure* and *Othello*. Such work is best undertaken after the class has already read the scene at least once and has a general idea of its content and context, probably after the initial read-through of the whole play and some preliminary discussion. Exercises should follow a general introduction to the kind of issues involved. They can be done assuming any kind of stage. Groups can be asked to consider which type of stage they think suitable to the scene, or instructed to assume a particular type of stage. Whichever type of stage they use, it would be productive to consider the possibilities for the scene of using different physical levels.

Act 2 Scene 2 of *Measure for Measure* is the scene in which Isabella, prompted by Lucio, comes to Angelo to plead for her brother's life. The first eighteen lines, before her arrival is announced by a servant, establish an uneasy atmosphere with the tension between the concerns of the Provost and the rectitude of Angelo. Isabella and Lucio enter. The Provost appears to be about to leave, but Angelo bids him stay (why?).

Enter PROVOST *and a* SERVANT.

Servant   He's hearing of a cause; he will come straight
          I'll tell him of you.
Provost   Pray you, do.

          Exit Servant

                         I'll know
          His pleasure; may be he will relent. Alas,
          He hath but as offended in a dream!
          All sects, all ages smack of this vice; and he   5
          To die for't!

Enter ANGELO

Angelo	Now, what's the matter. Provost?
Provost	Is it your will Claudio shall die tomorrow?
Angelo	Did not I tell thee yea? hadst thou not order?
	Why dost thou ask again?

Provost   Lest I might be too rash:
Under your good correction, I have seen,   10
When, after execution, judgment hath
Repented o'er his doom.

Angelo   Go to; let that be mine:
Do you your office, or give up your place,
And you shall well be spared.

Provost   I crave your honour's pardon.
What shall be done, sir, with the groaning Juliet?   15
She's very near her hour.

Angelo   Dispose of her
To some more fitter place, and that with speed.

Re-enter Servant

Servant Here is the sister of the man condemn'd
Desires access to you.

Angelo   Hath he a sister?

Provost Ay, my good lord; a very virtuous maid,   20
And to be shortly of a sisterhood,
If not already.

Angelo   Well, let her be admitted.

Exit Servant

See you the fornicatress be removed:
Let have needful, but not lavish, means;
There shall be order for't.

Enter ISABELLA *and* LUCIO

Provost   Save your honour!   25

Angelo Stay a little while. You're welcome. What's your will?

As with the scene from *Macbeth* discussed earlier (as with any scene), it's important to establish what the opening dynamic is (what we want it to be/what we find it can be). Choices concerning the positioning of the characters and the degree of their awareness of one another will affect our sense of the action of the scene. The first task for the class to consider, then, is the movement towards the key position at line 26. Practically, they investigate the possibilities, perhaps aiming to consider four different stage positions from which the remainder of the scene can follow. This needs to be done fairly swiftly, but in passing they should consider whether the Provost's brief soliloquy is shared directly with the audience or not, and whether Angelo should be played coldly or irascibly. (Does it bother him to have these questions asked? How is the audience to perceive him at this point?) There's no need to dwell on all the possibilities at this stage, as they can be reconsidered after the investigation of the whole scene, in which it will be apparent how our sense of the scene's development may alter our understanding of its beginning. The main thing is to fix possible stage pictures for the moment(s) at which Angelo first sees, and first addresses, Isabella.

The dialogue between them, which comprises the bulk of the rest of the scene, has two on-stage observers, and neither is silent throughout (both make comments, Lucio in some detail). In the Arden edition Lucio's comments are given as '*to Isab*' (in the New Penguin as '*aside to Isabella*') the Provost's as '*aside*'. These editorial interventions seem entirely reasonable, but – for instance – Lucio's short speeches *need* not be heard by Isabella. That most likely to do so is the longest, spoken after she appears to give up (almost as soon as she has started):

> Give't not o'er so. To him again, entreat him,
> Kneel down before him, hang upon his gown:
> You are too cold. If you should need a pin,
> You could not with more tame a tongue desire it.
> To him, I say.

However, this needn't determine the character and delivery of the others. (Nor does its being spoken directly to her determine how Isabella will hear it, at what level her mind is working.) It is at least possible that Lucio's subsequent lines comprise an independent commentary, anxious at first but growing in approval and admiration, while Isabella pursues the path of her own fluctuating/developing feelings. Played in this way the scene will appear differently from one in which Lucio is insistently, almost physically, prompting Isabella in her task, goading her externally into a discovery of what arguments she might use, how her feelings might go (there are also questions to consider about the relationships of the argument and feeling here).

> *Isabella* Must he needs die?
> *Angelo* Maiden, no remedy.
> *Isabella* Yes; I do think that you might pardon him,
> And neither heaven nor man grieve at the mercy.

Angelo	I will not do't.
Isabella	But can you, if you would?
Angelo	Look, what I will not, that I cannot do.
Isabella	But might you do't, and do the world no wrong,
	If so your heart were touch'd with that remorse
	As mine is to him?
Angelo	He's sentenced; 'tis too late.
Lucio	You are too cold.
Isabella	Too late? why, no; I, that do speak a word,
	May call it back again. Well, believe this,
	No ceremony that to great ones 'longs,
	Not the king's crown, nor the deputed sword,
	The marshal's truncheon, nor the judge's robe,
	Become them with one half so good a grace
	As mercy does.
	If he had been as you and you as he,
	You would have slipt like him; but he, like you,
	Would not have been so stern.
Angelo	Pray you, be gone.
Isabella	I would to heaven I had your potency,
	And you were Isabel! should it then be thus?
	No; I would tell what 'twere to be a judge,
	And what a prisoner.
Lucio	Ay, touch him; there's the vein.

Lucio's later lines ('Ay, well said', 'That's well said', 'Thou'rt i' th' right, girl: more o' that'), delivered when Isabella has, so to speak, found her stride, might be considered even more marginal, although not without function. If heard – or acknowledged – by Isabella, they would interrupt the flow and insistence of her arguments, disrupt whatever currents are passing between her and Angelo, perhaps even with comic effect. Are they, then, best delivered merely as 'aside', not to Isabella – and if so, should they be spoken directly to the audience?

These and related issues can be explored by the class through practical work. The scene is of a length that is manageable for groups to consider all of it with a particular set of instructions. Five basic tasks could be given, one per group:

1   Play the scene with Isabella and Angelo upstage in the *locus* (how will they get there?) and Lucio in the *platea*, directing his lines to the audience rather than to Isabella. Isabella and Angelo play without awareness of either Lucio or the Provost. Where are you going to

place the Provost? Isabella and Angelo will remain largely static, but you should consider whether there are any points at which they *must* move.

2 Explore the possible range of movement in this scene. Try all the possibilities that you can think of, and then decide on the moves that you think are best to bring out the drama of the scene. (What use might be made of different levels?)

3 Play the scene with Angelo and Isabella both aware of Lucio throughout. How will they respond to him? Try placing Isabella and Angelo downstage and Lucio upstage. Will this work? What are the best positions for playing the scene in this way? Does the scene afford any potential for comedy?

4 Pay particular attention to the use of pauses to bring out the psychological undercurrents (subtext) that can be discovered in the scene. Investigate all the possible pauses and then decide which ones you think it is most important to use. Also consider whether characters look at each other or not – and if they don't, where do they look?

5 Rehearse and play a version of the scene in which all Lucio's asides are cut. What difference does this make to the rhythm of the scene?

These group investigations should be followed by presentations and plenary discussion, the aim of which should not be so much agreement as a clear understanding of what is involved in the various choices that have been made. Such discussions can be fascinating but are doubtless hard work, requiring considerable skill in the teacher to keep the whole thing afloat and moving. This discussion should lead to and inform the next task, consideration of the movement into Angelo's concluding soliloquy:

Angelo	Well; come to me to-morrow.
Lucio	Go to; 'tis well; away!
Isabella	Heaven keep your honour safe!
Angelo	Amen:
	For I am that way going to temptation,
	Where prayers cross.
Isabella	At what hour to-morrow
	Shall I attend your lordship?
Angelo	At any time 'fore noon.
Isabella	Save your honour!

Exeunt all but ANGELO

Angelo	From thee, even from thy virtue!
	What's this, what's this?

This leads into considering the performance of the soliloquy itself. What positions and moves can we see in this passage? Does Angelo start speaking as soon as everyone has gone? From where does he speak? At what points in the soliloquy should he pause? How does he leave the stage at the end of the soliloquy? The class can consider two basic ways of playing the speech – (i) in the *locus*, with no awareness of the audience; (ii) in the *platea*, to the audience – trying them against the potential of the text. They may decide that a combination of the two is the most suitable. If so, they should work it out in detail. This section of work could conclude with a performance of the complete scene.

While it might be argued that spending so much time on the question of Lucio's asides takes attention away from the essential action of this scene, I suspect that, rightly handled, such an investigation (which anyway considers more than the asides) may sharpen our sense of that action. Shakespeare, after all, included Lucio in the scene. He did not include him in Act 2 Scene 4, the scene that the class could work on in detail next. In contrast to Act 2 Scene 2, Angelo and Isabella are alone on stage together, with only us as audience. What difference does this make? The scene begins with a soliloquy by Angelo (including a line we might now reflect on with a certain irony: 'let no man hear me') and ends with one by Isabella. Again, the movements from and to these soliloquies can be carefully considered.

With an even longer scene that a class has already studied to some extent, a similar investigation can take place with a sequence of shorter (overlapping) passages assigned to different groups for practical work. In *Othello* there are two scenes (Act 1 Scene 3 and Act 2 Scene 1) which move from a fully populated stage down to a dialogue between Roderigo and Iago before ending with a soliloquy by Iago (in each case moving from verse through prose to verse). The potential of the varying stage picture in scenes like this is well worth investigation. The *locus/platea* tool can be used to focus attention on the role of Iago throughout these scenes, and so to plot carefully the movement towards his soliloquies. The questions set can be quite detailed, asking for decisions about the delivery of particular lines, and focusing on moments when the stage picture definitely changes (i.e. with exits and entrances), or where it might change (with movement during or between speeches), with the relation of the actors to each other and the audience always well in mind. At any point in these crowded scenes, where is Iago? (Is it worth considering how visible Roderigo and his reactions should be?)

Act 2 Scene 1, the sequence of arrivals in Cyprus, can be divided as follows (line references are to the Cambridge edition):

Lines 1–82	the bringing of news: arrival of Cassio: arrival of Desdemona
Lines 83–122	greetings; more news; banter between Iago, Emilia and Desdemona

Lines 124–173   Iago's 'praise' of women; Iago's comments on Cassio; arrival of Othello
Lines 174–204   Othello and Desdemona, with a comment by Iago; the stage clears
Lines 205–266   Iago and Roderigo
Lines 267–293   Iago's soliloquy.

Specific points for consideration might include: the position of Iago and Desdemona in relation to the other on-stage groups during the conversation about women; the treatment of Desdemona's lines 'I am not merry, but I do beguile/The thing I am by seeming otherwise' (an aside or not? if an aside, to whom?); Desdemona's tone in responding to Iago's misogynistic merriment; the positions take up by Iago and Desdemona on Othello's entry; the positions of Iago and Roderigo as the stage empties. The group working on the penultimate (prose) section might be given this brief:

> Experiment with different ways of playing this section – for instance with Iago stationary (where?) and Roderigo moving, or vice versa; Iago playing with or without explicit acknowledgment of the audience; Iago improvising, or having all his arguments worked out already; Iago having difficulty, or easily having his way. Investigate possible variations of tone.

The group working on the soliloquy can be directed to attend, in addition to the considerations already outlined earlier regarding soliloquies, to moments in which shifts of thought and feeling may be apparent, for instance at the caesura in 'I dare think he'll prove to Desdemona/A most dear husband. Now do I love her too'. After these group investigations the class can attempt to put the sections together as a sequence, perhaps with a linking commentary from the teacher to draw out the implications of different choices, depending on what the students come up with.

The kind of classroom work outlined here is obviously very full and detailed, demanding for both teacher and class, and unavoidably time consuming. However, it shouldn't be assumed that the approach is only appropriate for such large-scale investigations, leaving little time for all the other things that have to be done (i.e. if classes are going to be ready for examinations), and so of little use. First, the range of questions can inform our own reading, thought and preparation outside the classroom, enhancing our own sense of the dramatic possibilities that they highlight. Second, the focus can be narrowed according to our present purpose. For instance, we might look at Act 2 Scene 1 of *Othello* during an investigation of the character of Desdemona, perhaps asking how her behaviour here can be related to her behaviour in later scenes, especially in Act 4. The question of how she relates to Iago, the on-stage audience and the real audience is clearly relevant here. Third, the questions about *locus* and *platea*, on-stage audiences and styles of delivery can be asked on smaller-scale occasions, more opportunistically and occasionally, especially with classes in Key Stages 3 and 4. What if, we might ask, the actress playing Juliet comes forward and shares her fears about taking the Friar's potion directly with the audience? From such brief considerations we might move to a fuller consideration of a manageable short scene.

Even without practical staging work, questions about silent observers can still be asked. In the first scene of *A Midsummer Night's Dream*, for instance, what does Hippolyta make of the exchanges between Egeus and Theseus? Year 9 pupils, asked to annotate the texts with the thoughts that go through her mind as the scene develops, came up with some interesting and amusing suggestions. Some Hippolytas, initially impressed that their husbands-to-be are treated with such respect and consulted on such matters, became bored as the scene goes on, retreating into thoughts of their own importance and of their forthcoming marriages. Others, watching keenly to see how the matter will be dealt with by the men who are to play such an essential role in their remaining lives, become increasingly disgusted, some with Hermia, some with Theseus. In this exercise, admittedly, the emphasis has shifted from performance to the kind of written 'empathic' approaches used in some of the early SAT questions, but the emphasis can easily be shifted back: how much of this should the actress playing Hermione *show*? Why did Shakespeare not make her reactions explicit? Aren't they important? In this way we can probe some implications of the silent character in drama. We are used to finding drama in the *exchange* of words, even when we are reading in a chair or at a desk, but can easily miss the possible significance of silent listeners when we read without visualizing how the scene might go on stage – and their silences, explored, can throw into stronger relief the words that are spoken. What might it be, for a given character in a given situation, to *hear* these words?

The Elizabethan/Jacobean theatre (and the assumptions and attitudes that audiences brought to it) is arguably the most important context in which to consider Shakespeare, and, as made clear in the foregoing, questions of theatrical performance bear strongly on interpretation of the plays. Context and interpretation, made unignorable in secondary schools by exam specifications in the early twentieth century, are the subject of the next two chapters.

Chapter 13

Context

We (literally) cannot read Shakespeare, or anything else, without context. There is the reader, a particular life embedded in a culture; there is the text, product of a particular life within a culture with a greater or lesser degree of continuity with that of the reader; and there are the circumstances in which and the purposes for which the reading is being done. We can't step outside this situation. What we can do is become more fully aware of and better informed about its various elements and the bearing they have on the sense we make of what we read. We can acquire 'contextual knowledge'. This can happen haphazardly, or we can choose to develop our understanding in particular respects; and we can be taught.

Some contextual awareness, an awareness of difference between us and Shakespeare, say, will come out as we learn more about the language and as we read the explanatory notes on words and phrases, allusions and the like; it's through an accumulation of these over time that we begin to develop confidence as readers of Shakespeare and to acquire a degree of contextual awareness. We mustn't underestimate this when considering grander schemes. Always particular, always local, knowledge acquired in this way has the advantage over specious generalizations of the 'In those days religion used to be important' variety that don't illuminate Shakespeare, history or the present. And through this knowledge we will build up a sense of differences and continuities between Shakespeare's age and our own.

Further contextual awareness will come to us as we look for answers to questions that arise in the course of our reading, such as: was this ever *really* found funny? How did they show ghosts when they didn't have special effects? How did Ariel appear invisible? Why is chastity considered such a big deal? Why do so many scenes end with rhyming couplets? Are we supposed to *like* Orsino? To admire Duke Vincentio? Isn't this misogynist? How was this originally received? Is it typical of its period or was it something quite new? Is the rest of the author's work like this? Why on earth was this ever considered immoral? What did anybody ever see in this that it should be nowadays considered a classic? What is a classic, anyway? Is Shakespeare *really* any better than his contemporaries?

(These, as teachers will recognize, are the sorts of question that can arise spontaneously in classrooms.)

We may begin to read around a bit, finding provisional answers in established critical texts, and with further study (and experience of life) find that they are indeed provisional, open to correction. As we grow in experience we may well come to question some of the established generalizations about an author, a genre, a period, and, prompted by a sense of dissatisfaction, a new piece of information, or a nagging question, go back to take another look. Hence those books that revise previous assumptions that arise every now and then, and sentences that begin 'It used to be assumed'. Accounts once authoritative become revised or discarded (although they often remain, unaltered, in print long after this happens; some, quite rightly, have a kind of classic status). Factors once thought marginal gain new prominence; others thought central are marginalized. During certain periods some questions simply don't occur to anyone, or if they do they are rejected as eccentric or unfruitful. And of course prejudice, belief and ideology will play important roles in these processes. The sense of context, although it has roots in early reading and reflection, is ideally a *late* development, maturing over a lifetime. (Yet our current exam assessment objectives ask for it in teenagers.)

Unfortunately, this developing contextual understanding sometimes takes turnings that prevent it illuminating a work of literature. Sometimes readers become more interested in the contextual information in its own right, and pursue it further, leaving the text (if only temporarily) behind, in which case the contextual element has become the subject and the passage in the text shrunk to the status of an example. Sometimes the contextual information is taken to be sufficient explanation for an understanding of what Shakespeare presents. A particularly good example of how an approach to Shakespeare via 'the ideas of his time' fails to do justice to the complexity and power of his plays is Lily B. Campbell's *Shakespeare's Tragic Heroes*.[1] She provides a detailed account of psychological theories during the period, illustrated by copious quotation – but then simply assumes it in her account of Macbeth, Hamlet, etc. The psychology accounts for the characters; Shakespeare merely provides illustrations (dramatic and vivid) of the theories; there is no *thinking* in his work. Understand the theories, understand the plays. Everything is explained, everything falls into place. In a number of accounts written along these lines, if the reader objects that it looks as if Shakespeare might not have thought quite like that, the riposte will be that he must have done, because he was an Elizabethan. The classic refutation of this approach is Wilbur Sanders' *The Dramatist and the Received Idea*.[2] More briefly, Helen Gardner points out in a still invaluable essay that

> even if we could discover a kind of highest common factor of contemporary beliefs and attitudes, it could not tell us what any individual

believed, and certainly not what Shakespeare believed. We do not know very much about Shakespeare outside his plays, but at least we know from them that he was not an average Elizabethan.[3]

Her account of what has been meant by 'the Elizabethans' is very funny and well worth bringing up to date.

Although it's true that sometimes what strikes us as deeply individual or novel is actually a commonplace of the period (we do need heading off from errors of understanding of this kind), the greatest objection to the 'contemporary ideas' approach is that it can give the impression that the meaning and power of Shakespeare's plays lies safely in the past. The plays, it can appear, may tell us about things, but they have nothing to say to us.

So context doesn't necessarily assist us in reading Shakespeare well; there are even occasions when it can prevent us doing so. It's not always the context that illuminates the plays; sometimes it's the other way round. The tendency to look outside the plays for a clue to their meaning can lead us to overlook what the plays themselves tell us. For instance, in relation to *Macbeth* we might talk about the institution of kingship, the divine right of kings and the crime and sin of regicide. But in the play itself we are taken into depth about what that wickedness can be:

> Besides, this Duncan
> Hath borne his faculties so meek, hath been
> So clear in his great office, that his virtues
> Will plead like angels, trumpet-tongued against
> The deep damnation of his taking-off;
> And pity, like a naked new-born babe,
> Striding the blast, or Heaven's cherubim, horsed
> Upon the sightless couriers of the air,
> Shall blow the horrid deed in every eye
> That tears shall drown the wind.

That tells us more deeply than any historical note what the horror of regicide – no abstraction, but the unlawful killing of *this* king, and soon – can feel like. The wrong teaching move here is to go off into the history; instead we should attend to the verse and what Shakespeare shows us in it.

As long as we are aware of this danger, we may not need to think very consciously about the uses of context in our occasional classroom use of cultural information (in our preparation, seeing where an explanation will be in order, or occurring unexpectedly, called up by a sudden memory, or in response to a pupil's question). But when exam boards' requirements foreground context (and interpretation – see the next chapter) they raise important (and for many teachers, anxious) questions of practice. What kinds of historical and cultural awareness? And above all, how much? (For instance, at what point in reading *Twelfth Night* does it become necessary to make much of Maria's description of Malvolio as 'sometimes ... a kind of puritan' and Sir Andrew's remark that he 'had as lief be a Brownist than a politician'? Are these incidental or essential to an understanding of the play?) If we overinterpret the requirements, we burden our pupils with unnecessary knowledge; if we make light of it, we (to put it bluntly) lose them marks. There is the anxiety of our pupils and students to be sympathized with, too; especially since they will, for the highest grades, have to show not just *insight* but also *originality* in their uses of context.

Without careful thought, these anxieties can lead to uses of context that are just plain unnecessary, and unilluminating. Sometimes in our attempts to meet the 'historical and cultural context requirement' we tack on bits of information which, although they extend our pupils' and students' historical sense (always a worthwhile thing to do), add nothing to, and can even detract from, their knowledge of the play. For instance, in relation to *Macbeth* we tell our classes about contemporary beliefs concerning witchcraft. Some attractive commercially available resources present us with brief texts, summaries and woodcuts, and very interesting they are too. But do they really help us come to terms with Shakespeare's witches? If we already 'know' what witches are, then we may fail to respond adequately to what Shakespeare shows us. Also in relation to *Macbeth*, we sometimes tell classes that Shakespeare was sucking up to King James by writing on a subject dear to his heart and presenting his ancestor Banquo, in whose posterity James stood. This conjecture might explain why *Macbeth* was written when it was, what produced at least part of the stimulus, but how does it illuminate the play? This approach fails to consider just how pleased James might have been to see his ancestor presented in a questionable light. (Consider Banquo's failure to act on the suspicions that he expresses in his soliloquy in Act 3 Scene 1; instead he conjectures that there might be some good to come to him from the Weird Sisters' predictions.) How does reference to James help us read *Macbeth* better? If 'context' is not fruitful in illuminating aspects of the play, it becomes inert 'background' and, in the pupils' essays, a bit of window-dressing. We're all familiar with the single sentence or paragraph that adds nothing to the candidates' understanding of Shakespeare but enables us to tick the 'context' box. It's a pity that over the years I have developed the impression that these sentences and paragraphs will serve the purpose, as the exam boards don't always seem to take their criteria that seriously.`

In the rest of this chapter I want to look at some of the ways in which contextual elements can be brought into specific studies in ways that are modest, manageable, fruitful and illuminating – ways that aid specific reading and can be adapted for the specific requirements of various schemes of assessment. The discussion is by no means exhaustive, but I hope it offers a useful range of ways in which contextual knowledge can be brought to bear in the classroom. Where possible the use of context is brought to bear on specific passages to aid re-reading and re-consideration of their significance, and comparison is frequently used as a tool that enables us to focus more closely on what Shakespeare wrote by examining it alongside what he didn't.

Sources and shaping

In an earlier chapter we have considered how looking at Shakespeare's dramatic shaping of narrative material into dramatic scenes might enhance reading. More specifically, it can on occasion be productive and interesting to look at elements of Shakespeare's actual source material and how he shaped it. Pupils and students are sometimes shocked to find that there *is* source material, that Shakespeare didn't invent his own stories. When I introduced an A level class to the speech from Golding's Ovid that lies behind Prospero's great speech abjuring his magic, they were appalled and instantly declared Shakespeare's speech to be of no value, as it was cribbed. Straight away this tells us something about different ideas of authorship, which might be worth discussing with certain classes. Our emphasis should be on what Shakespeare *makes* from his resources. This might be done very simply by highlighting a single element. For instance, we can tell classes which plot elements Shakespeare has changed or invented (this information is readily available in standard editions) and discuss ways in which they alter the balance and import of the play. Facts here may provide good jumping-off points for investigations which can lead quite deep into the play. A few examples: in Cinthio's *Gli Hecatommithi*, the source for *Othello*, the Ensign (Iago) does not hate Othello but lusts after Desdemona, and it is her destruction that he seeks. How does this information influence our reading of Iago's soliloquies? In Cinthio, the Ensign's wife (Emilia) has been in on Iago's plot from the beginning. Roderigo is entirely Shakespeare's invention. What structural and other differences do these changes make? In Robert Greene's *Pandosto*, the source of *The Winter's Tale*, Bellaria (Hermione) stays dead and Pandosto (Leontes) commits suicide. Has Shakespeare succeeded in reversing the tragic import of the original narrative? Autolycus and Antigonus are Shakespeare's additions; what role do they have in the transition from tragedy to comedy?

Sometimes it will be appropriate to deal with sources at greater length, even making them the basis a whole study. A useful example is provided in Michael Hayhoe's photocopiable resource *Creative Work Ideas for 'Macbeth'* (1986) which is, as far as I know, no longer easily available.[4] In it he provides a fictional letter from Holinshed to Shakespeare complaining of the latter's departures from the Macbeth story as told in Holinshed's chronicles. Specifically, Shakespeare's version differs in that, according to Holinshed:

1   Duncan was young and feeble.
2   Macbeth fought loyally in two campaigns.
3   Macbeth had a genuine grievance against Duncan, since Duncan had blocked Macbeth's *legal* path to the throne.
4   Banquo helped Macbeth to kill Duncan.
5   In fact, Macbeth seized power and ruled well for ten years before killing Duncan and then Banquo.
6   There was no banquet and Banquo did not have a ghost.
7   There was only one 'witch'.
8   Macbeth surrounded his castle with magical powers.
9   Macbeth did not hire murderers.
10 Macbeth fled from his castle and was pursued across country.
11 Lady Macbeth did not go sleepwalking, nor did she commit suicide.

The task is to provide Shakespeare's justification for these 'knavish errors'. Hayhoe remarks that 'Your teacher will negotiate with you how you are to present your findings' and suggests 'William's letter back to the old pedant, or a poster advertising the "new and correct" *Macbeth*, or a revised scene'. Clearly for assessment purposes these vary in appropriateness. The task lends itself well to group investigation, with each group taking one of the eleven objections and coming up with one or two possible answers which are reported back in a plenary session. The assessment task could be a group discussion of a section of the changes, individual presentations on one of them (with arguments for and against and a reasoned conclusion) or individual essays, either on a selection of the changes or on all of them. The governing question in each case should be 'What makes for a powerful and unified tragedy?', with emphasis on relation between characters, what is thrust into prominence, what makes for a strong scene, questions of pace and construction, etc. With some classes we might find ourselves discussing the *propriety* of dramatizing – interfering with – history in this way. (G. Wilson Knight went so far as to suggest that these alterations were the source of the curse on 'the Scottish play'.) With recent television films based on real and recent political situations, this could be quite a hot topic.

In some cases we can relate the question of shaping of sources to contemporary ideology. In *Richard III* we might look at how Shakespeare's presentation of Richard develops and emphasizes the view promulgated in Thomas More's history; or take edited extracts from the chronicles that relate to specific scenes and study how Shakespeare has shaped them, omitting, telescoping, inventing, and to what dramatic effect, learning about his craft as a writer.

Or we could focus on the presentation of Richmond as a Tudor hero. After Act 5 has been read, the teacher can present a brief introduction to the Tudor myth[5] as an introduction to an investigation of how Shakespeare presents Richmond and how, through the structure of scenes and use of language, he contrasts him with Richard. After some classwork on the alternating scenes, small groups could investigate how Richard and Richmond speak to their attendant lords and their troops; how they perform their military roles, and deal with the problem of Stanley; their language in relation to themselves, each other and England; the ghosts sequence (content, style and on-stage responses); the two orations to the armies; uses of parallels and variation in the language. After these have been presented, the class might discuss what impressions the audience receives of Richmond and how satisfactory an ending the act makes to the play as a whole.

This study should bring out clearly the ways in which our sense of the villainy of Richard and the heroism of Richmond are built up, and tie the context question firmly to questions of stagecraft. It's clearly a time-consuming piece of work, but with able classes we should not be short-changing on Shakespeare; we should aim at an appropriate depth of study. As presented here, the material is aimed at able pupils and higher grades, but it can easily be scaled down for the less able. It could be narrowed to any one of the group tasks listed above as preparatory to an essay. For instance, the task could be 'Compare Richard and Richmond's speeches to their troops. How does Shakespeare make Richmond sound more heroic and admirable than Richard? How would a contemporary audience respond, and why?' Or an essay could be set on the different ways in which the ghosts speak to Richard and Richmond and how the two respond to what they have heard. It's worth noting that although this investigation of Act 5 of *Richard III* nominally takes its stimulus from a contextual question, almost all the work is focused on reading what Shakespeare wrote. It could actually be done without explicit mention of context.

Other possible work on *Richard III* that uses a contextual element includes: techniques of persuasion (context: political situation, use of rhetoric); the role of women in the play (political status of women); a comparison of two soliloquies (the convention of the soliloquy and its different styles of delivery).

Genre

Questions of structure and dramatic emphasis might also come up in relation to another contextual element already touched on, genre. Students are sometimes specifically asked to work with a generic understanding of Shakespeare, a knowledge that he wrote in specific genres which have conventions, rules and histories. The Folio divides Shakespeare's plays into three genres: tragedies, comedies and histories. Later readers have been uneasy with this division for some plays (such as *Troilus and Cressida* and *Measure for Measure*), and categories such as 'problem plays' and 'last plays' have become more or less standard. Peter Hyland gives a well-balanced and useful account of genre in relation to Shakespeare, in which he argues, in effect, for retaining the Folio categories and makes the very useful point, one to pass on to students early on, that we should

> try to see each play as an individual work with a special relation to generic convention. What is important is not how a particular play fits into a genre, as if generic conventions were a strait-jacket, but how the author stretches and re-shapes the genre to suit his own needs ... the idea of a genre sets up certain expectations about a play ... but what is important is not so much how well the play conforms to these expectations, as how and why it teases and baffles them.[6]

Gabriel Egan also has some good points on genre and audience expectation in his book on Shakespeare in the 'Edinburgh Critical Guides' series,[7] which is particularly useful for offering a range of contextual considerations in relation to the interpretation of Shakespeare's plays.

There are a number of ways we can approach generic questions. We can investigate a genre in general terms, with no immediate reference to a Shakespeare play. A general introduction to the notion of literary genres could be followed up by working with the class to produce a sketch of the main elements of a particular genre, mapping out something elementary but useful, to be refined and supplemented at later dates. Comedy will probably prove the easiest for students to get going with, as there are plenty of contemporary examples. Tragedy may require more teacher input. If the students are familiar with *Educating Rita*, then they can revisit the conversation about the poor sod under the tree. Later developments could – should – include a development of the historical changes in ideas of the genre (and therefore in our responses to and valuations of particular plays). We may also include some key quotations from different periods, especially if they have a bearing on the particular text to be studied.

This is easy enough to do; harder is the question of how and where it has a bearing on our students' particular reading of Shakespeare. We might bring some examples of assumptions about genre to bear on our reading of a particular scene and see what emerges, the aim being to develop readings of, not theories about, the plays.

For instance, we might consider responses to the ending of *King Lear*. We can begin by referring to Shakespeare's departure from his sources. Notoriously, the ending of *Lear* is far more dreadful than that in the source, as Samuel Johnson memorably remarked (by introducing his comments we begin to bring into play another context, the history of reception):

> *Shakespeare* has suffered the virtue of *Cordelia* to perish in a just cause, contrary to the natural ideas of justice, to the hope of the reader, and, what is yet more strange, to the faith of chronicles.[8]

Widening the frame of reference, we can bring in Johnson's carefully phrased subsequent sentence to raise questions about art, justice and value, or about the morality of tragic form:

> A play in which the wicked prosper, and the virtuous miscarry, may doubtless be good, because it is a just representation of the common elements of human life: but since all reasonable beings naturally love justice, I cannot easily be persuaded, that the observation of justice makes a play worse; or, that if other excellences are equal, the audience will not always rise better pleased from the final triumph of persecuted virtue.[9]

After teasing out the assumptions of this formulation, we might tell them about Naum Tate's notorious rewrite of *Lear* (1681) with its happy ending, complete with marriage of Cordelia and Edgar, and perhaps even show them its last scene to compare with Shakespeare. Its final speech, by Edgar, reads:

> Our drooping country now erects her head,
> Peace spreads her balmy wings, and Plenty blooms.
> Divine Cordelia, all the gods can witness
> How much thy love to empire I prefer!
> Thy bright example shall convince the world
> (Whatever storms of Fortune are decreed)
> That truth and virtue shall at last succeed.[10]

So much for 'the gor'd state'. The comparison (placing texts alongside Shakespeare is making another context) could prove very illuminating, and we will have opened space for discussion of ideas of tragedy as a genre and about our responses to tragedy, and the fact that these both vary from period to period. As with Tate, changing generic ideas often influenced adaptation of the text. Garrick felt the need to add a dying speech for Macbeth; it's worthwhile discussing this with a class studying the play. Restoration and eighteenth-century rewriting of Shakespeare is a fascinating topic and affords a wealth of examples that we might bring into our teaching as a way of pointing up what Shakespeare has done.[11] For a modern idea of tragic response we might offer students an excerpt from Bradley on how 'we' feel at the end of a tragedy:

> the fact that the spectacle does not leave us rebellious or desperate is due to a more or less distinct perception that the tragic suffering and death arise from a collision, not with fate or a blank power, but with a moral power, a power akin to all that we admire and revere in the characters themselves.[12]

Ask them what they make of it in relation to the Shakespeare tragedy they are studying: do they indeed feel like that, and if not, why not?

Finally they might discuss Johnson's resolution of the question about the ending of *Lear*:

> In the present case the publick has decided. *Cordelia*, from the time of *Tate*, has always retired with victory and felicity.[13]

One question we might emphasize from this is whether it is the publick that should decide. Using some quickly imparted information and focusing on three brief extracts, we have opened up some questions of some importance: questions literary, moral, philosophical and even sociological (what is the role of tragedy within society?). Johnson is particularly fertile ground for widening the terms of reference (and not just on Shakespeare); his deeply felt views are sufficiently strange to us yet accessible enough to prompt thought in our students, especially on issues of morality and literature. As a reader of Shakespeare of peculiar intensity he is always worth attention, even when we feel unable to agree with him.

There's no guarantee, though, that a student able to refer to neo-classicism, poetic justice, Naum Tate and Bradley on tragic response will be able to read and write about *Lear* any better. An exam board gave an essay title 'Many definitions of tragedy claim that at the end of the play positives have emerged. Is it possible to see anything positive in the ending of *King Lear*?' There hardly needs to have been any context work, any study of the genre of tragedy to tackle it: all the theory needed is included in the question itself. The focus, a useful one, is entirely on the play. Using the contexts to frame the question does lead to an enhanced sense of literary history, and that in its own right is valuable, but the critical question which we must keep in our and our students' awareness throughout is prior: what will enable, and what hinder, the play having its full impact with a student? Once again, the questions are what and how much is presented to students, when, and how they are to use it.

Two further examples: if, as some theories of tragedy aver, the protagonist must be of high status in life, royal or aristocratic, for enough to hinge on his (it is usually his: there's fertile ground for discussion) life to engender tragic emotion, can there be domestic tragedy, tragedy of middle life? The question can be considered in relation to *Othello*. After all, politically Othello's downfall is just an incident; he is easily replaced. The state is not gor'd, there is no need for fundamental repair in the polis, or long recovery. Students might compare the closing moments of *Hamlet*, *Macbeth* and *Lear* (and it can be taken further if the class are also studying or have studied *Death of a Salesman*; why is it that 'Attention, attention must be finally paid to such a person?').[14] The view of tragedy that makes much of inexorable destiny might be read against *Othello* or *Romeo and Juliet*. Is it a sufficient sense of the tragedy of the lovers that they are 'star-crossed', necessarily doomed, or is the characters' own sense of destiny to some degree productive of it? This could lead to close reading of those parts in the play where destiny, fate, etc. are specifically mentioned.

This kind of approach could begin in lower school: a class reading *Much Ado* might focus on the element of opposition familiar in romantic comedies, considering the question: all romantic comedies have obstacles to be overcome before the happy couple(s) can be (re)united. What are these elements in *Much Ado*? Groups could then be set to research the following: Claudio's readiness to give up; his surliness; the speed with which he believes Don John's accusation against Hero; Beatrice's bitterness; Benedick's anger; Don Pedro's taste for manipulation; the malcontent Don John. After reporting back, a plenary discussion can consider how serious these elements are, whether there is any real sense of opposition, danger, darkness that might threaten the happiness of the conclusion, and to what extent should these elements colour a reading or performance of the play. Students who consider such questions earlier in their school career will be well prepared, for instance, for considering to what extent and in what ways *Measure for Measure* can 'really' be considered as a comedy. Does the convention of comic resolution via marriage override, or is it questioned by, the decidedly dubious matches that conclude *Much Ado*, *All's Well* and *Measure for Measure*?

Shakespeare's other plays, ghost scenes and contemporary beliefs

An important context of a Shakespeare play, one easily overlooked, is Shakespeare's other plays. This can be introduced almost in passing when, for instance, we remark 'This idea about appearance and reality comes up in quite a lot of the plays. For instance' followed by a brief selection of quotations. We can indicate how similar situations occur in varying treatments in different plays (referring to *Romeo and Juliet* when working on *A Midsummer Night's Dream* and vice versa). Regarding Claudio we might refer to other unsatisfactory men (or are *all* Shakespeare's men not good enough for their women?). Or we can make comparison the basic task of more developed work. One GCSE student in her essay on Richard and

Richmond ended by comparing Richard's and Richmond's final confrontation with that of Macbeth and Macduff to interesting effect. We could introduce this kind of comparison into our work more often. For instance, we might compare love duets from *Romeo and Juliet*, *As You Like It*, *Much Ado*, *Henry V* and *The Tempest* against a background of assumptions and conventions about love; or compare two villains' speeches (choose from Aaron, Gloucester, Edmund, Iago) in relation to one by an old Vice (for instance Politic Persuasion),[15] so bringing out Shakespeare's greater psychological subtlety. We could compare two scenes of murder (an interesting comparison is the killing of Clarence in *Richard III* and the murder of Thomas in *Woodstock*, a highly enjoyable history play which may or may not be by Shakespeare).[16] Or – the example that I'll develop in detail here – we could compare ghost scenes. This task can also make use of two other contexts: the contemporary stage and contemporary ideas about the supernatural. These may be used separately or combined in a single investigation.

Shakespeare abounds in such scenes, and they show considerable variety. Three that are particularly amenable to the approach outlined here are those from *Richard III* Act 5 Scene 3 (*lots* of ghosts), *Hamlet* Act 1 Scenes 1, 2 and 4–5 (just the one ghost, but offering a wealth of fascinating material), and *Macbeth* Act 3 Scene 4 (Banquo's ghost, with the old familiar question of whether it's 'real' or not).

For this work pupils will need a basic idea of the Elizabethan stage (see pages 93–4). In relation to the *Richard III* scene it's appropriate to mention the possibility of stage tents. It's also worth suggesting that the Shakespearean stage still retained a memory of the old symbolic division of the mysteries: above the stage, heaven; the stage, earth ('All the world's a stage'); below the stage, hell. (The latter I've seen revived effectively – indeed melodramatically – with a use of the trapdoor in *Richard III*: after each death, the corpse descended through it into a luridly lit scarlet afterlife.)

There's the context: the question is, how to present ghost scenes on such a stage effectively. Discussion of this question can involve consideration of how Shakespeare establishes atmosphere through verbal lighting effects, such as Horatio's lines on the dawn:

> But look, the morn in russet mantle clad,
> Walks o'er the dew on yon high eastern hill.

The deictic 'yon' involves the audience, and the personification offers so much more than a mere raising of artificial light can do. In relation to the Banquo scene we can look at the scene-painting that brings on Banquo to be murdered:

> The west yet glimmers with some streaks of day
> Now spurs the lated traveler apace.

To gain the timely inn, and near approaches
The subject of our watch.

We might also take the class on an excursion through darkness in *Macbeth*, noticing the tangible quality that it is given more than once ('Light *thickens*').

Looking at *Hamlet* Act 1 Scene 1 we might invite argument for and against using the balcony. (Is the ghost best played on the same level as the others? Would he be better above on the balcony or below on the forestage?) We can discuss the styles of speech and movement the actors playing the ghost might adopt (always on the lookout for clues in the text: 'See, it stalks away', 'We do it wrong, being so majestical'). We might mention the absence of 'exit' directions for ghosts, either singly or together, in the Folio text of *Richard III*. Should they stay on stage? How might they be grouped? Pupils can work on these and similar questions practically.

After this, a second question can be introduced: what do the modern stage and cinema offer for the presentation of Shakespeare's ghost scenes? It's important here to combat the tendency to be vague; it can help to drop in occasional bits of information about specific versions. For instance, in a production some years ago at Derby Playhouse, Richard dozed in front of the television in his tent and the ghosts came up on screen as Richard fidgeted in his sleep. The ghosts didn't say a word to Richmond. In one way this performance increased the subjectivity of the ghosts, who clearly now belong to Richard's imagination. (Or do they? Because there they are, on the television. What could be more real?) We can point out that the ghosts' lines to Richmond are often cut in modern productions and ask what effect this will have (apart from reducing the carefully planned symmetries of the final act) on the *meaning* of the scene. If we look at film versions we will find a tendency to rely on images, cutting down on the word count. What is gained and lost by this?

After investigation and discussion, an essay could be set: 'How does Shakespeare overcome the limitations of the Elizabethan stage to present convincing and dramatic ghost scenes? What might modern productions add to these scenes?' Studies can focus tightly on particular passages – the presentation of, say, ten lines of text in terms of its stage and cinematic potential. It's interesting that a number of pupils, having considered the matter in some depth, come round to thinking that Shakespeare's simple open stage might have some advantages over the technical superiority of the modern stage. Some comment that the words are thereby thrown into stronger relief, and indicate why this might matter (as conveying greater depth and range of *meaning*).

For the second proposed context – contemporary ideas about ghosts – pupils can be given the information that in Shakespeare's age there was (as, probably, in any age) a range of beliefs about ghosts. This may be represented schematically like this:

- Some people thought that ghosts had no real existence: they were simply frauds, tricks deliberately played on credulous people, or they were products of the imagination, illusions brought on by psychological states such as melancholy, madness or guilt.
- Others granted the objective existence of ghosts; Roman Catholics believed that the souls of some dead people were at times permitted to return for brief periods from hell or (more probably) Purgatory, to give comfort to people or to ask them for help.
- Protestants, who did not believe in Purgatory, did not share this belief and were inclined to believe that ghosts were devils that appeared in various shapes (perhaps by compressing the air about them into solid appearances) to tempt or test individuals, leading them into sinful actions in order to damn their souls. Roman Catholics also entertained this belief.
- Finally, some thought ghosts were angels who came to warn, encourage or test.

Perhaps after the pupils have investigated what they and their peers believe about ghosts they can be presented with this information, either as barely and schematically as above, or in a sequence of quotations from sixteenth- and seventeenth-century authors. This can lead into a close study of two or three ghost scenes. The immediate advantage is that they are looking for something, which obliges them to read closely. However, it's not enough to identify where the different view are expressed; the focus should be on what *dramatic use* Shakespeare makes of these ideas and how therefore his audience might respond.

The passages from *Hamlet* are most demanding both in range and content. Arguably *all* the contemporary ideas listed above enter into the play of thought and feeling, each contributing to the anxiety that is never resolved in the course of the play (although at times Hamlet takes it to be resolved):

> The spirit I have seen
> May be the Devil, and the Devil hath power
> T'assume a pleasing shape, yea, and perhaps
> Out of my weakness, and my melancholy,
> As he is very potent with such spirits,
> Abuses me to damn me.

There's a great deal to look at: Horatio's initial scepticism ("twill not appear'); the variety of language used of the ghost, suggesting uncertainties of conceptualization and response (it is first a 'thing' and then an 'apparition' that somehow 'comes'); the relating of legends; and, throughout, the overwhelming sense of spiritual *danger* that Hamlet staves off even as he articulates it:

> Be thou a spirit of health, or goblin damn'd,
> Bring with thee airs from Heaven, or blasts from Hell,
> Be thy intents wicked or charitable,
> Thou com'st in such a questionable shape
> That I will speak with thee.

Pupils can then look at how Hamlet's questions build up until at last, after the perilous shift to 'more removed ground', with (at first) stunning brevity the ghost speaks: 'Mark me' and the doubt is apparently – but temporarily – settled: 'I *am* thy father's spirit'. Then follows the business of the fellow in the cellarage. A detailed study can bring out here how Shakespeare has *used* the range of thought about ghosts in creating tension and meaning – inseparably, of course, from his superb handling of pace.

An essay question could be specifically angled to this investigation: 'What dramatic use does Shakespeare make of contemporary beliefs about ghosts in these scenes?' Comparison will bring out the different emphases between the scenes, the different ways in which contemporary beliefs come into play. And pupils might write about which they consider most effective.

A similar approach might be developed using Marion O'Connor's essay on iconomachy (opposition to image-worship) and the statue scene in *The Winter's Tale*.[17] This performs the useful service of investigating early modern sensibilities concerning images in a range of texts and bringing the findings to bear on a close reading of the statue scene, showing not 'what must be meant by the scene' (which would be making the 'background' determinative) but how a range of contemporary feelings are *in play* for the audience. This is much less familiar ground than ghosts, although some of our Muslim students may have interesting contributions to make, but is surely worth introducing to some degree when working on the play at A Level.

Changing values

Another contextual element that comes to play in interpretation, and which exam boards often focus on, is the question of changing values. A popular approach is to look at Shakespeare's sexual politics, to consider how he presents relationships between men and women in, say *The Taming of the Shrew* or *The Winter's Tale*, and how a modern audience responds to these relationships. Here 'context' is understood in terms of cultural opinions/beliefs about those relations, and the weight is thrown towards the modern context. The trouble with this kind of approach is that it can fail to move beyond clichéd and thoughtless assumptions about the benighted past in which 'they' were terribly religious and horrid to women and the enlightened present in which 'we' are all too sensible to be religious and invariably treat women with respect.

This continues to amaze me. Mixed-race classes will forget all about suicide bombing, honour killing, pro-life demonstrations, the Anglican controversies over sexuality. They will confidently aver that racism is a thing of the past while their TV screens, if not their own experiences, tell them differently. An A level class made up almost entirely of girls could see no point in the quotation I gave them (as prologue to a lesson on misogyny in Aphra Behn and Shakespeare) from Germaine Greer that 'Most women have no idea how much men hate them'. I think in some cases at least it must be that classes know the liberal ideology that school expects of them and don't expect either that or Shakespeare to have any bearing on their life, so they don't make connections, they aren't bothered. Perhaps what they need is to be shocked. An inspector once told me a wonderful story of teaching Shakespeare to adults somewhere abroad – I forget where. They were filled with admiration for *Antony and Cleopatra* – it was literature, culture – until they went to see a performance. Tight-lipped with disapproval, they stated the next day in class that it was *disgusting* that a man and woman of that age should carry on *like that*.

Rather than encourage glib generalizations, the teacher has to consider how to help students find a focus that will be genuinely fruitful. Supportive material, if any, will have to be carefully chosen and research carefully guided so that the candidate is not just left with heaps of interesting material of no very clear application, as is provided, for instance, in an edition of *The Shrew* which contain a wealth of texts related in some way to the (subject matter of the) play, including among much else tracts on wife- and servant-beating, a homily on matrimony and a lengthy 'Merry Jest of a Shrewd and Curst Wife Lapped in Morel's Skin, for Her Good Behaviour'.[18] Greatly interesting stuff, but I don't think it's clear just how it helps us read *The Shrew* today.

But there is, I think, a more serious objection to questions of this kind. It's arguable that Shakespeare *doesn't* present relationships between men and women in *The Taming of the Shrew*, *The Winter's Tale*, or anywhere else. He does nothing so general; his characters and situations, whatever relation they bear to the general, are all highly specific.

More to the point would be to consider those characters whose prominence in the play seems to grant them a positive role as a source of value, but who we find it hard to regard positively, for instance those unsatisfactory lovers. Or Prospero: for a long time it seemed natural to read him as a superhuman figure, awesome and good, and to find him the apex of a symbolic pattern. When I was teaching *The Tempest* in the late 1970s/early 1980s, it was clear that that time had passed. My students didn't like him; without benefit of the post-colonial readings not yet emerged from the pipeline, they found him tyrannical. There's a similar case with 'the old fantastical Duke of dark corners' in *Measure for Measure*. Is our modern (or postmodern) response anachronistic? Or was Shakespeare writing with irony? There is a range of important questions here.

Shakespeare's plays and other literary works

We shouldn't – once we start thinking seriously about it, we can't – consider 'context' as inert, lying before us, somehow simply available, or like a map that can be uncovered. Choices are always made, by us or for us, in the construction of a context in which to consider a literary work. Of course, unless we are lazy or serving a particular interest, the context that we construct will be in principle endlessly open to correction and extension. However much it is our construct, it will have a quality of 'thereness' which will operate as a corrective to – well, to what we might prefer to be the case. Inconvenient facts will obtrude themselves. While we shouldn't exaggerate our own role – or the role of others – we must be aware of it. In asking 'How does X look if read against Y?' some writers are quite specific about their role in contextualizing, making it clear that (and sometimes why) they have decided to read this X against this Y; others, for whatever reason, are much less so. Some contextualizing has a specifically political motive. Some is in service of a theory and knows what it will find. Some is heuristic, without an axe to grind. Some is basically a rhetorical device, a method of highlighting. (I suspect that in some of the contextualizing essays of the late twentieth century (Stephen Greenblatt *et al.*) an *aesthetic* element enters into the ordering and shaping of the material, making an essay that is elegant – the root word of 'elegant' being *legere*, to choose). The element of choice for us and our students is probably most evident when we ask them to compare a Shakespeare play with one or more works on the same 'theme', such as love, death or war.

This can have the major advantage of encouraging students to think across periods and genres – which is fine provided that the focus is right. Notoriously the 'thematic' approach invites vagueness rather than close attention, so care must be taken when devising – when assisting students to devise – tasks of this nature. Much may be gained by narrowing the focus. For instance, 'love' could be narrowed to *courtship*, which can be further narrowed by concentrating on the conscious, verbally adept and poised courtship, with much posing and (self?-) deception, in *Much Ado* and *The Importance of Being Earnest*. (*Much Ado* actually offers *two* patterns of courtship to be considered.) For contrast students might study the painful, almost silent re-courtship of Anne Elliot and Captain Wentworth in *Persuasion*. In all these cases we are looking at relationships between social convention, formality, restraint, and passion, in which language plays an essential part. Other possibilities include *Sons and Lovers* and *A Farewell to Arms*; or we might use a more recent novel in which the traditional sequence of encounter–love–courtship–marriage–sex is disrupted, inverted or otherwise edited, or a novel of homosexual courtship. (These latter suggestions might lead to reflections on whether or not the notion of 'courtship' is now quite dead.) There is ample scope for 'background' research – but much can be gained about assumptions and values from a close study of the texts themselves.

All well and good, so far; but how, given the specific concern of this book with teaching *reading* Shakespeare, might such a task help students to read Shakespeare better? I think the answer lies not in any contextual detours and backgrounds, or in any vaporous generalizations about 'relationships', but in the close comparison between carefully selected passages. Such a comparison of Wilde and Shakespeare can bring out a great deal about direct and indirect expression, about implications, about the arts of language, about superficiality and depth. While Shakespeare's texts can be seen to be fraught with sub-text (why else would people ardently debate the degree of love apparent/implicit in the exchanges of Beatrice and Benedick?), it may be questioned whether in Wilde there is any sub-text at all. (Maybe the lack of sub-text is in part what makes it so funny.) In *Much Ado* and *Persuasion* there is scope for consideration of the presentation of *buried* feeling.

Another possible text, increasing the contrast, is Henry James' *Washington Square*. Another way of narrowing the focus on 'love' is to look at adultery (*Antony and Cleopatra*, Dryden's *All for Love*). A unit on 'crawling towards death' might bring *Lear* alongside Tennyson's 'Tithonus' (or 'Ulysses') and Tillie Olsen's *Tell Me a Riddle*. And so on.

Further reflections

Context as an essential element in the understanding of Shakespeare has grown in prominence over the last thirty years, especially with the rise of New Historicism and Cultural Materialism. This isn't to say that it wasn't important before; under the general notion of 'background' it had been the leading concern of a number of books, perhaps the most widely used and influential being E. M. W. Tillyard's *The Elizabethan World Picture* (first published in 1943 and rarely, if ever, out of print since). But context certainly impinges more nowadays on our concerns as teachers, and is assumed to be essential rather than an adjunct, so that it can be perfectly natural to ask as a *rhetorical* question: 'What kind of understanding can a seventeen-year-old have of *Othello* without knowledge of Venice and the Turks, Moors, Machiavelli, the romance tradition, courtly love and so on?'[19] I think my answer must be 'A deep one', as such was exactly my first experience of *Othello* when I was a sixth-former. Studying *Othello* for A Level in the mid-sixties I don't think we said *anything* about the status of women. Bianca was just a whore (which, notice, is *Iago's* judgment). *The Female Eunuch* was yet to be published. And while we were aware of the issue of race, I don't think any of us thought it was anything other than incidental to the play's meaning. In teaching the play at A Level I have invited my students to consider the subtitle 'the Moor of Venice', drawing attention to the contemporary associations of each of the proper nouns and suggesting that the phrase, if not actually an oxymoron, is full of tensions; and we've considered the Turk as an enemy and his inscription into Othello's suicide speech, as well as issues of the status of women and of race. We've focused on the role of Bianca in a way that I would once have considered altogether disproportionate. We've done this because I think these things are important and interesting, and because they are concerns of my students and the society that they and I live in. Nonetheless, I persist in thinking that we got near to the heart of the play all those years ago without such contextual information, and what got me there was responding to the power of Shakespeare's dramatic writing. This doesn't mean that I was responding to timeless characters and situations (to whom and in which context is presumably unimportant), but to Othello and Desdemona and Iago; not to large generalizations about, for instance, love, but, to quote Robert Marchant, 'how love goes with this man'.[20] So my understanding of the play could later on accommodate what the New Historicists and Cultural Materialists came up with, as well as providing a touchstone against which to consider it.

Too much context, the wrong kind of context or context clumsily handled can take attention away from the power of Shakespeare's dramatic writing and the meaning it can have for us – which in all years of secondary Shakespeare should be our focus. We need to distinguish between what we need to know and what our students need to know. We might well need to revise and extend our knowledge of contexts in some detail, and there are plenty of resources to help us with this, most obviously in the introductions to the latest standard scholarly editions (Arden, Cambridge and Oxford). The 'Cambridge Student Guide' series offers compact information in relation to each of the plays in an accessible and useful manner. The series is well worth teachers' attention. Peter Hyland's book, already mentioned, is a very useful single-volume resource. But what our students need, and when they need it, is a separate question. And unfortunately, teaching being an art, there aren't any rules for this; the only time to introduce a specific contextual element is the right time.

Chapter 14

Interpretation

In his essay 'Text and context', Peter Winch writes of contextual 'surroundings' that they 'will of course be very various in kind and indeterminate in extent'. He goes on immediately to say 'Critical judgments made by others will frequently be an indispensable aspect of these surroundings.'[1] In the classroom, these others will be the teacher, fellow-students and critics variously encountered. In this context the class work together towards forming judgements. These days exam specifications do not say much, if anything, about critical judgement. They prefer to insist on *interpretation*. With Curriculum 2000, examination boards, to a greater or lesser degree, took on some of the preoccupations and assumptions of critical theory, including an emphasis on the indeterminacy of meaning of texts (a preoccupation not extended to the interpretation of their own syllabuses, of which the authors' intentions were certainly taken to be the determiners of the meaning). They specified that students must show an awareness of the range and variety of critical opinion, and that a work is susceptible of more than one interpretation. Plurality was insisted on – we were to deal not in interpretation but interpretations. Through encountering a range of interpretations and responses to the play being studied, students were to develop their own.

These specifications seem to assume an article of critical faith, and one that contrasts with an earlier view of interpretation, evident in some dictionary definitions of 'interpret': *explain, translate, expound the meaning of, elucidate, translate into intelligible or familiar terms*. In that earlier view, what gives value to an interpretation is not that it is mine (although, as Leavis insisted, a judgement is personal or it is nothing) but that it is right; that the aim of the critic is to say something cogent, not to provide a fresh and exciting viewpoint. On the older view the classroom is a place of collaborative debate – Eliot's 'common pursuit of true judgment' – and not, as might seem to be encouraged by Curriculum 2000, a little world of happily proliferating interpretations. Both ask a lot of the student, and may be the source of considerable anxiety, or just plain weariness/indifference: 'Can't you just tell us?' said a disconsolate student to me once. What worries me is that we might make so much of indeterminacy and multiplicity of meaning that our students will fail to develop a strong, personal, considered response and that we might be encouraging them in an easy and unphilosphical relativism. Also I'm concerned that we might thrust the literary work into a secondary place, rather than the primary one that it – surely? – should have in a study of literature. The work becomes an example, something on which we practise skills. But the literary work comes first, and our student's initial responses to it are important both in their own right and as points of departure for subsequent development ('At first I thought ... but later I came to see').

Thinking around literary theory is easier when the reader has first-hand acquaintance with a number of texts across a range of genres and periods. We might well think it best reserved for consideration later than A Level – at university. We need to think consciously about such things on our students' behalf – and we need to do so with this question uppermost in our minds: what of this framework helps them to read Shakespeare better (more attentively and responsively, with a well-attuned sense of what is and is not relevant)?

Interpretation in performance

In the earlier stages of work on Shakespeare, interpretation is best approached through practical investigations of performance, looking at the ways in which particular (at first quite short) passages can be performed with different emphases. Examples have been discussed in Chapter 12, developing from basic questions about stage grouping, movement, tone and pacing, and going on to consideration of the dramatic meaning of whole scenes. Such investigations will at first encourage a focus on (a) the motivation and interaction of characters, and (b) the impact of the moment on the audience. Exam boards and some critics may object to (a) that it commits the category error of treating characters in a play as real people, but (b) keeps us firmly in check over this. And surely the primary impact of a play is as an imitation of a human action, so to regard the characters in some sense as people is not too grievous an error for a fourteen-year-old.

A particular advantage of this approach is that pupils will quickly become aware of both the potential of the text for different emphases in performance *and* a degree of resistance from the text. We can't just do it any way we like. Pupils might be invited to play against the text – do 'To be or not to be' or 'To-morrow and to-morrow' like a stand-up comic – and see how far they can get. Even on the simplest level they will find limits: a low ability group working on five lines or so of a scene (there's no reason they shouldn't be given *very* short extracts to focus on) made the discovery that one character couldn't be already on stage and that she must enter some distance away from the others 'because it says "*Yonder* she comes." '

Later we might approach whole scenes with a more explicit emphasis on different readings. For instance, a class studying *The Shrew* might focus on different ways of playing Act 4 Scene 5 before debating which seems the truest to the text and the play as a whole. This is the scene in which Petruchio insists that the moon – or the sun – is what he says it is, and Katherina agrees ('But sun it is not when you say it is not,/And the moon changes even as your mind'). Groups are each given a specific brief for how to present the scene:

A   Petruchio is aggressive and inexorable, without a trace of humour. Katherina is afraid and gives in completely, doing whatever he says. He pushes her to the limit, and she just obeys, like an automaton. If she expresses anything, it is exhaustion. Petruchio wins.

B   Petruchio has nearly had enough of the whole business. He is weary and beginning to wonder if it's worth it. When Katherina starts agreeing he can't believe his luck and gets quite lively. He is curious to find out how far she will go, and then has to stop her when it seems there's no limit. Katherina is deliberately pushing it, seeing how far *he's* prepared to go. She wins.

C   Petruchio is applying his it-will-be-what-I-say-it-is method in a deliberately 'over the top' manner. Katherina decides (when, exactly?) that she can beat him at his own game. She doesn't give in, but decides to show that anything he can do she can do better. He is amazed and decides to push her further, upon which she goes further than he expects. He is delighted. Both win – or think they have.

D   Petruchio and Katherina are from the beginning of the scene enjoying themselves, at the expense of anybody and everybody else; playing their own private game, the rules of which only they understand. In this game they express their love and understanding of each other, and they don't care what anyone else thinks. It isn't about winning any more. (If this is so, at what point do they learn to play?)

Sometimes it's productive to bring the focus even tighter, on a particular moment: for instance, on the performances possibilities of the kiss in Act 5 Scene 1 of *The Taming of the Shrew*:

Petruchio	First kiss me, Kate, and then we will.
Kate	What, in the midst of the street?
Petruchio	What, art thou ashamed of me?
Kate	No sir, God forbid, but ashamed to kiss.
Petruchio	Why then, let's home again …

Kate	Nay, I will give thee a kiss. Now pray thee, love, stay.
Petruchio	Is not this well?

A detailed comparison of the handling of this moment in film versions by Miller and Zeffirelli and a stage performance can bring out a great deal about possibilities of meaning in the play as a whole. In particular the moment's potential for reluctance, passion, intimacy, reserve, display, manipulation, sarcasm, tenderness can be discussed, as can its potential contrast with the previous kiss (if there is one) in Act 2 Scene 1. How might the kiss work as a sign between the couple, to their on-stage audience, to the theatre audience? Also students can be asked to consider what limits on interpretation at this point are suggested by the qualities of the lines themselves. What is the range of possibility in terms of intonation, really? (Personally, I find the greatest encouragement to a non-misogynist reading in this moment.)

It's worth mentioning in this connection that, while we often show the class a video at an early stage, largely to establish the storyline and mood(s) of the play, there is a lot to be said for leaving it until a more strategic moment. In work on theatrical performance, it can be interesting to delay the video version of a scene until the pupils have already investigated some possibilities in depth and detail, and then watching *two* versions. Pupils can prepare for watching the scene by thinking about where they would use close-ups, long shots, etc. After they've watched the video it's worth drawing their attention to any cuts that have been made in the text and asking them why – apart from requirements of length – they have been made specifically in this way.

Interpretation of characters

These investigations can move into written form. After a character has been considered in a number of scenes, pupils can reflect on their overall sense of that character. They might further be prompted to consider different perspectives on the character expressed in the play itself. For instance, a Year 9 class were asked to consider Beatrice in relation to two descriptions given of her in *Much Ado* – 'base and bitter' and 'pleasant spirited'. The best work on this showed an awareness that the phrases themselves have their origins within the drama and may tell as much about the speakers as who is spoken about:

> [Earlier in the essay] Beatrice has been shown to be base and bitter, yet witty, but by no means is she unfriendly towards *everybody*. Indeed Don Pedro describes her as a 'pleasant spirited lady', bearing in mind his proposal has just been turned down. This could affect his statement because he is talking to Leonato, in front of Hero. He would

naturally be politer to such closer relatives and could be trying to hide a disappointment at Beatrice's answer. 'Pleasant spirited' could be out of gratefulness that she didn't refuse him in a harsher manner. (Megan)

This shows an excellent sense of the dramatic context of the utterances, and rightly avoids seeing them as supradramatic, authoritative descriptions, of which one is simply 'right'.

Such approaches can build up to an even fuller consideration of how a character might appear to us in a performance/reading of the whole play. Work with one Year 9 group on Orsino in *Twelfth Night* began with finding out what range of opinion there was within the class. After working on ways of staging the first scene, pupils were asked to write brief answers to the question 'What is Orsino like?' Here is a selection of responses:

- Orsino seems to be a high-class person because he gives orders and he is called my lord.
- Orsino is very self-pitying and feels very sorry for himself. We [girls] think he should get up and fight for his girl – and get a grip!
- Orsino seems like an emotional man who is used to getting what he wants because of his position.
- Orsino seems to be the type of person who gets tired of some things easily. He is quite a romantic person as he says a lot of pleasant and sweet poetic sort of things.
- Orsino was a confident and emotional person who enjoyed getting his own way. His emotion and confidence is shown by his thoughtful speeches, line 1–line 15 etc.
- Orsino seems to be a very understanding, but indecisive man. He is very understanding that Olivia feels she should be in mourning for 7 years.
- Orsino seems to be a pleasant man (he is not angry at Valentine for the news he brings) and well educated (compares himself to Actaeon). He is wise and thoughtful, but also he is prone to follow his emotions (he keeps on loving someone who will not love him for at least seven summers).
- Orsino is emotional, caring and big-headed. He can become unhappy quickly, he cares for people but in doing so he compares himself to gods and famous important people.
- Orsino seems to be sensitive, but determined. He is easily angered and frustrated and his moods can change dramatically in a short space of time.

It's notable that, although there are some hints that Orsino is self-indulgent in his emotions, there's nothing here about being in love with being in love.

On the whole, his expressions of love are taken as sincere enough. The teacher's immediate follow-up might not be to ask 'Which is right?' but 'Why do you think so?', encouraging reference to the text.

After reading more or all of the play, pupils can be asked to tease out their readings of the character further, and the question of 'being in love with being in love' can be raised explicitly (since it is a frequently repeated idea and for some readers constitutes an important part of the play's meaning). They may be helped by being given a sketch of three suggested readings of Orsino and asking them to explore and consider the evidence:

A   A big-headed arrogant man, in love with being in love, insensitive and fixed in his opinions, regarded by his followers with wariness and dislike.
B   A genuine lover; poetic, generous, passionate and caring, regarded by his followers with affection and concern.
C   An unstable, rather wimpish character, in love with being in love, looked down on by his followers.

A PGCE student, Bina (to whom thanks), provided an excellent worksheet showing how textual evidence may be used in support of contrasting/contesting views, giving her class some alternative readings on the pattern shown in Figure 14.1.

A more sophisticated approach – perhaps with the addition of a contextual element with brief observations about conventions of love poetry – might focus specifically in the quality of Orsino's 'pleasant and sweet poetic sort of things'. (Similarly, GCSE candidates might consider Romeo's speeches in Act 1 Scene 2 against the charge of self-indulgence.)

	Orsino – arrogant, in love with being in love, self-important	Orsino – sincere, romantic, deeply in love with Olivia
If ever thou shalt love, In the sweet pangs of it *remember me:* For *such as I am, all true lovers are, Unstaid and skittish*, in all motions else, Save in *the constant image of the creature That is beloved.*	*Remember me* – draws attention to himself, not Olivia who he says he loves *Such as I am, all true lovers are* – holds himself up as the ideal example of a 'true lover'	*Unstaid and skittish* – hard to admit when you're a prince – embarrassed that his love makes him behave strangely? *Constant image of the … beloved* – suggests he's always thinking about Olivia

Figure 14.1 Notes for exploring the character of Orsino.

This approach led to some very perceptive work from a different Year 9 class, as these examples show:

- Orsino seems very noble and arrogant in this scene. He ushers his attendants away quickly – 'Stand you awhile aloof' – then proceeds to order Cesario off to Olivia's court – 'Good youth, address thy gait unto her.' He continues by saying 'Stand at her doors,/and tell them, there thy fixed foot shall grow/Till thou have audience'. These lines suggest that Orsino is very eager to have attention and be heard, but he isn't going to listen to what Olivia has to say – he wants Cesario to stand at Olivia's door until she pays some attention to Orsino's love, being fixed on his opinions and stopping until Olivia agrees. Then, Orsino tells Cesario to be quite rude to Olivia – 'Leap all civil bounds' – to be heard, showing he is never going to stop, even if he offends Olivia by not being courteous. (Ellie)
- What I think is worthy of note ... is that if Viola was handsome and good-looking, why would Orsino send her to entice his love? Surely he is making a mistake? Doesn't he realize that by sending a beautiful young man he could be heading towards an even bigger problem? ... I think this could explain that Orsino isn't really in love but in love with being in love because if he felt really deeply about Olivia, as he says then he wouldn't make a stupid mistake and he would have thought it all out which he clearly hasn't. (Aliah)
- He could be saying that his love for Olivia is so strong that he needs music to 'feed' it, which would be character B. Or Orsino could be saying that he needs the music to feel as if he really loves Olivia and to help him wallow in self-pity that she won't return his love, in which case it would be C. He also says 'O, it came o'er my ear like the sweet sound/That breathes upon a bank of violets', but then, only one short sentence after, says 'Enough, no more;/'Tis not so sweet now as it was before'. This change of opinion shows Orsino's indecisiveness which could also refer to his love for Olivia, strong and passionate one minute, bored of her the next. (Emma)

The essays from which these quotations are taken are long, well sustained and clearly argued throughout, as were those of most of the class. Clearly these pupils have already developed habits of close attention and are able to weight evidence thoughtfully and argue cogently.

'Originality'

However, for the highest grades exam boards ask for *originality* in interpretation. This mustn't be taken too literally as has often been pointed out. There's certainly no point in urging our students to come up with an entirely novel reading, which is likely to be ungrounded and merely eccentric. Again, a judgement is personal or it is nothing, but just because it is personal doesn't make it a (sound) judgement. The classroom should be among other things a testing ground for readings, in which individual contributions are respectfully considered but not simply endorsed. I don't think we should talk about originality at all, much less make it an aim; as teachers we are looking for judgements that are personal (inhabited) rather than original in the sense of unprecedented.

Nonetheless our pupils and students do at times come up with provocative and suggestive readings which, however partial they may be, should be taken seriously and made part of the class's discussion, the common pursuit of true judgement. In the year that I ran the scheme of work on *Richard III* described in the previous chapter, the class produced a number of outstanding essays. One student (quite genuinely, I think; he wasn't trying to be either awkward or clever) argued that Shakespeare is actually *undermining* Richmond – but only implicitly, as 'Queen Elizabeth … was Henry the Seventh's (Richmond's) grand-daughter, so Shakespeare may not have been able to talk freely about his true feelings towards Richmond's motives'. Unfortunately his argument turned on an unhistorical equation of Richard's and Richmond's killing in order to become king. One thing we do sometimes have to explain is that not all killing was regarded as murder. Iago appeals to this distinction: 'Though in the trade of war I have slain men,/Yet do I hold it very stuff o' the conscience/ To do no contrived murder.' He's a hypocrite, of course, but here he's saying something he has no doubt will be regarded favourably, a commonplace. Similarly Macbeth's murder of Duncan is quite different in his own mind and everybody else's from his 'valiant' slaying on the battlefield. However, we may not want to stop here; we may want to suspect with Wilbur Sanders[2] that the emphases of Shakespeare's language actually lead us to *question* that distinction. It remains the background against which we read, but we need to be alert to the possibility that Shakespeare is not just assuming the commonplace. My student's argument might be in need of a development of this kind, if it is available in this case. Nonetheless, he is clearly beginning to use context in quite a sophisticated manner. The argument could be developed to suggest how 'hero' and 'villain' might not be neatly independent concepts – the one requiring the other, and maybe partaking of some of his qualities. Close textual analysis might attempt to show that hypocrisy can be detected in Richmond's speeches.

Turning points

Again narrowing the focus but keeping the whole play in view, using the scene as a potential focus of the significance of the whole play, we might consider dramatic moments (such as the second kiss in *The Shrew*) that are turning points. For instance, in the Folio in the final Act of *The Tempest* Ariel describes the distresses that Prospero's enemies have fallen, and there follows this remarkable exchange.

> *Ariel*   your charm so strongly works 'em
> That if you now beheld them, your affections
> Would become tender.
> *Prospero*   Dost thou thinke so, Spirit?
> *Ariel*   Mine would, Sir, were I humane.
> *Prospero*   And mine shall.

Is this a moment of *conversion*, Prospero turning from his intended and fury-driven revenge, or of *confirmation*, Prospero assuring the spirit that his revenge has a limit, even that his intention has all along been reconciliation, not revenge? Our answer will depend in part on how we interpret the continuation of Prospero's speech:

> Hast thou (which are but air) a touch, a feeling,
> Of their afflictions, and shall not my selfe,
> One of their kinde, that rellish all as sharpely,
> Passion as they, be kindlier mou'd than thou art?
> Thogh with their high wrongs I am strook to th' quick,
> Yet, with my nobler reason, gainst my furie
> Doe I take part.

There's a grammatical question here concerning Prospero's verbs: does he mean that he *characteristically* (i.e. habitually) sides with his nobler reason, or that from now on he will? Our students' consideration of the possibilities can move out into a reading of earlier and later scenes, which may help determine the issue or suggest that Shakespeare leaves it undecided. Either way we can consider this a moment at which a limit to what it is to be human(e) is tested and defined (we might compare Macbeth's 'I dare do all that may become a man,/Who dares do more, is none'.); and this can lead us on to consider the nature and limits of humanity in relation not only to Ariel but also to Caliban (in what does his monstrosity consist?) and the biologically human characters Sebastian, Alonso and Antonio. And, of course, we can consider the subsequent separation of *humane* into our *human* and *humane*. So attention to a few lines leads us into larger matters of interpretation but keeps us from unanchored generalities.

Where there are particular moments in the drama over which strikingly different critical views exist it's worth pausing at that point in the study and introducing them for consideration. Take the scene in which Hamlet declines to kill Claudius when he finds him at prayer:

> Up, sword, and know thou a more horrid hent
> When he is drunk, asleep; or on his rage,
> Or th' incestuous pleasure of his bed,
> At gaming, swearing, or about some act
> That has no relish of salvation in't,
> Then trip him, that his heels may kick at Heaven,
> And that his soul may be as damn'd and black,
> As Hell, whereto it goes.

We might just present for discussion Johnson's memorably phrased reaction:

> This speech, in which Hamlet, represented as a virtuous character, is not content with taking blood for blood, but contrives damnation for the man he would punish, is too horrible to be read or to be uttered.[3]

Is Hamlet represented as a virtuous character? Is *our* sense of virtue incompatible with such a degree of revenge, as Johnson's was? Is Johnson going too far in saying the speech is too horrible to be read? Is that an appropriate response to a scene in a play? Or we might open it up further, introducing from other critics the view that Hamlet is making excuses, that he doesn't really mean it. How might such an argument be conducted? Where else in the play might we find support for it? Or we might use a contextual approach, perhaps, bringing in contemporary ideas of revenge as they bear on this one particular point. Could an audience at the time have taken this speech at face value and still found Hamlet heroic? Or is Hamlet actually not heroic at all?

In some cases we might need to consider turning-points that occur only in performance, there being no textual warrant for them. There are, for instance, productions of *The Taming of the Shrew* which introduce a crucial moment which is nowhere indicated in any texts of the play – an immediate, astonished response of mutual love between Kate and Petruchio in Act 2 Scene 1, from which all afterwards depends, and casts all the subsequent scenes between them as a delighted voyage of discovery, a shared game of parody and affection. And when in the final scene Kate offers to place her hand under Petruchio's foot, does he accept the gesture? Or – for instance – applaud with ironic appreciation, burst out laughing or take her in his arms? (In Jonathan Miller's production for the BBC she places her hand on his.) Consider also the much-discussed ending of *Measure for Measure*; what if in performance it is clear that Isabella *doesn't* accept the Duke's proposal? A general principle might be raised here: if there is no warrant in the text for these and other performances,[4] is there any warrant for them at all?

Range and variety of interpretation

We – and our students – will need to judge carefully the extent to which we wish to highlight a range of readings. Sometimes, as with context, a few strategically placed sentences, a relevant paragraph, will be enough. But we must remember that for the higher grades our candidates are required to demonstrate 'interpretive skills', and sometimes we may want to build a whole unit around the question of alternative readings. Such an approach is pretty straightforward with plays about which there are long-standing critical controversies. *Othello* is an obvious case. Is he the noble hero or a deluded egoist? And do we approach this internally or externally (approached through generic assumptions, or through close reading)? We can also set up opposed pairs of interpretation in relation to *The Tempest*. Is Prospero the godlike hero (the artist, the playwright himself) or the oppressor of Ariel and Caliban? Is Caliban the devil or an abused slave? Given that there has been, roughly speaking, a chronological shift from the first of these alternatives to the second, why is that so? Or is the play misread in these political terms, being in reality a symbolic representation of the real world, a mystery play?[5] With *Romeo and Juliet* we might consider if the protagonists are romantic hero and heroine or adolescent pains in the butt; and after Zeffirelli and Luhrmann we might want to investigate what textual evidence there is for considering whether Mercutio is gay or not, and think about what's involved in so representing him. Looking at *Macbeth* we might consider different valuations of Malcolm (heaven's agent or shallow self-seeker?). And so on. We should also note that while dichotomies can prompt useful discussions our students do need to be aware that they might well be false.

Such issues could be explored through debate, with pairs of students researching a particular view via brief reading suggestions made by the teacher and then presenting the view to the class. Individual students then write reflective comments on the interpretations, weighing up which seem the most persuasive – and considering which, if any, is just plain unacceptable. (It's worth throwing in the occasional googly simply to raise the issue of whether there are limits to interpretations, whether it's possible simply to be wrong.)

If there isn't time for reading around, students can be given a view to consider on the spot. With only, say, fifteen or twenty minutes' consultation with the text, working in pairs or threes, students might prepare arguments for and against the following propositions:

1   Iago is a repressed homosexual deeply attracted to Othello. (This proposition was greeted with hoots of laughter, but the 'for' team

actually found that they could come up with a surprising amount in support, even though they remained skeptical. We followed up by looking at some clips of Ian McKellan's deeply repressed Iago.)[6]

2 The marriage between Othello and Desdemona is unwise and unlikely to be successful.

3 Othello's race is of no significance for an understanding of the play.

4 Othello is presented as self-approving and self-dramatizing.

These statements involve various kinds of assumption that can at some point be made explicit: the first statement is in danger of the 'real person' fallacy; the fourth avoids it by the phrase 'presented as' – which some students will tend to overlook; the third involves cultural issues past and present.

Or we can present students with a schematic account of a full range of critical opinions in relation to the play they are studying. This may (as with the *Hamlet* example) focus on a particular scene or speech. Barbara Hardy remarks on Kate's final speech in *The Taming of the Shrew* that 'Generations of playgoers and readers have accepted [Kate's final] speech with varying responses of acquiescence, anxiety, fury and cynicism'.[7] Students can be told that critics vary widely in their understanding of the last scene and of Kate's speech in particular. While they disagree, they tend to see their own view as the *obvious* one. The range of views can be charted as follows:

1 Kate's speech is to be taken 'straight':

a The play is patriarchal, but inoffensive because it is in no way threatening to women of today; the play is sexist but a harmless 'romp'.

b The play is patriarchal and offensive; it celebrates the destruction of a woman who is brought into mindless conformity with patriarchal values. 'Kate's life is finished, because she concedes her voice.'[8]

c The play is patriarchal, but so is Nature. This is how things are meant to be between a man and a woman.

d The play is patriarchal, but, within limitations, the ending is positive: 'the girl has found herself at last ... her "real" nature will flourish in the role she has learnt no longer to resist'.[9]

2 Kate's speech is to be taken ironically:

a because we know from other plays that Shakespeare had a positive view of women, or because we regard him as ideologically sound, so he *can't* have meant Kate's speech to be taken at face value.

b because irony is implied in the speech itself.

   c   because the speech is to be understood as Kate's counter-testing of Petruchio. She shows how well she can play his game, and he realizes that he has gone too far. There is a private understanding between them that leaves the other characters far behind.

   d   because doubt is cast on the reality of Kate's conversion by the response of the other characters, especially in the concluding couplet.

   e   because the Sly 'closure' reminds us that we have only been watching a play, and encourages us to mock the tinker who has taken its apparent 'message' seriously.

Or, more generally, they can be presented with the range of views on the principal characters in the play as a whole:

1   Kate's shrewishness

   a   is just what the characters in the early scenes say it is
   b   has been much exaggerated
   c   stems from neglect by her father and/or favouritism towards Bianca
   d   is a form of self-defence
   e   is to be taken seriously as an aberration, perhaps medical in origin
   f   is a donnée, to be taken at face value.

2   Petruchio's 'cure'

   a   is motivated by his desire for a rich marriage
   b   began as a. but was fired by love on first seeing her
   c   is almost medical/technical, carefully planned
   d   is wildly improvised, made up as he goes along
   e   is cruel
   f   is kind.

Individually or in pairs, students could take a particular view and revisit the text for evidence, or discuss the full range. This can lead to some very orderly, considered essay writing.

Students can also be told about the ways in which directors over the years have cut and re-arranged the text, introduced 'business' and emphasized lines in particular ways, in order to bring the play into conformity with one or other of these interpretations. They might also consider David Garrick's rewriting of the final scene, in which Kate's notorious speech is cut and redistributed, with the lines from 'Such duty as the subject owes the prince' to 'to love, to honour, and obey' (suitably emended) delivered as the play's final lines by Petruchio to the audience.[10] If they're studying *Othello*, they can consider the significance of the nineteenth-century reluctance to provide the full tragic loading of the bed in the last act; instead Desdemona, Emilia and Othello died decorously on separate little mats, and so no object is present to 'poison sight'. What's involved in such a choice? Once students have been alerted to this technique of 'interpretation', they can investigate it further by considering what cuts and other alterations in the text they could make to support a particular view of the play – and discuss the morality of doing so.

Using critics

As outlined above, we can do a lot of work on interpretation without naming any particular critic. (Some of the 'Cambridge School Shakespeare' editions do this particularly well and afford a useful model). There's a tendency for teachers to present critics' views in the form of snippets, one-liners. But for some students, as they develop as readers, this will not be enough. We will want to recommend some reading for specific individuals. Sometimes this will be a matter of a class approach where different critical essays are assigned to members of the class to summarize and present to the others. I'm thinking more, though, of things that will engage with the direction a particular student's thoughts are moving in, or will prompt them to consider something that they will benefit from in some way. At a certain point in my A level study of *Othello* one of my teachers suggested that I read F. R. Leavis's essay 'Diabolic intellect and the noble hero'.[11] I did so, and was gripped by it (as I had already been by the play; I hope that otherwise my teacher wouldn't have made the recommendation). It wasn't suggested to me that I read anything else. As far as my own development as a reader went, that one recommendation was enough, and it was also enough for the then requirements of A level. In the years after A level, in reading round I encountered opposed views in Helen Gardner and others, became aware of a wider range of readings, but whatever sense I have of the play now, Leavis' essay will always be a lively and living factor. A critical account can be influential and enable the student to read – although of course it can also prevent him/her from reading, as s/he accepts an interpretation from an apparent expert.

As students express interest in knowing more about a particular view among those represented, their reading can be directed accordingly. When they read a complete critical essay, it's a good idea to encourage them not just to pick out quotations, but to summarize and evaluate the argument as a whole. Sometimes it will be appropriate to introduce substantial passages of criticism for the whole class to read, ponder and debate. Where a critic offers a sustained reading of a speech or a passage we can ask students to put their own reading up against it: do they read the passage in the same way? Has the critic overemphasized anything, or passed anything over? A good example is Bradley on the last moments of *Othello* ('there is almost nothing here to diminish the admiration and love which heighten pity'),[12] useful because it directs the students to a reconsideration of the passage, but mainly because I think it's fairly clear that we *don't* see what Bradley describes. This helps sharpen a sense of what we do see. We might (if we are pursing more general questions) ask *why* he produces what strikes us as a misreading but the immediate aim is to sharpen our own reading. (We might even argue that there is a place for the occasional deployment of very *bad* criticism.)

It can also sometimes be illuminating to put alongside each other not only opposed readings, but opposed readings by two critics who might be assumed to be arguing from similar premises. A particularly striking example is the very different line taken on *The Shrew* by two committed feminists, both fully engaged and cogent. Germaine Greer:

> Kate ... has the uncommon good fortune to find Petruchio, who is man enough to know what he wants and how to get it. He wants her spirit and energy because he wants a wife worth keeping. He tames her as he might a hawk or a high-mettled horse, and she rewards him with strong sexual love and fierce loyalty ... The message is probably twofold: only Kates make good wives, and then only to Petruchios; for the rest, their cake is dough.[13]

Stevie Davies (who, incidentally, uses a lot of contextual material):

> I cannot tamely represent the comedy as a light-hearted romp nor persuade myself that its author intended a subversive critique of the values his plot endorses. Women endured centuries of purgatory to redeem themselves from the abusive attitudes enshrined in *The Taming of the Shrew* ... Kate's life is finished, because she concedes her voice ... Bonding between hero and heroine in *The Shrew* is predicated on bondage.[14]

Which is right? Can they both be right? How can they have come to have such different views? Are they both reading the same play?

It's worth mentioning that in addition to critics we can make use of the published accounts by actors of their thoughts in relation to specific parts and plays.

'Critical approaches'

Exam boards ask older students for a more conscious, even theoretical awareness of 'interpretation', and some knowledge and use of specific critical interpretations. While we might feel – I feel – that university is soon enough for this, and that too early an emphasis on it might detract from students forming their own impression of books, while the boards require it we have to work with it.

We might decide to tackle the question of interpretation explicitly – 'theoretically' – with our students, independently of the in-depth study of any text, as part of a prolegomena to the study of literature. This won't work with all classes, but some such invitation to discussion as the following can be fruitful with students with a taste for philosophical/general argument:

> What different people might read a text in different ways?
>
> - interpreting it differently (disagreement about meaning)
> - evaluating it differently (disagreement about value)
>
> Of course these are interrelated: but the distinction is worth making as a starter.
>
> Come up with as many suggestions as you can, considering
>
> - different kinds of reader
> - different purposes in reading
> - different periods
> - different contexts.

This could be done in relation to a specific short text, introduced for the purpose; a text which seems to stand in need of interpretation because the meaning is not 'on the surface', perhaps a short a poem by Blake, Emily Dickinson or ee cummings, or even a children's book such as Maurice Sendak's brilliant *Where the Wild Things Are.*

This can be followed, either immediately or at a later stage, by a consideration of different kinds of critical interest (feminist, Marxist, etc.). This is often dealt with under the rubric of 'approaches', but this can be very misleading and is a metaphor best avoided. It's better, I think, to focus on how attitudes and beliefs might inform valuations of texts, direct emphases, and so on. Particularly useful to teachers and students is Peter Barry's *Beginning Theory,*[15] which contains summary lists of what different kinds of critics characteristically do. These can easily be adapted for our students. For instance, we can give them thumbnail sketches of invented critics. This approach is highly artificial, in danger of confounding people with positions and encouraging stereotypical thinking, but can be productive. Something along the following lines might do (the list can be tailored specifically to the teacher's current requirements):

- Gabriella is a feminist. In reading she is on the lookout for examples of sexist views of women, of the mechanisms of patriarchy, positive representations of women, false and limiting ideas of women's roles in literature and society. She celebrates strong women in literature.

- Miles is concerned with the moral tendency of literature. He is on the lookout for attitudes and values and how they are expressed. In particular he is concerned with how literature can deprave and corrupt its readers, or enhance their moral sensitivity, implicitly as well as explicitly.
- Ronald is a reader who enjoys literature for its formal qualities as art. He looks for qualities of language – for conscious patterns, formal symmetries, rhetorical devices, wit, ingenuity and inventiveness.
- Raymond likes to relate the content and attitudes of the work to the social situation of the period. In particular he looks for power relations, how they appear and what lies behind them. He highlights literature's progressive (i.e. revolutionary) tendencies and laments its repressive/conservative elements.
- Chloe likes to be entertained.

These 'characters' could be introduced after a particular passage (an opening scene, perhaps, or a turning-point or major dramatic confrontation) has been read and there has been some initial discussion. The students could then be asked to write about the scene from the point of view of two of them, either in two separate pieces or in a dialogue. (Some students – perhaps after a little research on their 'position' – may be able to handle this more easily in role-play.) This will work better with some scenes than with others, most obviously where 'issues' are writ large.

I didn't include in my *critical personae* a deconstructionist – they can wait until university, if they haven't gone by then. Nor did I include a psychological critic, because it requires much more explanation (unless we just say 'Sigmund looks for hidden meanings, usually sexual' and see what ensues). The psychological/psychoanalytic kind of reading may be better introduced as part of the sustained study of a major text – for instance when discussing the notorious handkerchief in *Othello*. After reminders of where it occurs in the play and what is said about it (a homework task, perhaps) the students can be introduced through a short lecture to some of the ways in which it has been 'read', along these lines:

> The handkerchief is most obviously a plot device, and as such considered a contemptible absurdity by Thomas Rymer in 1643 ('This may be a warning to all good Wives, that they may look well to their Linnen … This may be a lesson to Husbands, that before their Jealousie be Tragical, the proofs may be Mathematical'), and by Samuel Johnson in 1776 as 'merely a trick, but a very pretty trick', but not until later considered as a locus of meaning. We might look for meaning at the level of individual psychology – Othello's: why is the loss of the handkerchief so terrible to him – especially when we reflect that there are reasons for thinking that in Act 3 Scene 4 he is

telling porkies? Does he take it for the 'ocular proof' that he has demanded, a sign – 'like the raven o'er the infected house'? If his account can be taken at face value, might not this be evidence that Othello *did*, as Brabantio suspected (or rather *knew*, as the only possible explanation of his daughter's aberrant behaviour), use charms to seduce Desdemona? (We might note the suggestiveness of Emilia's use of the word 'conjured'.) And might not this knowledge be an element in Othello's unspoken mind? Or, if his account is honest and also objectively true, might there not *be* magic in the web, and the curse be working itself out in Othello's mind? Or maybe we should be going deeper into subjectivity, the mind of Othello, or even of the play: the handkerchief is spotted with strawberries, symbolic of lust (compare the other occurrence of 'spotted' in the play – 'Thy bed lust-stained shall with lust's blood be spotted'). From here we move into questions about those bedsheets (which Desdemona asks to be laid on what will be her deathbed) and the speculations of, among others, Stanley Cavell:[16] has Othello taken Desdemona's virginity or not? Does he know if he has? How are these speculations related to the monster that Iago begets in Othello's thoughts? Is the bed, central in Othello's mind, also central, as has been suggested, on the stage throughout the last act?

If we've taken the trouble to present students with a digest of psychoanalytical ideas, we could follow it up with specific questions: Does Othello repress/project/sublimate? Does he live in a world of false images of himself and others? Is Iago anal? Does he have a repressed motivation which is given away in the lexis and texture of his utterances? Do you see evidence of the death-wish? Or of the libido? Note Othello's claim to be low in libido when asking the Senate to agree to Desdemona's request that she should accompany him to Cyprus:

> Let her haue your voice.
> Vouch with me Heaven, I therefore beg it not
> To please the pallate of my Appetite:
> Nor to comply with heat the young affects
> In my defunct, and proper satisfaction.

The difficulty of this passage (Furness' Variorum edition has four pages of notes) has led some readers to see evidence of parapraxis. Does the fact that psychoanalytical theory belongs to a later period than *Othello* make such readings anachronistic?

Or, more briefly, we could tell them about the Oedipus complex and ask them if Hamlet lusts after his mother.

Resources

Preparation of these approaches is demanding and time-consuming for the teacher, but there are plenty of published materials that can help us with the work. Scholarly editions come now with some account of the history of critical (and theatrical) interpretations. As already mentioned, the Cambridge Schools Shakespeare editions of the plays have short sections at the back which highlight some of the critical issues without getting bogged down in particularities of who exactly said what, when and where. The format and focus varies from play to play. Some (not all) offer a brief selection of paragraphs from particular critics. The 'Cambridge Student Guides' each include a section on the play outlining something of the critical history and what is made of the play from various critical stances (including something they call 'Traditional Criticism' – or reading, as it used to be called). The English Centre provides resources on some of the plays. All of these are useful starting places for the teacher. There are books on the performance history of individual plays, as for instance the old Macmillan *Text and Performance* series and Manchester University Press's *Shakespeare in Performance* series. Julie Hankey has edited a superb resource, an edition of *Richard III*[17] which as well as a fine introduction give detailed notes on particular performances on the page opposite the text. (She's done the same for *Othello* but I haven't yet been able to see that.) We should be reading around – even if it means only the occasional browsing in the six volumes of Brain Vickers' *Shakespeare: The Critical Heritage*,[18] or reading reviews in the *TLS* and elsewhere, which will enable us to say occasionally to our students: 'So-and-so has just published a book claiming that such-and-such – can we see any cogency in this?'. Occasionally a book (such as A. D. Nuttall's *Shakespeare the Thinker*)[19] will come to our notice that seems likely to deserve our full attention. Over the years, we should be building up our own knowledge, looking for materials we can use. There's no reason that a member of the department might not have as a professional target for a year the developing of materials on the plays to be taught in the following year (and – let's be wildly idealistic – being given some time in which to do it). There must be ways of establishing reading as part of our professional duties.

Above all we should be renewing our experience of the plays. As long as we don't reduce our teaching to formulae, one of the delights of teaching Shakespeare is that the process can continually enlarge, extend, deepen, challenge and correct our own experience of Shakespeare, so that we are teaching from our own involvement rather than simply passing on chunks of processed information. The plays must continue to have an impact on us if we are to enable them to have an impact on our students; we must be thinking about the plays if we are to encourage and enable our students to read them with consideration.

Chapter 15

Talk

With the development of A Level English Language and Literature syllabuses, students were asked to use the concepts and terminology of conversational analysis[1] in relation to plays, Shakespeare's included, in order to show how the characteristics of speech are used by the dramatist to produce 'particular dramatic effects.' In this chapter I want to explore some of the issues, critical and pedagogical, that are raised by this approach to the reading of Shakespeare play.

Non-fluency features

Approaching the question in general terms, it seems likely that if one comes to the study of a Shakespeare play fresh from an examination of some of the typical features of speech – in particular those that distinguish it from writing, such as lower lexical density, frequent coordination of clauses, utterances that are less than complete according to a 'written' grammar and 'non-fluency features' ('ums' and 'ers', false starts, self-interruptions, changes of direction in mid-sentence, etc.) – then asking what features of real-life speech occur in the play may lead very quickly to the judgement that the dialogue in Shakespeare's plays is *nothing* like real-life conversation. General support for such a view may be found in linguistically inclined critics: Lance St John Butler, for instance, writes that 'literary texts bear little, if any, resemblance to natural speech as recorded and transcribed. One can find almost nothing in any literary text that remotely resembles a real conversation.'[2] And Ronald Carter and Walter Nash: 'a literary conversation is unnatural, an artifice; and the essence of its artificiality is the subordination of conversational features, having an immediate pragmatic import, to the larger aesthetic design, the planned plural significance, of a text.'[3] If this is so, it would appear that the main emphasis in analyzing Shakespeare's speech should be on this difference and artificiality – and that if typical characteristics of everyday speech are absent it will be hard to discuss the dramatic uses to which they are put.

In order to develop this view we might start by noting the presence of the blank verse convention. People don't talk in sustained passages of iambic pentameter and they didn't in Shakespeare's day. Although it can be granted that the rhythms of a flexible iambic pentameter such as those found in the mature Shakespeare can come close to the rhythms of English speech and can feel very natural (it has even been asserted that the steady five-beat lines mime the human heartbeat, and examples are frequently given of 'real-life' pentameters), it still remains the case that Shakespeare's language has a recurrent element of artifice that should not be underestimated, especially when to metre are added the arts of language – such as pervasive metaphor, and the complex syntactical and rhetorical patterning discussed on pages 39–45.

We might further note the non-naturalistic conventions of soliloquy and aside and the fully formed sentences of much of the plays' prose. The following example from Iago, which, while not typical, is characteristic, lacks altogether the false starts and grammatical incompleteness typical of (some) utterances transcribed from real life:

> if we will plant nettles or sow lettuce, set hyssop and weed up thyme, supply it with one gender of herbs or distract it with many, either to have it sterile with idleness or manured with industry, why, the power and corrigible authority of this lies in our wills. If the balance of our lives had not one scale of reason to poise another of sensuality, the blood and baseness of our natures would conduct us to most preposterous conclusions. But we have reason to cool our raging motions, our carnal stings, our unbitted lusts, whereof I take this, that you call love, to be a sect or scion.

The periodic nature of the first sentence, the sequence of phrases in apposition, the careful balancing of phrases throughout, the development of the 'garden' analogy, the neat 'return' of the final subordinate clause to the speech's starting point are far removed from what we have come to think typical of sustained spontaneous spoken language. It's a wonderful text for performance, though; its fluency is exhilarating (this is part of its danger) and its energy and clarity may easily on stage give the illusion of being speech-like. The fluency gives added pleasure to our knowledge that Iago is improvising, as – in quite different but equally uninterrupted style – he is in his misogynistic quayside couplets in Act 2 Scene 1.

Even given drunkenness, a subject for which a modern writer would almost certainly deploy the 'realistic' resources of phonetic spelling, frequent self-correction, etc., in *Othello* Shakespeare does no such thing. When Cassio is drunk, there is no evidence in the writing of slurring, etc., and the expression of the thought is perfectly clear. Instead, Shakespeare offers greater, funnier and more thought-provoking evidence of drunkenness in the *content* of Cassio's speeches, adding unexpectedly to the characterization that has already taken place:

> Cassio   Well, God's above all; and there be souls must be saved, and there be souls must not be saved ... For mine own part, no offence to the general, nor any man of quality – I hope to be saved.
>
> Iago   And so do I too, lieutenant.
>
> Cassio   Ay, but by your leave, not before me. The lieutenant is to be saved before the ancient.

What is it about Cassio that leads him, under the influence of drink and so quickly, to such class-inflected eschatological considerations? If we play up the manner of delivery rather than the matter, we may lose something of subtlety and significance. There are matters of choice here for the teacher as well as for the actor and director. (Of course in other plays at times Shakespeare *does* use phonetic means to convey characteristics of an individual's speech, most notably in the dialect of Captain Jamy and Fluellen in *Henry V* and Edgar's remarkable burst of yokelese in *King Lear*. In these cases the dramatic purpose is different.)

It is possible that the non-fluency features, while of real existence and some importance, may be given too much attention in this context; surely non-fluency features are of interest to the dramatist only insofar as they are carriers of significance? Marginal hesitations and slips of the tongue may carry a wealth of meaning, but a range of tiny false starts and extra-linguistic sounds may be of no importance, as is indicated by the fact that we don't attend to them and in effect either delete or even fail to hear them, considering them if anything simply as 'noise'. (It can come as quite a surprise to examine closely a recording of a conversation that sounded perfectly 'clean'.) Further, we may underestimate the extent to which some real-life speech, especially in formal circumstances, has many of the qualities of prose (that is, of writing). For instance, most students will have heard a lot of connected discourse from their teachers that is not – or at least not obviously – marked by the non-fluency features that we may tend to make much of in introducing this topic. Listening to Radio 4's *Today* programme – a fruitful source of examples for analysis and discussion – gives at least the impression that some speakers are very fluent even in response, whereas others (or the same speakers on other occasions, for instance when flummoxed or on the defensive) are less so. Conversation analysis, quite rightly in its own terms, focuses on the features that I listed earlier, as they had previously been neglected in the study of language, but their intrinsic interest – and their easiness to teach – can lead us to assign to them too great an importance, and too easily to assume that their absence is a significant measure of lack of realism (rather than of naturalism).

When Elizabethan and Jacobean writing, in both prose and verse, has been celebrated for its closeness to speech – a commonplace of twentieth-century criticism – that closeness has surely been found in the frequent use of active verbs, concrete nouns, directness, forceful and idiomatic phrasing, the absence of abstract terms and weak generalization, the *tones* of speech, giving often the sense of being in direct contact with the very genesis and evolution of a thought as it occurs to the speaker – all of which are quite compatible with more formal and rhetorical elements. Also the writing is such that in performance it necessitates the use of tongue, teeth, etc. – it cries out for, is often best realized in, performance. And this bodily quality can actually be lacking in some real-life speech, which can be bloodless and inexpressive, coldly efficient, as well as inarticulate and lacking fluency.

However, all that being said, there actually *are* some instances of non-fluency in Shakespeare's dialogue; although they are not to be exaggerated, when they occur they are significant, for instance, self-interruptions, such as Desdemona's self-correction during her singing of the 'willow' song ('Nay, that's not next' – we might compare Portia's 'One half of me is yours, the other half yours,/Mine own I would say' in the *Merchant* and Leontes' self-betraying 'O, I am out' in *The Winter's Tale*). A minor celebrity among examples of this (surely comparatively rare) feature of Shakespeare's speakers is this exchange between Brabantio and Iago in the first scene of *Othello*, quoted here from the Longman Literature School Shakespeare edition:[4]

Brabantio:	Thou art a villain.
Iago:	You are – a senator.

The commentary has at this point: 'It is likely that Iago is about to call Brabantio something more insulting; he achieves the same effect by pausing and then referring to his title.'[5] This seems a moment of naturalist representation of speech. But as has been pointed out, this celebrated moment is an editorial invention, even though it often appears as part of the text. (It does not do so in the Cambridge edition.) H. H. Furness' note on the line reads: 'It was Upton who suggested the dash after these words, which is found in all editions since Capel's time, except Knight's.'[6] While a variant of this kind may quite properly be produced by an actor in performance, it is a potential in the text, not a feature of it; it is among the possibilities. (More to the point for students might be to note the use of 'you' and 'thou' in this exchange – Brabantio's 'thou' is the contemptuous talking down appropriate to a villain, Iago's 'you' the casually insulting assumption of social equality. As often in the play, terms of address are significant.) Even if we accept the punctuation, it might be that Iago's hesitation is less a non-fluency feature than a deliberate ploy to get Brabantio going: it is apparent throughout the play that Iago is very much in control of his language, able to manipulate it through a series of styles and registers and to exploit some of the features of conversation to his own advantage in a way that is quite beyond the other characters. This ties in interestingly with A. D. Nuttall's thought-provoking observation that Iago's is an 'over-evolved' nature: 'Iago's is a literature as yet unwritten, the literature of existentialism, according to which any assumption of the motive by the ego is an act of unconditional, artificial choice.'[7] The relationship that Iago has with his motives and his self is like the relationship he has with his language.

Actors may find places of hesitation that are in no way suggested by the text. David Garrick gives an account of his pausing as indicated in Hamlet's 'I think it was to see – my mother's wedding'. He did not make a 'real stop (that is close the sense) but I certainly suspended my voice, by which your ear must know the sense is suspended too; for Hamlet's grief causes the break, and with a sigh, he finishes the sentence – "my mother's wedding"'.[8] This strikes me as quite arbitrary (why not break after 'mother's'?) and contrary to the run of the verse, although it makes good psychological sense.

Even without Garrick's inventions, I have the impression that interruption and self-interruption are more frequent in *Hamlet* than in *Othello*. A particularly splendid example of self-interruption occurs in Act 2 Scene 1 of *Hamlet* when Polonius completely loses his way in his discourse to Reynaldo.

> Polonius   And then, sir, does he this. He does: what was I about to say?
> I was about to say something where did I leave?
> Reynaldo   At 'closes in the consequence',
> At 'friend or so', and 'gentleman.'
> Polonius   At closes in the consequence, ay, marry;
> He closes with you thus: 'I know the gentleman ...'

It's easy to note this as (for Shakespeare) a fairly extreme piece of naturalism, but we need further to consider whether it has any dramatic significance beyond this. Is it merely a bit of humorous characterization, giving a typical instance of Polonius' bumbling? Is it significant that Polonius' fluency and memory should desert him at just *this* point in his discourse? Is this a local effect, or does it serve 'the larger aesthetic design'?

A speech in which the immediate dramatic purpose of naturalistic self-interruption is more evident is Hamlet's first soliloquy, in which the continuous interruption is evidence of (creates the illusion of) emotional pressure and a drive towards incoherence that is only just held off. After a sequence of exclamations ending in the question 'Must I remember?' Hamlet manages each time to complete his main clause in spite of the invading emotions given in the interceptions. There is complete control in that the grammar is never disrupted; the parentheses are kept in order, main clauses are completed, there is, eventually, no breakdown. (How untidy this speech will appear depends in part on how it is punctuated. It's arguable that much use of dashes will imply a greater drive to incoherence, commas and – more so – brackets a neater containment. See the appendix to this chapter.)

This kind of self-interruption may be distinguished from that found in Hamlet's soliloquy at the end of Act 2 Scene 2, in which Hamlet's discourse does seem to break down altogether, if only temporarily. The speech can be seen to lead up to this breakdown. The sequence of rhetorical questions is cut across by the interjection 'Ha!', and then after a sequence culminating in exclamations the verse again comes to a shuddering halt on an incomplete line:

> Remorseless, treacherous, lecherous, kindless villain!
>
> O, vengeance!

Then Hamlet's quieter reflection leads into a climax of self-insulting, followed by things that aren't words at all:

> Must, like a whore, unpack my very heart with words,
>
> And fall a-curing, like a very drab,
>
> A scullion!
>
> Fie upon't! foh! About, my brain! Hum, I have heard

Is this to be interpreted as a blank verse line at all? Students might profitably discuss – and try out – what an actor might make of this moment in the text.

These examples of inarticulate interjections may just be taken as instances of extreme naturalism for immediate dramatic effect, but in some cases reflection may take us further. Such moments of inarticulacy, of the inability to continue with sense, seem to be of particular significance in *Othello*. The most familiar example is Othello's collapse in Act 4 Scene 1:

> Lie with her? Lie on her? We say lie on her when they belie her. Lie with her!
>
> Zounds, that's fulsome! Handkerchief – confessions – handkerchief! To confess and be hanged for his labour. First to be hanged and then to confess. I tremble at it. Nature would not invest herself in such shadowing passion without some instruction. It is not words that shakes me thus. Pish! Noses, ears, and lips. Is't possible? – Confess? Handkerchief? O devil!

It is commonplace to note the breakdown of Othello's language here, his lurching into prose, his loss of syntactical control, the descent into interjections, the distance he has travelled (and how quickly) from his characteristically rolling cadences. However, we shouldn't fail to note the two perfectly formed sentences, the first of some magnificence. What we are seeing here is not so much verisimilitude as art, although clearly related to the common real-life experience of being stuck for words. We probably can't say quite the same about Hamlet's last words as recorded in the Folio: 'The rest is silence. O, o, o, o', which is why perhaps the second part is sometimes edited out of the modern text altogether.[9]

There are other moments in which language fails, or the speaker deserts the resources of language, even being reduced to (or taking refuge in) non-lexical sounds, interjections. Such moments of inarticulacy – of utterances on the borders of language – are quite frequent in the play, and deserving of attention. Consider this, for instance:

> Desdemona   If you say so, I hope you will not kill me.
> Othello   Hum!

('Hum' is from the Quarto, which gives no exclamation mark; the Folio has 'Humh'. Malone suggested 'Humph!', which strikes me as comical. Do different renderings of the interjection give different degrees of inarticulacy? Do some versions make something approaching a *semantic* difference?) What is an actor to make of a moment like that? Or this?:

> Emilia   She was too fond of her most filthy bargain.
> Othello   Ha!   (Folio: Hah?)

Some students read this as an angry reaction to 'her most filthy bargain' ('How dare you call me that?'), some as horror at the suggestion that 'she was too fond' (not really registering the insult) – although the alliterative linking of 'fond' and 'filthy' suggests to me a more complex reaction.

It is not only Othello who is reduced to inarticulacy. Consider Emilia with Bianca in Act 5 Scene 1:

> Emilia   Oh, fie upon thee, strumpet!
> Bianca   I am no strumpet, but of life as honest
>   As you that thus abuse me.
> Emilia   As I? Foh! Fie upon thee!   (Quarto: 'Fough, fie'.)

Students quickly note the contrast between Emilia's intemperate exclamations and Bianca's dignified, well-turned response. (Also once again the 'thee'/'you' distinction is in significant play.) The sub-text here may involve Emilia's recollection of her speeches to Desdemona in the previous scene outlining circumstances in which she would be prepared to commit adultery;

her inarticulate exclamation may not be so much disgust at Bianca as shocked self-discovery. And such an idea may well enter into an actress's performance of the lines.

In each case (we are not looking for a general formula to cover all cases) we can ask of these interjectors: what kind of limit they have come to? Is this a momentary failure, through, for instance, pressure of emotion, or something more essential? Or has the character arrived at a point at which nothing *can* be said? How do we interpret – how do we perform – such moments?

Patterns of exchange

In considering interruptions and interjections we have moved beyond the individual speech (and its natural fluency or lack of it) to the larger conversational unit of exchange. Exchange – initiation and response – is the fundamental unit in both conversation and drama, so it is here perhaps that an approach based on features of real-life talk will prove most illuminating. A question to be kept in mind, though, is how much technical terminology and analysis will prove helpful, will enhance our grasp of the drama. Does this framework help us get a better grasp on what is going on in a given Shakespeare scene? What illuminates what?

Unlike some of Shakespeare's plays (such as *The Shrew* – leaving the Induction on one side – with its opening exposition by Lucentio, and *Twelfth Night* and *Measure for Measure* with their Ducal monologues), *Othello* begins with exchanges – begins, indeed, in mid-exchange; the audience has to struggle to keep up before the pace steadies with Iago's expository but still passion-fuelled narrative. And in light of the foregoing it's also worth noting the presence from the very beginning of interjections/expletives (although they do not appear in the Folio) and the way in which they disrupt the iambic flow with their strong initial stresses:

Roderigo	Tush, never tell me, I take it most unkindly
	That thou, Iago, who hast had my purse
	As if the strings were thine shouldst know of this.
Iago	'Sblood, but you will not hear me

We might note also the identifying use of one character's name, the deictic 'this' and the first appearance of the 'you/thou' distinction, not that this complex opening exchange is, for clarity, the best place to begin an exposition of what are called 'interactive features' – although Shakespeare thought it the best way to start his play.

In considering the nature of exchanges, the notion of the adjacency pair – such as greeting and acknowledgement, question and answer, statement and comment – gives a useful start as a unit of analysis. The opening scenes of *A Midsummer Night's Dream* afford a range of material for considering conversational exchanges in relation to discourse analysis. In the first scene the dialogue is clear, orderly and largely arranged in adjacency pairs, even when more than two characters are present on stage. For the most part each contribution is a sustained speech. There are clear appellations and nominations – the directedness of the speech is always explicit. The purposes of exposition are smoothly effected as the dialogue quickly establishes situation and characters:

Egeus	Happy be Theseus, our renowned Duke!
Theseus	Thanks good Egeus. What's the news with thee?
Egeus	Full of vexation, come I, with complaint
	Against my child, my daughter Hermia.
	Stand forth Demetrius! – My noble lord,
	This man hath my consent to marry her.
	Stand forth Lysander! – And, my gracious Duke,
	This man hath bewitched the bosom of my child.

There is an editorial question here. The text I've used for this quotation (from the Cambridge edition) agrees with most modern editions in making 'Stand forth, Demetrius!' and 'Stand forth, Lysander!' part of the dialogue. However, in the Folio they are given as stage directions. In either case the clarity of exposition is apparent.

After Theseus has given his judgment the pace alters from these sustained speeches to the shorter exchanges between Hermia and Lysander, characterized by passages of stichomythia. There has been one brief but telling instance, in which the second line artfully reworks the first as a riposte or correction, in the earlier dialogue:

Hermia	I would my father look'd but with my eyes.
Theseus	Rather your eyes must with his judgment look.

This can be dramatic without being naturalistic – the drama residing in the tension of opposites and the rapidity of the thought mimed by the lines. This contrasts with the Lysander-Hermia exchange, in which the artfulness and artificiality to which the device is liable is all too evident, with its grammatical parallelism and its pairing of opposites. This is less dramatic than the previous instance, as the movement of the thought is slower. Instead there is mutual development of an idea, a developing duet on a theme set up by Lysander:

Lysander	Ay me: for aught that I could ever read,
	Could ever hear by tale or history,

> The course of true love never did run smooth,
> But either it was different in blood:
>
> Hermia   O cross! Too high to be enthrall'd to low.
> Lysander   Or else misgraffed, in respect of years:
> Hermia   O spite! Too old to be engag'd to young.
> Lysander   Or else it stood upon the choice of friends.
> Hermia   O hell! To choose love by another's eyes.

The mutuality is further highlighted by the continuous punctuation, Lysander's colons indicating a rising intonation that invites Hermia's continuation. (See the Appendix on punctuation, however.) The effect is less of rapidity than ease of movement, of cooperation rather than antagonism.

Stichomythia occurs again in the later dialogue with Helena, which works towards a more oppositional feel:

> Hermia   I give him curses, yet he gives me love.
> Helena   O that my prayers could such affections move.
> Hermia   The more I hate, the more he follows me.
> Helena   The more I love, the more he hateth me.
> Hermia   His folly Helena is no fault of mine.
> Helena   None but your beauty, would that fault were mine.

Here the artificiality is further emphasized by the rhyming couplets, which reinforce the 'insulation' of each adjacency pair. Couplets also appear in more complex dialogue, for instance the marvellous exchanges in *Twelfth Night* Act 5 Scene 1 lines 119–34, in which the natural movement of passion is beautifully articulated through the formality of the shaping and restraining couplets.

Such effects are obviously amenable to analysis (because more obviously 'effects') and imitation. Stichomythia, although I suspect usually thought of as a fairly primitive device, is not confined to early Shakespeare. It can also be found, for instance, in Hamlet's encounter with his mother:

> Hamlet   Now mother, what's the matter?
> Queen   Hamlet, thou hast my father much offended.
> Hamlet   Mother, you have my father much offended.
> Queen   Come, come, you answer with an idle tongue.
> Hamlet   Go, go, you question with an idle tongue.

Do Hamlet's substitutions and reversals strike us as incisive wit or as annoyingly smart petulance? Here a consideration of the style of the dialogue involves us in questions of interpretation of character.

Elements of stichomythia occur in a more complex passage of exchanges between Othello and the enraged Emilia in the last act of the play, a sequence of devastating force, an analysis of which can show just how much interplay – interdependence – there can be between formal and naturalistic and simple and complex elements in Shakespeare's dialogue:

Emilia	Why, how should she be murdered?
Othello	Alas, who knows?
	You heard her say herself it was not I.
Emilia	She said so; I must needs report the truth.
Othello	She's like a liar gone to burning hell:
	'Twas I that killed her.
Emilia	O, the more angel she,
	And you the blacker devil!
Othello	She turned to folly, and she was a whore.
Emilia	Thou dost belie her, and thou art a devil.
Othello	She was false as water.
Emilia	Thou art rash as fire to say
	That she was false. O, she was heavenly true!

We could begin by noting the parallel syntax, Emilia's echoing and completing of Othello's lines. We can observe here another feature of real-life exchanges observed by linguists, that of 'latching', distinct from interruption but on occasions bordering on it, which occurs when a responding speaker does not allow the usual pause at the end of the previous utterance. This may be seen in Shakespeare's text where characters share half-lines, or even shorter divisions of the line. This ensures pace – neither character is taking time to think here. The imagery of patterned opposites (heaven–hell, angel–devils, water–fire, false–true), the first pair bracketing all the others, so that Emilia's last line here gives formal closure to the pattern, clearly belong to 'the larger aesthetic design, the planned plural significance' of *Othello*, a field of imagery that pervades the play. We might also note the skill of Shakespeare's variation, avoiding monotony. Also worth noting is the linguistic parity of the speakers – in spite of the contrast in gender, status, stature (Othello does not fall back on physical threat until later in the exchange) – and Emilia's *moral* superiority. Yet for all this closely worked art, the exchange has the forward momentum and naturalness of a *row*, and there is psychological depth in Othello's move from flat denial to boasting responsibility in a way that goes beyond emblematic patterning. Othello does not resume the pattern (although the 'hell' note sounds again) but moves on to self-justification:

Cassio did top her: ask thy husband else.
O, I were damned beneath all depth in hell

But that I did proceed upon just grounds
To this extremity. Thy husband knew it all.

A complex sentence between two simple sentences, the first of an appalling directness that he has learned from Iago. Does the complex sentence betray in its awkwardness of construction an uneasiness in Othello? From here Emilia is reduced to 'iteration', and Othello's role develops in power, the reciprocal balance of the earlier exchanges quite gone:

Emilia	My husband?
Othello	Thy husband.
Emilia	That she was false to wedlock?
Othello	Ay, with Cassio. Nay, had she been true,
	If heaven would make me such another world
	Of one entire and perfect chrysolite,
	I'd not have sold her for it.
Emilia	My husband?

With 'entire and perfect chrysolyte' (at the other extreme from 'Ha!') we are back with Othello's characteristic grandeur of speech. But who is he talking to, saying this? Emilia? The lines savour more of soliloquy. And anyway, Emilia is still responding to what Othello said several lines previously. That Othello might be diverted into contemplation at this point may be convincing psychologically, but there is nothing particularly naturalistic in the rendering.

And so it goes on, to culminate in:

He, woman;
I say thy husband. Dost understand the word?
My friend, thy husband, honest, honest, Iago.

The repetition issues, with telling double irony, from Othello's exasperation at what appears to be Emilia's stupidity, but is also the culminating moment of the structural dramatic irony of Iago's 'honesty' ('the larger aesthetic design' – although it should be clear by now that in some works 'aesthetic' is too narrow, too limiting a word. And if we talk about 'planned plural significance' we don't necessarily mean that Shakespeare sat down and worked it all out like a problem in (moral) geometry – but the patterns are observably there).

As well as the adjacency pair, there are further terms of discourse analysis that students might be expected to be familiar with and able to apply.

Dramatic dialogue may be considered in relation to the notion of 'the floor', the 'rules' of turn-taking and the so-called 'maxims of conversation'. The factors involved in turn-taking, other than adjacency pairs, which have already been discussed, are: [10]

- *Current speaker's rights*
  Whoever is speaking has the floor by right of possession.
- *General 'script' or framework*
  Many speech situations have an in-built structure or procedure, in which roles, register and even particular sentence shapes are defined in advance, certain conventions of power relations, lexical fields, registers, forms of address, sequences, and so on, that can be expected to apply. Consider, for instance, a visit to a shop or to the doctor; military or political situations; the courtroom; even the love scene. The situations work because of the assumptions. Departures from these conventions will disrupt the whole situation. (Hence the judge's power to clear his courtroom of those who depart from the script.) One way of focusing on speech in *Othello* might be to ask when characters are most securely in and when most distant from their 'scripts'. What about Desdemona's failure to capture the import of the relevant military language and the disciplinary assumptions that it involves? Or Othello's attempt to balance the language of command and the language of love within the same situation? We might argue that Iago takes Othello into linguistic situations he has not been in before.
- *Eye contact and body language*
  These can help maintain the current speaker's position, signal the willingness to speak next, or authorize the next speaker.
- *Grammatical and syntactic structure*
  A change of speaker usually occurs at the end of a sentence or shorter but complete grammatical unit (or one that can be interpreted, willfully or otherwise, as complete). It is felt to be more acceptable to insert a contribution at a point of potential closure, for example, at the end of a clause, than to cut into a grammatical unit. Students might be given a transcript of sustained speech and asked to identify the Transition Relevance Points (TRPs).
- *Stereotyped tags*
  'That's about it really'; and trailing away ...
- *Intonation, volume and speed*
  In Shakespeare this is to a large extent dictated by the verse; prose leaves far more room for variation and interpretative possibility.[11]
- *Pre-sequences*
  For example, 'When I've finished making this point I'd like to hear what you have to say, Janet.'

- *Status, age, power, gender, personality*
  Questions about who initiates and who responds, and how – and where the balance shifts within a series of exchanges – may help illuminate the dynamic of a given scene.

In addition to these terms, conversation analysis also makes use of the 'conversational maxims' associated with H. Paul Grice and Robin Lakoff. These maxims formulate certain regularities and assumptions that appear to be at work in 'succesful' conversation. The 'co-operative principles' outlined by Grice state that contributions to conversation should be orderly, relevant, truthful, of ordinate length, lacking obscurity or ambiguity. Lakoff's 'politeness principle', stated as 'rules', goes: don't impose, give options, make the person you are speaking to feel good.

When we are considering a drama script (especially one like Shakespeare's in which stage directions are few and most of which are editorial anyway) some of the elements outlined above can be a matter of direct observation (adjacency pairs and TRPs can be readily identified in the text); others will be a matter of inference; and some may be entirely matters for actors' and directors' choices. For instance, how far 'intonation, volume and speed' can be determined by the writer (beyond the effects of 'latching' already mentioned and those of suspended half-lines to be mentioned shortly) needs careful consideration. Physical factors such as body language and eye contact are very much the business of the actor and director, and the extent to which they are implied or necessitated by the script is also a matter for debate. (How could Desdemona and Othello *not* be making eye contact during their reunion in Cyprus? Any eye contact made between them in the final acts of the play will be very different.)

When considering Shakespeare's handling of these matters, students can also be invited to look at examples in which expected closures are postponed, refused or frustrated, and the dramatic effect of these disruptions. Students might also consider whether violation of the maxims is *inherently* dramatic? (Setting-up tensions, new expectations, etc.)

A useful text for study in this respect is the beginning of Act 1 Scene 2 of *A Midsummer Night's Dream*, which also makes a contrast with the preceding scene (not only in the transition from verse to prose). Bottom and Quince's running battle for the floor, their challenge for pre-eminence, comes out very clearly in an analysis using this framework – but it needs to be asked whether they can't become equally clear without it (especially in a good performance). Bottom's persistent (would a linguist say systematic?) flouting of the rules of turn-taking and the maxims of ... well, all of them probably, together with Quince's repeated attempts at re-insertion, are a plentiful source of comedy. Does discourse analysis help us to get a firmer (i.e. more explicit) grasp of the nature of that comedy here?

As the convener of the meeting and the titular head, Quince quite properly opens the proceedings with 'Is all our company here?' The expected response, closing the adjacency pair opened by Quince's question ('Yes, Peter Quince', 'Flute's not here yet,' or whatever), is not forthcoming, as Bottom immediately interrupts – in the name of propriety and good order(!):

> You were best to call them generally, man by man, according to the scrip.

Quince responds with a fuller beginning, expanding his contribution (with some threat to the maxim of quantity) perhaps in an attempt to establish his authority:

> Here is the scroll of every man's name, which is thought fit, through all Athens, to play in our interlude before the duke and the duchess, on his wedding-day at night.

This, however, is still not good enough for Bottom, who becomes more explicit about procedure, coaxing Quince along the lines he deems to be correct:

Bottom	First, good Peter Quince, say what the play treats on, then read the names of the actors, and so grow to a point.
Quince	Marry, our play is, the most lamentable comedy, and most cruel death of Pyramus and Thisby.
Bottom	A very good piece of work, I assure you, and a merry. Now, good Peter Quince, call forth your actors by the scroll. Masters, spread yourselves.
Quince	Answer as I call you. Nick Bottom, the weaver.
Bottom	Ready. Name what part I am for, and proceed.
Quince	You, Nick Bottom, are set down for Pyramus.
Bottom	What is Pyramus? a lover, or a tyrant?
Quince	A lover, that kills himself most gallant for love.

Quince's line, which closes the adjacency pair quite satisfactorily, is followed by Bottom's splendid violation of the maxim of quantity. Students working with the passage could look for the moments at which Quince might try to regain control, the TRPs, all moments of potential comedy:

> That will ask some tears in the true performing of it: [TRP] if I do it, let the audience look to their eyes [TRP]; I will move storms [TRP], I will condole in some measure. [TRP] To the rest: [TRP – *rising intonation, indicative that Quince should pick up the cue and continue; instead of which Bottom splendidly interrupts himself*] yet my chief humour is for a tyrant: [TRP] I could play Ercles rarely, or a part to tear a cat in, to make all split. [TRP]

> The raging rocks
> And shivering shocks
> Shall break the locks
> Of prison gates;
> And Phibbus' car
> Shall shine from far
> And make and mar
> The foolish Fates.
>
> This was lofty! (TRP) Now name the rest of the players. (TRP) This is Ercles' vein, a tyrant's vein; (TRP) a lover is more condoling. (TRP)

At last, Quince regains the floor, only to find Flute breaking the pattern before Bottom seizes the floor again.

Consider two further examples, one from *Hamlet* and one from *Much Ado*. Claudius, in his tightrope-walking manoeuvres to keep Laertes on side, infuriates him by his apparent digression about Hamlet and the Norman who allegedly excelled him in swordsmanship, so that Laertes breaks in with obvious rudeness/irritation:

Claudius	... this report of his
	Did Hamlet so envenom with his envy
	That he could nothing do but wish and beg,
	Your sudden coming o'er to play with him;
	Now, out of this.
Laertes	What out of this, my lord?

In terms of discourse analysis this is clearly an abrupt interruption, as there is no real TRP after 'this', even though the Folio gives a full stop after 'out of this'. (There's one after 'to play with him', however.) The interruption actually occurs after Claudius has already begun to answer the question that Laertes inserts.

More amenable to a sustained analysis is Beatrice's interruption in the first scene of *Much Ado*, which is her first line in the whole play. That it's an interruption can easily be missed, as the previous utterance is not only grammatically complete, but in its formal antithesis can be seen as an elegant closure to the sub-sequence opened by Leonato's reference to Claudio's uncle:

Leonato	He hath an uncle here in Messina will be very much glad of it.
Messenger	I have already delivered him letters, and there appears much joy in him; even so much that joy could not show itself modest enough without a badge of bitterness.

Leonato	Did he break out into tears?
Messenger	In great measure.
Leonato	A kind overflow of kindness: there are no faces truer than those that are so washed. How much better is it to weep at joy than to joy at weeping!

If anyone is licensed to speak next, it is clearly the Messenger. He and Leonato are not just exchanging information, but engaging in a mutual show of rhetorical elegance which began with Leonato's sententious 'A victory is twice itself when the achiever brings home full numbers' and continues with the Messenger's balanced alliterative figures 'he hath done in the figure of a lamb the feats of a lion'. Leonato's artful antithesis might prompt either admiration or competition, depending. But instead Beatrice cuts across/breaks in with:

I pray you, is Signior Mountanto returned from the wars, or no?

Even if the onstage positioning makes it fairly easy to manage, this is technically an interruption. Beatrice's abrupt question (with its surprisingly frank bawdry – do the men recognize it?) appears not be received as such – there is no rebuke, and the Messenger simply closes the adjacency pair as best he can:

I know none of that name, lady: there was none such in the army of any sort.

'Of that name, Lady' can easily be given an amused or disapproving intonation. It's worth considering just how rude Beatrice's 'Signior Montanto' is (and to what extent we want pupils to be aware of this). Annotators usually explain 'Montanto' as a fencing term involving an upward thrust; it may also refer to social climbing – actresses sometimes pronounce it 'Mount on to'. A modernizing gloss might be 'Mister Likes-to-get-on-top'.

Leonato appears to ask for further information. Is that because he's genuinely puzzled, or because he knows perfectly well what Beatrice is up to? If the latter, then Hero's explanation must be to the Messenger; which makes sense, as it is he that replies. Hero is also technically interrupting, as Leonato's 'niece' nominates Beatrice to reply:

| Leonato | What is he that you ask for, niece? |
| Hero | My cousin means Signior Benedick of Padua. |

This is Hero's first line in the play, her only line in this scene, and might be regarded as to some degree transgressive, especially if Hero plainly understands her cousin's joke. The Messenger closes the sequence by answering Beatrice's initial question:

O, he's returned; and as pleasant as ever he was.

There are further intonation possibilities here for the actor: 'O, he's *returned*' (reassuring, sensing Beatrice's anxiety); 'O, *he's* returned' (sensing Beatrice's sarcasm and anticipating a bit of fun).

We should also note that, more than grammatical and semantic elements, questions of status, age, gender, power and personality may be determinative of what counts on a given occasion as an interruption and therefore as aggression or rudeness.

An analysis of this kind might seem too finicky for the classroom, especially with younger pupils. However, some of the same issues can be approached by working in the terms discussed in Chapter 12; we can look at potential stagings of the sequence, the directing and acting of specific lines, with considerable success. Once the visual element is brought in, a number of possibilities becomes clear. Work of this kind, that can go very successfully in Key Stage 3, needs none of the specific terms of conversation analysis (although awareness of them can help the teacher to devise the sequence). And, especially at A Level, we need to ask: can such analysis add anything to *critical* reading?

That at times it can do so can be made apparent through an analysis of a passage from *Othello*. In Act 1 Scene 3, the play's first formal situation, power rests with the Duke, invested in his formal position (he is given no proper name), and the senators. However, their power may be compared with the power of Brabantio's animus, of Othello's confidence in 'my parts, my title and my perfect soul', of Desdemona's confidence in her love – all variously apparent in the qualities of their language. Similarly, *formally* Brabantio as senator and father has power in relation to Desdemona and Othello, but the language and interplay between the characters severely qualifies its status.

In this scene we can see a number of the 'turn-taking' factors in play. The Duke's clear authorization of Othello to speak, spoken perhaps (in the absence of a term of address) as a challenge rather than an invitation (although there may also be a note of *dismay*) – 'What in your own part can you say to this?' – is followed not by the anticipated closing of the adjacency pair by Othello but by Brabantio's interruption. It looks like an adjacency pair on paper, but isn't so.

| Duke | What in your own part can you say to this? |
| Brabantio | Nothing, but this is so. |

As the interruption is not a complete blank verse line, a pause is implied before the start of 'Most potent, grave, and reverend signiors'; similarly, a few lines later the implied long pause after the First Senator's 'But, Othello, speak' (again, a straightforward authorization, granting the floor through nomination) implies that Othello is in no hurry to comply – feels, that is, no urgency. This in itself is an index of his power. (Compare the speed with which he responds to Iago's hints and suggestions in Act 3 Scene 3.) At the end of Othello's speech (on a half line) Brabantio again takes up the discourse, taking his cue from the grammatical and syntactical structure which makes it possible, intonation and volume apart (there seems to be small sign of trailing away), to read Othello's words as a closure:

> Othello   ... what drugs, what charms,
> What conjurations and what mighty magic –
> For such proceedings am I charged withal –
> I won his daughter.
> Brabantio   A maiden never bold.

When the First Senator instructs Othello to speak there is a half-line pause (although the Folio has a comma) where Othello might have responded instantly; instead the Senator elaborates his request in two further questions, clarifying what he wants to know:

> But, Othello, speak:
> Did you, by indirect and forcèd courses
> Subdue and poison this young maid's affections?
> Or came it by request and such fair question
> As soul to soul affordeth?

Now Othello does reply, but not to answer directly; instead he requests that Desdemona herself be sent for, and only after some lines of business later and further prompting from the Duke ('Say it, Othello') does he actually begin his narrative. Detailed critical accounts of Othello's power – and questions about his self-image – in this scene usually concentrate on his sustained speeches; it is at least interesting that such analysis can be supported by a close description of the exchanges of which they are an integral part. Does his delay imply merely a relaxed confidence, or is there an element of stage management, of arrogant, even insolent *display*? Here an approach based on conversational analysis may feed usefully – but not decisively – into a literary critical approach.

    The exchange of couplets between the Duke and Brabantio is also worth a moment's attention. Couplets have an obvious artificiality, and on the page these are very unlike real-life speech. In performance, however, we can feel the pointed animus of Brabantio's riposte to the Duke's (at best well-intentioned but badly judged, at worst sanctimonious) 'sentences'. His lines have something of the force of an improvisation. His final line 'I humbly beseech you, proceed to th'affairs of state' – (which may be read as prose) prepares for the Duke's drop into prose exposition, with less elevated language ('slubber') before Othello lifts the register again in verse with his grander phrasing (while still conducting business). Throughout a sequence like this we can see Shakespeare's art while still feeling the exchanges as in a sense 'natural'.

Pragmatics

Another element of conversation analysis is pragmatics, the study of how utterances in particular contexts are intended and (mis)understood. Pragmatics is a complex field of study, bordering on both psychology and philosophy,[12] and it's a matter of judgement to what depth it should be entered into with any particular class. Here I'm only concerned with its bearing on *Othello*. In a play in which so much depends on what is intended, understood, misapprehended, where the possibility, the suspicion, the certainty of hidden and implied meanings, of lies and innuendo gathers in importance towards the dénouement, so that for some speakers sincere statement becomes all but impossible, sensitivity to pragmatics may be of the utmost importance.

It's easy enough for students to understand that even straightforward sentences can have a range of meanings according to particular contexts – how, for instance, 'Shut the door' can mean anything from 'You are the kind of inconsiderate twerp who habitually lets in drafts' to 'You are in imminent danger of sexual harassment'. To take some isolated examples from *Othello*: in Act 5 Scene 2 Emilia's line 'She said so; I must need report the truth' could be read as 'If she said so, I'll have to report that; I can't deny it' or – making more of a potential contrast between 'she' and 'I' – 'I won't lie for you'. On the page, the ambiguity stands; in performance, nuances of tone and emphasis may settle the matter. At the beginning of the 'whorehouse' scene Desdemona says to Othello 'What is your pleasure?' How easily might Othello hear that as the enticing offer of a prostitute ('that cunning whore of Venice')? (It's curious that Iago should ask Desdemona the same question later in the scene, where such overtones are improbable.) In Act 5 Scene 2 it's possible to hear Desdemona's 'Will you come to bed, my lord?' as an attempt at seduction. An actress might make something of that; is it impossible that the bewildered Desdemona might fall back on the offer of, the desire for, physical intimacy as a sign or enactment that all is now all right between them? We can ask such questions as the specific examples come up in class.

The sustained sequence in *Othello* to which pragmatics most obviously applies is the great and terrible 'temptation' scene in Act 3 Scene 3, by the end of which Othello, whose love and trust of Desdemona had appeared absolute ('My life upon her faith'), is convinced she is adulterous and determines her death. How has this come about? Does the framework offered by pragmatics help us get deeper into this scene?

Such a framework begins with the maxims of Lakoff and Grice (see page 164). These are interesting not as a bland set of rules, but as an aid to understanding what happens when we understand speech that doesn't follow them closely. It seems that we tend to read such departures as meaningful (rather than as irrelevant or rude). I say 'Are you coming to the pub?' and you say 'It's Tuesday', and I understand that I am being rebuked for forgetting how important your weekly badminton is to you. (Your tone of voice will convey the degree of your disappointment or indignation and the depth of my offence.) Sometimes we detect (or suspect) that there is an unstated meaning, and we ask 'What are you getting at?' Detecting hints and suggestions, we make inferences. The developed exploration of these matters involves a terminology that distinguishes and analyses the roles of presupposition, implication, implicature and entailment: the situational elements and logical structures that enable our inferences.

A sustained account of the 'temptation' scene that uses the framework of conversational maxims can be found in Brian Vickers' *Appropriating Shakespeare*.[13] He has no difficulty in showing that Iago violates the maxims – and students, when asked to do this, have no difficulty either. He remarks that 'Grice's fundamental idea, "that the very act of communicating creates expectations which it then exploits" … is one that Iago realized long ago'. And not Iago alone, surely? This is something of which we all have at least a dim awareness, and theoretical understanding of it predates both Iago and Grice, as Vickers later makes clear: 'Classical rhetoric and modern speech-act theory are at one in describing the process by which an unscrupulous speaker can violate the conventions of speech exchange in order to plant suspicion in the speaker's mind.' After he has conducted his analysis Vickers adds: 'While accepting the value of speech-act philosophy in its task of reconstructing the norms of social intercourse, and while drawing on pragmatics for its analysis of the process of interpretation, we see that these models are much simpler than Shakespeare's.' Yes – and this is surely the point. The danger is of taking Shakespeare's dialogue merely as *illustrations* of the linguistic terms, rather than by a close and responsive reading to follow the intricacies and nuances of the dynamics of the interaction.

Vickers' account is one-sided; it makes Iago's success merely a matter of technique and leaves out any thought of what predisposition Othello may have to be invited. Surely some men would have got wind of what Iago was up to and dismissed it, whether angrily or with irony, depending on personality? Also it ignores the range of tones potential in Othello's responses – for instance 'O misery', which, unlike the preceding 'Ha!' is extra-metrical, and so may be taken to allow the actor a wide degree of latitude (we could ask students to suggest a range of paraphrases for the phrase). In Oliver Parker's film, Laurence Fishburne's Othello is only partly attending to Iago and his responses don't suggest the smallest awareness of personal danger, so Iago has to work harder. This involves no forcing of the text. (A productive question for students to consider is at what point Othello is – or begins to be – persuaded. A number of possibilities can be discussed.)

From this discussion it's clear that while a theorized pragmatic framework *can* be useful in getting into the depth of this scene, it is not indispensable, whatever the requirements of a particular exam might be. At worst, it can inhibit or even prevent a fully responsive reading; rather than use the terms to think about the dynamic of the scene, we may merely use the scene as an illustration of the terms.

The most natural way for students to think about these things is in terms of psychology and sub-text, and to a large extent these matters can be grasped and discussed without any specific linguistic terminology. It's perhaps telling that discourse analysts at times fall back on common language when analysing the drama. Vimala Herman, a very technical analyst, generalizes some of the issues in common-language, non-technical terms:

> The expressive power of the not-said, the indirect, the unfinished, the elliptical is integral to the pragmatic understanding of language. The unsaid can function as a weapon and could be used for power, manipulation, deceit as much as tact, consideration and kindliness, or it can signify just plain emptiness.[14]

This strikes me as a useful formulation and one that we might ask students to explore in relation to selected passages of the text.

When Malcolm Coulthard, in a standard introductory text on discourse analysis, analyses the 'temptation' scene, his description, apart from a few references, is conducted in common language: no specialist linguistic terms are used – or needed. He focuses on *questions*, suggesting that 'Iago rouses Othello's suspicion by a sequence of unanswered questions, not simply because the questions are unanswered but because they are avoided clumsily and in fact deliberately so, in order to suggest that Iago is concealing something'.[15]

His approach could be carried wider into the play, looking at the sheer *range* of purposes for which questions are used. In Act 1 alone they are used for rhetorical effect ('And what was he?'), to express disgust ('What a full fortune ...?'), to elicit instant information/clarification ('Is it they?', 'What is the news?' and the ubiquitous 'What's the matter?'), to cause alarm ('Are your doors locked?'), to express confusion and indignation

('Why, wherefore ask you this?'), to indulge personal curiosity ('Ancient, what makes he here?'), to issue a challenge ('Where hast thou stowed my daughter?'), to unsettle ('Whither will you that I go/To answer this you challenge? … What if I do obey? How many …?'), to express surprise: ('How? The Duke in Counsel?/In this time of the night?'). Later in the play we encounter questions that are rhetorical ('what should such a fool/Do with so good a wife?'), those that are not so much rhetorical as arising out of bafflement ('Are there any stones in heaven/But what serves for the thunder?'), questions that simply cannot be answered ('Where should Othello go?') and the question that Othello can't bring himself to ask directly in so many words, and which receives no answer ('Will you, I pray, demand that demi-devil/Why he hath thus ensnared my soul and body?').

For some syllabuses students will *have* to analyse, at least in part, using the terminology of conversation analysis. What we need is the right balance, with the framework enabling rather than preventing a grasp of the particularities of the drama, and complemented with other terms and considerations from the common language. In getting students to analyse the 'temptation' scene to bring out what is involved in it, we might divide it among several groups with a set of working questions along these lines:

1 What might Othello's expectation reasonably be after each of his turns?
2 How does Iago's response differ from what might be expected?
3 In what ways does Iago violate the maxims of conversation?
4 How might (specific selected lines) be spoken?
5 Look at the length of speeches; where do they begin to get longer, and why? (The length of speeches might be considered in relation to the maxim of quantity: don't make your turn longer or shorter than necessary.)
6 What part is played by questions, statements, assertions, requests, and exclamations in this passage?

I have to admit, though, that on the two occasions that I used this approach I was disappointed by the outcome. However, I still think that there's some mileage in the approach, especially if a class just aren't *getting* it. Such analysis would need to be complemented by a study of the orchestration of the whole very long scene, its dramatic pacing and structure.

Above all, though, don't we want our students to *feel* it? I don't just mean emotionally, but also intellectually. When I was gripped by *Othello* in the sixth form, I'd never heard of pragmatics, maxims, implications and entailments; but I did feel intensely the power of the writing, and I'm sure that it was above all in the movement of meanings, the sense of significances suddenly opening up, of things happening too quickly to be controlled, of precipices barely skirted, of boundaries crossed: qualitatively different from the dynamic and logical relations that pragmatics tries, necessarily bloodlessly, to give a general account of. We haven't really read the 'temptation' scene until we come to the end of it thrilled and appalled. We haven't really read *Othello* until we've seen something of its depth and danger, until we've begun to consider what it might have to say to us about love, for instance, or become aware of the possibility entertained by Edward Pechter[16] – that Iago poisons our minds in the first scene and we never recover from it. Reading Shakespeare isn't always safe.

Appendix to Chapter 15
Punctuation

As I've indicated parenthetically throughout, punctuation raises editorial questions. It differs considerably, with variations of both rhetorical and grammatical pointing, from edition to edition.

Students need to be aware of the following:

- Punctuation in Shakespeare's day was rhetorical – pointing as a guide to delivery – rather than grammatical. (Of course the categories overlap to a large extent in practice.)
- Punctuation in all editions after the Quartos and the first Folio is editorial; it doesn't have the authority of deriving from a manuscript by Shakespeare.
- By the time of the eighteenth-century editors, the function and rules of punctuation were conceived grammatically rather than rhetorically.
- Nearly all modern editors assume that the punctuation is for them to decide.
- Some modern editors mark as exclamations things that are not so marked in the earlier editions.
- Differences of punctuation can bring about not just differences of emphasis, but differences of meaning.

The frequent use of exclamation marks in modern editions suggests at times an exclamatory abruptness or intensity and a particular rhythmic emphasis. For instance the opening line of *Henry VI Part 1* appears in the Cambridge edition like this:

Hung be the heavens with black! Yield, day, to night!

This renders the line as a pair of exclamations – to my taste, a little showy and outward, rather than an expression of a deeply felt grief, rhetorical in the bad sense. Contrast the Folio's

Hung be the heavens with black, yield day to night;

Here we surely hear a more subdued rhythm, a strong sense of inevitability –
like it or not, the heavens will be hung with black, the day will yield to
night; emotion is not displayed, but felt.

We might compare two versions of Juliet waiting for the consummation
of her marriage:

> 1   Come night, come Romeo, come thou day in night,
>   For thou wilt lie upon the wings of night
>   Whiter than new snow upon a raven's back:
>   Come gentle night, come loving backbrow'd night,
>   Give me my Romeo ...

> 2   Come, night! Come, Romeo! Come, thou day in night;
>   For thou wilt lie upon the wings of night
>   Whiter than new snow upon a raven's back.
>   Come, gentle night; come loving, blackbrow'd night,
>   Give me my Romeo.

Which is the more intimate, the more urgent, the more sexual?

A particularly remarkable set of variants can be find in the New Variorum note for *Othello* Act 5 Scene 2 line 344, of which the following is a
selection (the first is from the Folio):

> 1   Oh Desdemon! Dead Desdemon: dead. Oh, oh!
> 2   O Desdemona, Desdemona, dead, O, o, o.
> 3   O Desdemona! Desdemona! dead? O, O, O!
> 4   Oh Desdemon! dead Desdemon: dead. dead. Oh, oh!
> 5   O Desdemona! Desdemona! dead? O!
> 6   O Desdemona! Desdemona! dead! Oh! Oh! Oh!
> 7   Oh Desdemona! Desdemona! dead, dead! oh, oh!
> 8   O Desdemone! dead, Desdemone? dead? dead? oh, oh?

Sometimes a difference of punctuation gives not so much a nuance or subtlety of emphasis as a plain difference of meaning. Most editions have in
the last scene of *Hamlet*:

> *Laertes*   This is too heavy. Let me see another.
> *Hamlet*   This likes me well. These foils have all a length?
>   [*They prepare to play.*]
> *Osric*   Ay my good lord.

In the Folio, Hamlet's line is

This likes me well, these foils have all a length.

It may be worth giving a lesson or part of a lesson to establishing and exploring this point and its implications, considering (and trying out) some short passages according to the different ways in which they have been punctuated. Students could also be asked to decide and defend their own punctuation of a given passage.

Epilogue: finding value in Shakespeare

Struggling through Act 3 Scene 2 of *Much Ado* one morning with a Year 9 class of middle ability, I was asked by one of the girls, a genuine question without animus, 'Why are we studying this?' Later in the same lesson, after I had attempted to explain Don Pedro's remark that Beatrice 'shall be buried with her face upwards' (who knows, perhaps in the hope of at least the response of coarse laughter), another girl (or perhaps the same one, I can't remember), screwing her face up in distaste, asked 'Why *are* we studying this?' In the circumstances, it seemed an entirely reasonable question.

There are different kinds of answer. The immediate and pragmatic is that it is required; it is part of the National Curriculum, established by law. (Although as far as I can gather, there's never actually been a statutory requirement that knowledge of Shakespeare be *examined*.) So we can pass the buck – look, we're all in this together, we have to do it, let's make the best of it, etc. We can also say that it will help them to get good examination results, whereby they will be better qualified. (And so on the way to a better job, more money, the best house, the best car and the perfect husband, as one very intelligent girl said to me, apparently without a trace of irony.) But, they will say, why Shakespeare? Couldn't we study something else, something that has some application in our lives? What's the *use*?

Well, less pragmatically, we can argue truthfully that in the process of studying Shakespeare they will develop their knowledge of the English language, of literature and history. We can also say that they will develop their use of intelligence, their abilities to read and to argue, to develop a case using evidence.

That is, we will be talking about transferable skills, instrumental values: the value of the activity that we are seeking to justify lies outside the activity, in what we can get from having done it, and which we might conceivable have got by some other means. It's a way of arguing that we are very used to, and it may serve to quiet some of the objections our pupils raise. But I think that, while not without value, it misses the point.

Compare the case of a man who plays football for his health, to keep in with the boss or because the girl he fancies likes footballers. Wouldn't we say that he didn't really understand (appreciate) football? Even, if we're a certain kind of philosopher, that he wasn't really playing football at all? The nature, the value of the game inheres in the game itself, in the playing of it. (And the watching – being a football fan is not a transferable skill.)

Having started with an anecdote, I want to proceed with three more – rather more encouraging this time, and leading into an account of what might be the value of reading, studying (and therefore teaching) Shakespeare, although one that has the immediate disadvantage that we can't give to our pupils, for reasons that will be obvious, but which, for reasons that will also be obvious, if we get the teaching right we won't have to.

After a workshop session on *Macbeth* which had focused on Act 1 Scene 7 I noticed one of my GCSE students sitting quietly, reading the text with intense concentration, mouthing to herself some of the following words, as if (it seemed to me) she was seeing them for the first time:

> I have given suck, and know
> How tender 'tis to nurse the babe that milks me:
> I would, while it was smiling in my face,
> Have plucked my nipple from his boneless gums
> And dashed the brains out, had I so sworn
> As you have done to this.

I don't, of course, know what she was thinking. She may, for instance, have been reading with disbelief, with horror, or with relish. (As someone – it was either Wilbur Sanders or Ian Robinson, but I've lost the reference – remarked, it can never be *safe* to really hear the tone we find in Lady Macbeth's lines in this dreadful scene.) But she was certainly finding herself up against something.

The same girl, when she came to write her sustained piece of narrative coursework, presented a work divided into three sections, each with a title: 'Grows … Lives … and Dies'. In Year 9 she had read in *A Midsummer Night's Dream*:

> Thrice blessed are they that master so their blood,
> To undergo such maiden pilgrimage,
> But earthlier happy is the rose distill'd,
> Than that which withering on the virgin thorn,
> Grows, lives, and dies, in single blessedness.

Whether or not she had grasped, consciously or unconsciously, the wonderful poise of Theseus' comparison of the married and the single life, or whether the final line on its own had lodged on her mind, again I don't know, but clearly she had been arrested by something here, and the line had entered into her thinking.

I remember a girl in another (less able) GCSE class who suddenly got the point as I was labouring to conduct them through the progress of the argument of Romeo and Juliet's shared sonnet in Act 1 Scene 5, trying to bring out the physical implications (the implicit stage directions) in the lines:

Juliet	Good pilgrim you do wrong your hand too much
	Which mannerly devotion shows in this,
	For saints have hands, that pilgrims' hands do touch,
	And palm to palm is holy palmers' kiss.
Romeo	Have not saints lips and holy palmers too?
Juliet	Ay pilgrim, lips that they must use in prayer.
Romeo	O then dear saint, let lips do what hands do,
	They pray, grant thou, lest faith turn to despair.

As the penny dropped she cried out vigorously (words to the effect of) 'The cheeky so-and-so! I'd slap his face for him'. (Compare the response of pupils when they are taken line by line through Feste's catechizing of Olivia in Act 1 Scene 5 of *Twelfth Night*. I have even heard an intake of breath on 'I think thy brother is in hell, Madonna.')

And on another occasion in yet another GCSE class I remember seeing a girl at her desk intent on a Penguin copy of *The Taming of the Shrew* (the class was engaged in planning and writing coursework essays) and feeling a rush of irritation that she was looking things up in the notes rather than using her own ideas, developing her own response. As I approached her, words of admonishment at the ready, I saw that she was actually just reading the play. Because she liked it, as it turned out.

In each case the pupil is engaged, at whatever level and however momentarily, with the text of a Shakespeare play in a way that would make it utterly beside the point to ask why what they are doing is worth doing. When we are enjoying something, we just don't ask. By 'enjoying' I don't mean having fun with; while I've nothing against fun (although I do think it seriously overrated), I am very suspicious of the unspoken and deceptive argument 'We have fun when we do Shakespeare, therefore Shakespeare is fun'. A lot of Shakespeare is no fun at all. 'Involvement' and 'engagement' might be less misleading, but I want to hang on to 'enjoy' in a broader sense than it currently has. (My dictionary indicates the potential range: *to joy or delight in, to feel or perceive with pleasure, to possess or use with satisfaction and delight; to have the use of.*) This enjoyment, involvement, engagement is the aim of our teaching, and it has many forms, and opens into many awarenessses. Among these is a discovery of a language which simply says more, which suddenly engages with, articulates or brings into existence our sense of something. The Savage in Huxley's *Brave New World* finds the language that articulates (but also to some extent produces) his disgust at his mother's promiscuity. Gloomy teenagers wonder 'What should such fellows as I do, crawling between Heaven and earth?' Sometimes the experience can be fun: we fire off Shakespearian insults enthusiastically. Sometimes it's a delighted discovery of a moment of beauty:

> When you do dance, I wish you
> A wave o' th' sea, that you might ever do
> Nothing but that: move still, still so:
> And own no other function. Each your doing
> (So singular, in each particular)
> Crowns what you are doing, in the present deeds,
> That all your acts, are queens.

After lengthy discussion of the meaning of these lines from Act 4 Scene 4 of *The Winter's Tale*, I asked the class if there wasn't something further we ought to say about them. No, they said, what? 'They're very beautiful, aren't they?' A girl sitting near me – Simone – breathed out with a kind of relief: 'Yes'. So it's all right to say that kind of thing, then. Reading this speech, a young reader may find for the first time what it can be to contemplate another human being with delight. Saying this begins to anticipate my fuller argument, as follows.

In reading, contemplating the text, trying it out to see what it involves, we are coming to terms with it, interpreting, going into a sense of what is realized and realizable there. All this is of course *active*, but it is also a matter of *attention*; we are not *constructing* meanings in quite the way that some writers suggest. There may be here something of the ambiguity of the old word *invenio*; while there is scope for invention – we may suggest, for instance, that a given line might work better done in this way – what we are doing as we do so is discovering more closely the text's potential (for performance), as we find that the line can or can't go like that. With a text of the quality of Shakespeare's, such performance-exploration can be utterly absorbing – felt to be of value in the doing of it. And as we try to characterize just what it is that is happening in the drama, we might also find ourselves asking what it is for a man or woman to do what is being done here – find ourselves, that is, closely occupied with questions of value.

One way in which I can make sense to myself of talking of Shakespeare's plays conveying value is to say this: I find that attention to certain moments in Shakespeare may enhance or refine our attention to qualities that I suppose we must call moral. Attention to Paulina in *The Winter's Tale*, or to Perdita's wonderfully courteous 'these are flowers/Of middle summer, and I do think they are given/To men of middle age', or to Cordelia's unfathomable words to her father, 'No cause, no cause', may extend or enhance our grasp/conception/apprehension of *kindness*, for instance; in these moments we are shown or we can see what (some of the things that) kindness can be, of what it can be to be kind. It would be a mistake to call these *examples* of kindness, as if kindness was something that we had already fathomed. They are more than reminders; they afford opportunities for the extension of our knowledge. The philosopher John Wisdom is hardly alone in pointing out the importance of literature in affording us this 'greater apprehension':

> words, even when they are about things very familiar to us, sometimes remind us of something in them which we have come to neglect and, what is more, sometimes show us something in them that we have never remarked. Hate and love we knew before Plato, Flaubert or Proust wrote about them. Nevertheless, these men and others have given us a greater apprehension of the varieties of hate and love, of their entanglement with each other, and of their relations with honesty, honour, degradation, war and peace.[1]

What this may not make sufficiently clear is that there will be nothing of generality in this learning and that it is hard to say what place such learning might have in our lives. Some remarks of Rush Rhees' may be helpful here, not so much in clarifying the difficulty as in helping us to see that there is one (a possibility of misunderstanding, that is):

> 'A work of art shows me itself.' I suppose the sense of this is: it does not show me something that might be shown in another way.
>
> The force, the humour or the irony of what was said or done – this cannot be expressed in general terms.
>
> ... I do not try to put what I have learned in general terms ... It does not show me how I might see any *other* events, the lives of other characters.[2]

Some will object to 'shows me itself', saying that the active role of the reader in the construction of meaning is being effaced, and that this is an instance of ideological mystification. It is commonplace that perception is an active process. However, I try to relate the two sides of my experience by asserting that while in perception the mind may well (in Wordsworth's phrase) half create what it sees, that making belongs beyond the individual will; we do not (always) choose so to make. What we perceive lies over against us, and is not directly subject to our will. Of course that parenthetical 'always' reminds us that there are distinctions to be made. There are occasions on which we are aware of our activity in the making or finding of meaning, particularly where the meaning is not immediately apparent. We might say not just 'I don't understand it' but 'I can't make anything of it'. Nonetheless, in the process of our making something of it, meaning *dawns*. As Roger Nash observes, 'when meaning dawns in a poem, it seems beyond the control of the reader's will. But its occurrence requires his strength to remain sensitively open to possibilities of meaning in the work'.[3] Our observations and critical judgements, when right (but also unfortunately sometimes when wrong), have the force of recognitions.

The remaining sensitively open, I've argued, can be an activity. In the doing of it, things occur to us. In our active trying of the text, we come to recognitions. (I don't think the relation between our activity and what I am inclined to call *disclosures* is ascertainable, however – it isn't certain how, or even that, one *produces* the other; I don't presume to know what the relationship is. This is an area where I am aware of further thinking to be done.) Of course what we bring to bear on our reading of the moment, our interests (so to speak), have a bearing on what is salient ('shows itself') in the text. When Kiernan Ryan uses 'salience' as a verb, speaking of the duty of the radical critic to 'retrieve and salience the subconscious progressive impulses of the work'[4] he is not talking of the active consideration so much as of electing from among the possibilities that have become apparent. That new possibilities do, and rightly do, become apparent is a particularly attractive element in Ryan's subsequent work; he makes it abundantly clear that Shakespeare goes on having meaning for us in the present and for the future. This being so, I don't think that to talk of the work of art 'showing itself' is necessarily to talk from within mystification.

It follows from Rhees' remarks about particularity that we are far from the ubiquitous concept of 'skills' and its conceptual cousin, information. '[The] crucial difference between becoming educated and acquiring sundry skills is ... that skills can be acquired without making much difference to the person who acquire the skills.'[5] Similarly, information, which we deploy our skills on, is also something which we can have more or less of, but the having of which need not change us, or have much bearing on our life. The notion of educational thought whereby knowledge (reduced in the process to information) and skills are separated and set over against each other is a serious misconception outside the limited sphere in which it is properly applicable. It isn't information that is to be had from reading Shakespeare, but knowledge. The plays are not vehicular in the sense of conveying to us what could equally be known from another source. What is known is known only in particular readings. We are far, that is, from the world of PHSE; I am not proposing (for instance) a course on kindness, or the good. What may be had from Shakespeare in the way of learning value is in a sense more incidental and accidental – although not any less valuable for being so – than something of that sort. As my quotations from Rhees may begin to suggest, and a sustained look at the essay

('Art and philosophy') from which they are taken will confirm, the question of the *application* of what we so learn – of the place that it finds in our lives – is by no means easy, and the likely answers are unlikely to satisfy educationalists who hold instrumentalist views. They will want to know what difference it makes. If I understand Rhees, he says that the knowing just *is* the difference. But shouldn't an advance in moral knowledge show in moral *fruits*? (We might begin to answer this objection by saying that while there is no guarantee that an apprehension of, say, Cordelia's kindness will make us kind, it may lead us to recognize that we are not kind. Macbeth knew, and knew deeply, what kindness involves.)

I don't think that the values found in reading Shakespeare are our constructions. I do think that in valuing we are shown value, and that we may come to recognize values as having a claim on us. That is, they do not occur to us as *options*. When that happens I would prefer to talk of *absolute* values rather than of universal values, the term preferred by the writers of the Cox Report when justifying the place given to Shakespeare in the National Curriculum:

> Many teachers believe that Shakespeare's work conveys universal values, and that his language expresses rich and subtle meanings beyond that of any other English writer. Other teachers point out that evaluations of Shakespeare have varied from one historical period to the next, and they argue that pupils should be encouraged to think critically about his status in the canon. But almost everyone agrees that his work should be represented in the National Curriculum. Shakespeare's plays are so rich that in every age they can produce fresh meaning and even those who deny his universality agree on his cultural importance.[6]

This says nothing of the argument, common at the time, that Shakespeare as he had been valued was the *production* of an ideologically determined valuing, that it was not the plays that could 'produce fresh meaning', but we who produce meaning in or by them, in accord with an ideology. The plays were sites of struggle for the erection of contesting and contested meanings. Cox misrepresented 'many teachers' when he said that 'even those who deny his universality agree on his cultural importance'. It looks as if this 'cultural importance' is the same sort of thing suggested in the first quoted sentence, but it all too clearly isn't. *That Shakespeare has been culturally important* is what they asserted, and what they would make the subject of study. This is not the same as saying that Shakespeare is of value to our culture, and can be quite compatible with a denial of that assertion. So Cox asserted as one thing being done differently what could be more accurately represented as two different things; the committee's way of putting it suggested that no important difference was involved. One group could work for the perpetuation of an unjust society through the propagation of idealist myths of eternal value embodied in Shakespeare's wonderful language, and the other side for the undoing and abolition of the same, and the demands of the National Curriculum concerning Shakespeare – the test case for an understanding of literature, as both sides recognized – would be satisfied. You can do it your way, and you can do it yours; it's all right as long as it's Shakespeare.

I certainly don't think values such as kindness and courage (to say nothing of such less fashionable virtues as chastity and patience)[7] should be stigmatized as bourgeois. If universal (some added, eternal) means appearing everywhere and always in the same form, then I suppose it may not make sense to call them universal and eternal. But aren't they what philosophers call universals? And aren't universals realized on specific occasions in specific ways? In which case Shakespeare can teach us – or rather his plays can be occasions for our learning – about universals.

Is kindness an eternal or universal value? It isn't hard to imagine a society in which it counts for very little – although dwelling on what kindness can mean in Shakespeare may lead us to consider such societies somehow lacking. I think values are real, and that there is such a thing as loss of value. Asked to choose between a life in which I know what is shown in, say, Cordelia, Perdita and Hermione (I don't find it accidental that they are all women) and one in which I don't ... but then, I am not personally offered such a choice. The question is whether or not my pupils should be granted the opportunity of learning what they can represent.

But this raises the question of time: how much of the curriculum can we give over to something as uncertain and accidental as what I'm suggesting? And it raises the further question: to whom is what I've been outlining available? Who are the 'we' of the preceding paragraphs? How many of our pupils arrive at (or are granted) the moment that can be characterized as the work of art showing itself? (The moment can't be infallibly produced by pedagogical technique, but we can bring about circumstances more or less propitious.) For many the approach to Shakespeare is laborious, and there is little to persuade them that the labour is worthwhile. Terry Eagleton's remark that we can imagine a society with no use for Shakespeare was well publicized in the 1980s; less publicized but more to the point was Malcolm Evan's additional remark that:

> If Shakespeare's expensive life-support systems in English education and subsidized 'culture' were turned off now ... this society might well emerge sooner than expected, *and it has always been here, at least in part, for most British men and women*.[8]

Those who find value in Shakespeare in the way I have been discussing may only be a few, and they will – and Evans intimates that they should – become fewer. (Further, I must consider the possibility that the claims

I have been making are just hyperbolical and inapplicable to the lives of our young people, although I don't think they are.) An answer to this objection can only be worked out in practice, in work done by teachers who remain convinced that Shakespeare continues to belong to the good of the language, that the possibilities of continuity remain (and, if they are socialist teachers, that such continuity does not necessarily involve the perpetuation of injustice).

And anyway this learning of value takes place in the surrounding of much else that is worthwhile – other forms of engagement, involvement and enjoyment, even fun, as I hope has been evident from the examples of classroom encounters and children's work that I have recorded throughout this book. Any further articulation of the argument needs to proceed along narrative lines: *stories* of finding value in Shakespeare.

Notes and references

Prologue

1 I discuss some of the methods alluded to here in '"I was Macbeth's Kilt-maker" or, What are we making of Shakespeare?' in *The Use of English*, Spring 1993.

1 Admitting the difficulty

1 Frank Whitehead, *The Disappearing Dias*, London: Chatto and Windus, 1966, p. 133. Quoted in Martin Blocksidge (ed.), *Shakespeare in Education*, London: Continuum, 2003, p. 8.
2 Charles Barber, *Early Modern English*, Edinburgh: Edinburgh University Press, 1997.
3 N. F. Blake, *Shakespeare's Language: An Introduction*, London and Basingstoke: Macmillan, 1983.

2 'All these old words'

1 Charles Barber, *Early Modern English*, Edinburgh: Edinburgh University Press, 1997, pp. 152–7.
2 Adamson, Hunter, Magnusson, Thompson and Wales (eds), *Reading Shakespeare's Dramatic Language – A Guide*, London: Thomson Learning, 2001, pp. 226–31. Also of interest to those concerned with the *religious* use of 'thou' is Peter Toon and Louis R. Tarsitano, *Neither Archaic nor Obsolete: The Language of Common Prayer and Public Worship*, Denton: Edgeways Books, 2003, pp. 64ff.
3 See the discussion of deferential uses of personal pronouns in John E. Joseph, *Language and Politics*, Edinburgh: Edinburgh University Press, 2006, pp. 68–73.
4 Charles Barber, *Early Modern English*, Edinburgh: Edinburgh University Press, 1997, p. 217.
5 C. S. Lewis, *Studies in Words*, Cambridge: Cambridge University Press, 1967, p. 4.
6 Ibid., pp. 12–14.
7 Roger Warren and Stanley Wells (eds), *Twelfth Night*, Oxford: Oxford University Press, 1994, p. 170.
8 Roma Gill (ed.), *Oxford School Shakespeare: Hamlet*, Oxford: Oxford University Press, p. 128.

3 Case study: 'virtue'

1   Melvyn Bragg, *The Adventure of English*, London: Hodder & Stoughton, 2003, pp. 57–8.

4 Grammar

1   N. F. Blake, *Shakespeare's Language: An Introduction*, London and Basingstoke: Macmillan, 1983.
2   Charles Barber, *Early Modern English*, Edinburgh: Edinburgh University Press, 1997.
3   A. P. Rossiter, 'Poetry and gagaram: an enquiry into meaning', in *Our Living Language: an Englishman Looks at his English*, London: Longmans, 1953.
4   Charles Barber, *Early Modern English*, Edinburgh: Edinburgh University Press, 1997, p. 173.
5   Ibid., p. 191.
6   N. F. Blake, *Shakespeare's Language: An Introduction*, London and Basingstoke: Macmillan, 1983, p. 126.
7   Rex Gibson, *Teaching Shakespeare*, Cambridge: Cambridge University Press, 1998, pp. 177–8. No direct quote involved.

6 Allusion

1   Ian Robinson, 'UCCA to what?', *The Use of English*, Summer 1983, p. 30.
2   Roma Gill (ed.), *Oxford School Shakespeare: Twelfth Night*, Oxford: Oxford University Press, 1997, p. 3.
3   *Twelfth Night*, Cumbria: Coordination Group Publications, 2002, p. 1.

7 Rhetoric

1   Two useful books: Brian Vickers' compendious *In Defence of Rhetoric*, Oxford: University Press, 1989, and (much more brief) Peter Dixon, *The Critical Idiom: Rhetoric*, London: Methuen, 1971.
2   Dominic Palfrey, *Doing Shakespeare*, London: Thomson Learning, 2005, pp. 39–57.
3   Jazz lovers, take note.

8 Paraphrase

1   Michael Pafford, 'Shakespeare rules O.K.?', *The Use of English*, Summer 1985, p. 52.
2   Examples of the use of paraphrase to clarify or disambiguate grammar can be found in N. F. Blake, *Shakespeare's Language: An Introduction*, London and Basingstoke: Macmillan, 1983, pp. 94, 107, 116 and 134.
3   *Twelfth Night*, Cumbria: Coordination Group Publications, 2002, p. 3.
4   As in most editions. The Folio allocates from 'Paddock calls' to the end of the scene to '*All*'.
5   The whole scene is on page 21 of Alan Durband, *Shakespeare Made Easy: Macbeth*, Cheltenham: Stanley Thorne, 1990.
6   Ibid., p. 25.
7   Ibid., p. 27.

10 Long speeches

1   Pamela Mason, 'Cambridge Student Guide: Othello', Cambridge: Cambridge University Press, 2002, p. 81.
2   Ibid., *Student Guide*, p. 81.
3   Rex Gibson, *Teaching Shakespeare*, Cambridge: Cambridge University Press, 1997, pp. 61–6.
4   On 'shall' and 'will' in Shakespeare, see N. F. Blake, *Shakespeare's Language: An Introduction*, London and Basingstoke: Macmillan, 1983, pp. 93 ff.
5   Dorothy Boux's *All the World's a Stage: Speeches, Poems and Songs from Shakespeare*, London: Shepheard-Walwyn (Publishers), 1994, presents a range of excerpts in a variety of calligraphy, each page nicely designed, which I can imagine being attractive for some young readers. Making a nicely produced book of Shakespeare extracts might be a good group activity for Key Stage 3 pupils at some point.
6   Fred Sedgwick, *Shakespeare and the Young Writer*, London: Routledge, 1999.
7   Barbara Hardy, *Shakespeare's Storytellers*, London: Peter Owen, 1997.
8   Roma Gill (ed.), *Oxford School Shakespeare: Much Ado*, Oxford: Oxford University Press, 2004, p. 9.

11 Narrative

1   Charles and Mary Lamb, *Tales from Shakespeare* (1807), Hertfordshire: Wordsworth Classics, 1994, p. 136.
2   This expository urge can also be found in the invented and/or expanded stage directions of some editions/versions produced for classroom use. I've discussed this in 'A local habitation and a name', *The Use of English*, Spring 2001.
3   Jennifer Mulherin, *Shakespeare for Everyone: Twelfth Night*, Bath: Cherrytree Books, 1988, p. 28. And no, we don't.
4   Jennifer Mulherin, *Shakespeare for Everyone: Macbeth*, Bath: Cherrytree Books, 1988, p. 26.
5   Garfield's versions came in two large books, illustrated by Michael Forman: *Shakespeare Stories*, London: Gollancz, 1985 and *Shakespeare Stories II*, London: Gollancz, 1994. A brief selection, *Six Shakespeare Stories*, was published as a Heinemann New Windmill in 1994. I've discussed Garfield's Shakespeare stories, especially his *Much Ado*, and versions by Marchette Chute and E. Nesbit, in detail in '"The least part of Shakespeare": telling Shakespeare's stories' in *The Use of English*, Autumn 2007, pp. 4–13.
6   This exchange is a useful one to use as a class warm-up early in the study of the play, one half asking the question, the other responding. Such rituals of entry may well be worth developing as a classroom device.

12 Theatre

1   Roma Gill (ed), *Oxford School Shakespeare*, Oxford University Press.
2   I record a debt here: the train of thought developed in this chapter was triggered by Christopher Parry's excellent essay 'What is Mamillius doing?', *The Use of English*, Summer 1979.
3   Veronica O'Brien's *Teaching Shakespeare*, London: Edward Arnold, 1982, has some useful suggestions along these lines.
4   Rex Gibson, *Teaching Shakespeare*, Cambridge: Cambridge University Press, 1998, pp. 177–8.

5   Dover Wilson (ed.), *New Shakespeare: Hamlet*, Cambridge: Cambridge University Press, 1951.
6   Walter Raleigh (ed.), *Johnson on Shakespeare*, Oxford: Oxford University Press, 1925, p. 80.
7   Alan C. Dessen, *Recovering Shakespeare's Theatrical Vocabulary*, Cambridge: Cambridge University Press, 1995, pp. 93–4.
8   Nicholas Brooke (ed.), *Macbeth* Oxford edition (1990), p. 203.

13 Context

1   Lily B. Campbell, *Shakespeare's Tragic Heroes: Slaves of Passion*, London: Methuen, 1930.
2   Wilbur Sanders, *The Dramatist and the Received Idea: Studies in the Plays of Marlowe and Shakespeare*, Cambridge: Cambridge University Press, 1968.
3   Helen Gardner, 'The historical approach', in *The Business of Criticism*, London: Oxford University Press, 1959, p. 34.
4   I last saw it as part of 'The Shakespeare Workshop Series', general editor Peter Jones, in the early 1990s.
5   Schools' editions will probably help here, and there's still E. M. W. Tillyard, *Shakespeare's History Plays*, London: Chatto and Windus, 1944, often reprinted.
6   Peter Hyland, *An Introduction to Shakespeare*, Basingstoke: Macmillan, 1996.
7   Gabriel Egan, 'Edinburgh Critical Guides', Edinburgh: Edinburgh University Press, 2007.
8   Walter Raleigh (ed.), *Johnson on Shakespeare*, Oxford: Oxford University Press, 1925, p. 161.
9   Ibid.
10   James Black (ed.), *The History of King Lear*, London: Arnold, 1975, p. 95.
11   A selection of Restoration adaptations is available from Everyman: Sandra Clark (ed.), *Shakespeare Made Fit: Restoration Adaptations of Shakespeare*, London: Dent, 1997.
12   A. C. Bradley, *Shakespearean Tragedy* (1904), London: Macmillan, 1957, p. 26.
13   Walter Raleigh (ed.), *Johnson and Shakespeare*, Oxford: Oxford University Press, 1925, p. 161.
14   Arthur Miller, *Death of a Salesman* (1949), Harmondsworth: Penguin, p. 44.
15   In John Philips, *The Play of Patient Grissell*, c.1565.
16   Peter Corbin and Douglas Sedge (eds), *Thomas of Woodstock, or, Richard the Second, part one*, Manchester: Manchester University Press, 2002.
17   Marion O'Connor, '"Imagine Me, Gentle Spectators": Iconomachy in *The Winter's Tale*', in Richard Dutton and Jean E. Howard (eds), *A Companion to Shakespeare Works Volume IV: The Poems, Problem Comedies, Late Plays*, Oxford: Blackwell, 2003, pp. 365–88.
18   Frances E. Dolan (ed.), *Texts and Contexts: The Taming of the Shrew*, Boston and New York: St Martin's Press, 1996.
19   Sean McEvoy, 'Shakespeare at 16–19' in Martin Blocksidge (ed.), *Shakespeare in Education*, London: Continuum, 2003, p. 104.
20   Robert Marchant, *Tragedy against Psychology*, Retford: Brynmill, 1984, p. 33.

14 Interpretation

1   Peter Winch, 'Text and Context', *Philosophical Investigations*, vol. 1 no. 1 (January 1982), p. 44.

2 Wilbur Sanders and Howard Jacobson, *Shakespeare's Magnanimity*, London: Chatto & Windus, 1978.

3 Walter Raleigh (ed.), *Johnson on Shakespeare*, Oxford: Oxford University Press, 1925, p. 161.

4 In the sixteenth and seventeenth centuries 'perform' had a meaning (deriving from the Old French *parfournir*, 'to accomplish completely') of 'to complete by adding what is wanting'.

5 As argued in Colin Still, *Shakespeare's Mystery Play*, London: Palmer, 1921, and further developed by Michael Srigley in *Images of Regeneration: A Study of Shakespeare's The Tempest and its Cultural Background*, Uppsala: Uppsala University, 1985.

6 In the film directed by Trevor Nunn.

7 Barbara Hardy, *Shakespeare's Storytellers*, London: Peter Owen, 1997, p. 173.

8 Stevie Davies, *Penguin Critical Studies: The Taming of the Shrew*, Harmondsworth: Penguin, 1995, p. 23.

9 David Williamson, 'Re-teaching ... Shakespeare?', *The Use of English*, Summer 1991, p. 33.

10 Useful texts on performance of *The Shrew* include Graham Holderness, *Shakespeare in Performance: The Taming of the Shrew*, Manchester: Manchester University Press (1989) and Toni Haring-Smith *From Farce to Metadrama: A Stage History of The Taming of the Shrew 1594–1983*, Westport: Greenwood Press (1985).

11 F. R. Leavis, 'Diabolic intellect and the noble hero', in *The Common Pursuit* (1952), Harmondsworth: Penguin, 1962.

12 A. C. Bradley, *Shakespearean Tragedy* (1904), London: Macmillan, 1957, p. 161.

13 Germaine Greer, *The Female Eunuch*, London: Paladin, 1971, p. 209.

14 Stevie Davies, *Penguin Critical Studies: The Taming of the Shrew*, Harmondsworth: Penguin, 1995, pp. viii, 23, 91.

15 Peter Barry, *Beginning Theory: An Introduction to Literary and Cultural Theory*, Manchester: Manchester University Press, 1995.

16 Stanley Cavell, *Disowning Knowledge*, Cambridge: Cambridge University Press, 1987, pp. 125–42.

17 Julie Hankey (ed.), *Plays in Performance: Richard III*, Bristol: Bristol Classical Press, 1988.

18 Brian Vickers, *Shakespeare: The Critical Heritage*, Volumes 1–6, published over the years by Routledge, the final volume in 1981.

19 A. D. Nuttall, *Shakespeare the Thinker*, New Haven and London: Yale University Press, 2007.

15 Talk

1 There's an excellent introduction to conversation analysis in Aileen Bloomer, Patrick Griffiths and Andrew John Merrison (eds), *Introduction to Language in Use*, London: Routledge, 2005.

2 Lance St John Butler, *Registering the Difference: Reading Literature through Register*, Manchester: Manchester University Press, 1999, p. 50.

3 Ronald Carter and Walter Nash, *Seeing Through Language,* Oxford: Blackwell, 1990, p. 92.

4 Robert Southwick (ed.), *Othello*, London: Longman 1993, p. 17.

5 Ibid., p. 16.

6 Howard Furness (ed.), *A New Variorum Edition of Shakespeare: Othello* (1886), New York: Dover, p. 22.

7   A. D. Nuttall, *A New Mimesis: Shakespeare and the Representation of Reality*, London: Routledge, 1983, p. 142.

8   Quoted in George Taylor, ' "The just delineation of the passions": theories of acting in the age of Garrick', in Kenneth Richards and Peter Thomson (eds), *The Eighteenth Century Stage*, London: Methuen, 1972, p. 54.

9   Discussions of this may be found in Simon Palfrey, *Doing Shakespeare*, London: Thomson Learning, 2005, pp. 289–90 and Terence Hawkes, *That Shakespeherian Rag*, London: Routledge, 1986, pp. 73–4.

10 This list is based on materials from the Language in the National Curriculum project.

11 John Barton, *Playing Shakespeare*, London: Methuen, 1984, and Peter Hall, *Shakespeare's Advice to the Players*, Theatre Communication Group, 2003, are particularly useful on how verse directs the actor.

12 See, for instance, Stephen C. Levinson, *Pragmatics*, Cambridge: Cambridge University Press, 1983.

13 Brian Vickers, *Appropriating Shakespeare: Contemporary Critical Quarrels*, New Haven and London: Yale University Press, 1993, pp. 74–91.

14 Vimala Herman, *Dramatic Discourse: Dialogue as Interaction in Plays*, London: Routledge, 1995, pp. 243–4.

15 Malcolm Coulthard, *An Introduction to Discourse Analysis*, London: Longman, 1985, p. 185.

16 Edward Pechter, *Othello and Interpretative Traditions*, Iowa City: University of Iowa Press, 1999.

Epilogue: finding value in Shakespeare

1   John Wisdom, *Paradox and Discovery*, Oxford: Blackwell, 1965, p. 139.

2   Rush Rhees, *Without Answers*, London: Routledge and Kegan Paul, 1969, pp. 145, 148, 145.

3   Roger Nash, 'God and beauty', *The Gadfly* 6.4 (November, 1983), p. 17.

4   Kiernan Ryan, 'Towards a socialist criticism: reclaiming the canon', *LTP: Journal of Literature Teaching Politics*, no. 3 (1984), p. 5.

5   Ian Robinson, quoted in Roger Elliott, *'Discourses That Pretend to Inform and Instruct'*, Gringley-on-the-Hill: Brynmill, 1987, p. 4.

6   *English for Ages 5 to 16: Proposals for the Secretary of State for Education and Science and the Secretary of State for Wales*, Department of Education and Science, June 1989, paragraph 7.16.

7   I'm thinking here of Miranda and Hermione. For the former, see my article 'Is Miranda wet?', *The Use of English*, Summer 1984.

8   Malcolm Evans, *Signifying Nothing: Truth's True Contents in Shakespeare's Text*, Sussex: Harvester, 1986, p. 255.

Index